ABOUT THE PROGRAMME

Introducing *Rapid Writing* 2
Rapid: the whole family 3
Supporting the struggling writer 4
Writing Logs: key features 8
Guided writing sessions: key features 10
Using the *Rapid Writing* Pupil Software 12
Scope and Sequence: Writing Log 7 (Units 1–10) 14
Scope and Sequence: Writing Log 8 (Units 11–20) 16
Scope and Sequence: Writing Log 9 (Units 21–30) 18

GUIDED WRITING SESSION NOTES

Units 1–10 (Writing Log 7) 20
Units 11–20 (Writing Log 8) 60
Units 21–30 (Writing Log 9) 100

WRITING ASSESSMENT USING *RAPID WRITING*

Rapid Writing and Assessment for Learning 140
Rapid Writing and Assessing Pupils' Progress 141
Assessment of unaided writing 142
Correcting common errors 146
Progression in writing skills 148
Words for spelling 149
My writing progress charts 150

About the programme

Introducing *Rapid Writing*

Rapid Writing is a collection of resources to support you in your work with children who find writing difficult. It provides:

- Finely-levelled fiction and non-fiction writing tasks to build children's skills
- Colourful Writing Logs that scaffold children's work and provide evidence of their progress
- Essential skills practice software for rehearsal of the basics
- Fantastic text-to-speech technology to help children hear their own writing
- Detailed teaching support for guided writing sessions
- Independent tasks to help assess children's writing

Who are the target pupils?

Rapid Writing is designed to support children aged 7–11 years who are working within National Curriculum levels P8 to 3C.

Guided Writing with *Rapid Writing*

The *Rapid Writing* materials are designed to be used with small groups of children during a 30-minute guided writing session. Each session is based around one Writing Log page. The page is bright and enticing, and provides a scaffold for children's writing. Each session follows the same format:

- The sessions start with warm-up work focussing on letter formation and spelling of words that the children will use in the writing session.
- The children orally rehearse each sentence before writing it. This reinforces the importance of the sentence as a means of ensuring written text makes sense.
- Then the children are encouraged to write the rehearsed sentences themselves.
- Finally, children are asked to review and improve their work, and to evaluate their writing.

Each *Rapid Writing* guided session has been developed to ensure that pupils make steady progress in their writing skills. Some of the features that ensure this progress are:

- Limited number of words in each writing session
- Gradual build-up in progression of sentence complexity
- Drawing on characters and non-fiction contexts that children will engage with, especially if they have met them before in the *Rapid* reading books
- Short, achievable writing tasks to break down the barriers to writing
- Handwriting and spelling are practised at the start of the session, and reinforced by being used in the sentence

Rapid Writing Pupil Software

The *Rapid Writing* Pupil Software is designed to help children practise the essential skills needed for writing in a supportive and fun environment. Some of the ways it does this are as follows:

- The software includes short, enjoyable tasks that ensure repeated practice of word and sentence level skills.
- Each software session is linked to the preceding guided writing session, so that children can have confidence through recognising the context and vocabulary used.
- Children collect medals as they progress, to ensure that they remain motivated by repeated success.

The *Rapid Writing* Pupil Software also features a number of activities that use text-to-speech technology, which reads back children's work as they type it. This fantastic software allows children to create their own texts, providing a rewarding experience. Being able to hear their own work read back to them will reinforce the habit of rereading to ensure that what they have written makes sense.

About the programme

Rapid: the whole family

All of the *Rapid Writing* books can be used completely independently of the reading books in the *Rapid* series. However, the contexts and characters used in the *Rapid Writing* books are drawn from those in the reading series, and there are a number of benefits in children having had previous exposure to those reading books:

- Children may approach the writing task with more confidence after they have successfully read and enjoyed the reading text to which it links.
- They will be more familiar with some of the vocabulary used, reducing the need to spend time introducing vocabulary.
- Children may recognise the characters, stories and non-fiction contexts, and will be able to draw on their familiarity with the material.

Because the focus in the writing sessions is sometimes different from that in the reading, there will be some twists on the original text, which children will enjoy spotting!

The chart below shows how the *Rapid Writing* and *Rapid* reading books correlate in terms of National Curriculum levels:

Rapid Writing level	Rapid reading book level	England and Wales National Curriculum Level	Northern Ireland Curriculum Level	Scotland Curriculum Level
Stage 1: Writing Log 1	Starter 2 Yellow	P8/1C	Within Level 1	5–14 Towards level A; CFE early
Stage 1: Writing Log 2	Stage 1 Blue Stage 2 Green	1C/1B	Towards Level 2	5–14 Towards level A; CFE first
Stage 1: Writing Log 3	Stage 3 Orange	1A	Within Level 2	5–14 Towards level A; CFE first
Stage 2: Writing Log 4	Stage 4 Turquoise	1A/2C	Within Level 2	5–14 Towards level B; CFE second
Stage 2: Writing Log 5	Stage 4 Turquoise	2C	Within Level 2	5–14 Towards level B; CFE second
Stage 2: Writing Log 6	Stage 4 Purple	2B	Within Level 2	5–14 Towards level B; CFE second
Stage 3: Writing Log 7	Stage 6 Gold	2B	Within Level 2	5–14 Towards level B; CFE second
Stage 3: Writing Log 8	Stage 6 Gold	2B/2A	Within Level 2	5–14 Towards level B; CFE second
Stage 3: Writing Log 9	Stage 6 Gold	2A/3C	Within Level 2	5–14 Towards level C; CFE second

About the programme

Supporting the struggling writer

Rapid Writing and guided writing

Research suggests that working together with other children can be a very effective way for children to improve their writing skills. Working in a small group provides a safe environment for children to develop their ideas and try sentences out orally before committing them to paper. In addition, seeing writing modelled by an 'expert writer' will help them recognise and emulate good writing practice.

How should the guided writing sessions be organised?

Ability range of the children

Rapid Writing is intended for children who are finding all aspects of the writing process difficult. The chart on page 3 shows how each Writing Log relates to National Curriculum levels for England, Wales, Scotland and Northern Ireland. When children are working in a small group, it is helpful if they are working at approximately the same level. This helps children work together effectively and helps teachers provide the right amount of support to make sure all children can progress.

Group size

Rapid Writing has been designed for an adult to work with a small group (between three and six children), though it can be used more flexibly as a whole-class or one-to-one intervention, depending on the school's needs.

Frequency of sessions

Each writing task (unit) is taught across two 30-minute sessions. Ideally teachers will timetable for both sessions to take place within one week.

Rapid Writing, spelling and phonics

The *Rapid Writing* approach to spelling and phonics works on the basis that children will already have had exposure to a range of spelling and phonic work during their early years. Throughout the programme, word-level work is directly linked to the sentences the children write during the main part of the session – it is spelling FOR writing. The progression in these words can be seen in the charts on pages 14–19.

The word-level work in *Rapid Writing* follows the basic principle that where a word has a straightforward grapheme-phoneme correspondence (GPC), it is taught using phonic strategies. Words that have a less straightforward or irregular GPC, are treated differently. Strategies for teaching these types of words include using the letter names (rather than the letter sounds) or using mnemonics as a memory aid. However, if children have the necessary level of phonic knowledge, certain words that are taught as 'irregular' here could be taught phonically instead.

About the programme

Rapid Writing: the teaching sequence

Every unit in *Rapid Writing* follows the same format. During the 30-minute session, children practise all the elements of the writing process, from handwriting and spelling to constructing and punctuating sentences, and ensuring that their sentences link for continuity. They will be rehearsing all the skills necessary for creating an extended piece of writing when back in the classroom.

Guided Writing Session
↓

Warm up
Children practise handwriting (Writing Logs 1 and 2 only) and spell some of the words they will need later in the session.
↓

Introducing genre
Discussion of the text type that children will be writing; explaining its purpose and form.
↓

Collecting ideas
Talk for writing (text level): children discuss ideas for their writing, using the picture stimulus and prompts from the adult.
↓

Scaffolding ideas
Partner talk for writing: with guidance from the adult, children rehearse orally the sentence(s) they will write.
↓

Demonstration writing
The adult models the writing, sentence by sentence.
↓

Memorising sentences
Children are encouraged to recall the sequence of words in the sentence before writing them down.
↓

Independent writing
Children work, sentence by sentence, to complete their writing.
↓

Checking accuracy
Children are encouraged to check the word order, spelling and punctuation of their sentences.
↓

Reading own writing
Working with a partner or the rest of the group, children read their work with fluency and intonation.
↓

Reviewing the session
Together the group recaps the genre and purpose of writing.
↓

Reflecting on learning
Children recap the skills they have learnt and assess their own work.
↓

Pupil Software Session
↓

Reading own writing
Children rehearse the skills they have acquired during the guided writing session.
↓

Applying skills
Children use their skills and knowledge of text type and genre to complete more open-ended writing activities.

About the programme

Handwriting

We recognise that schools will have their own handwriting policy, following particular principles of letter formation and joins. Schools should follow their own handwriting policy. It is easy to adapt the *Rapid* handwriting suggestions to fit any handwriting style.

Writing Logs 1 and 2 of *Rapid Writing* include a handwriting activity as part of the warm-up work at the start of a session. This section is intended to help children become 'tuned in' to the writing task, and to aid them with the spelling of the focus words when they come to practise them. The letters and joins that are focused on are those used for the main writing activity; they are also those that children often find particularly difficult.

For children who struggle with forming and joining letters, we recommend the following teaching practices.

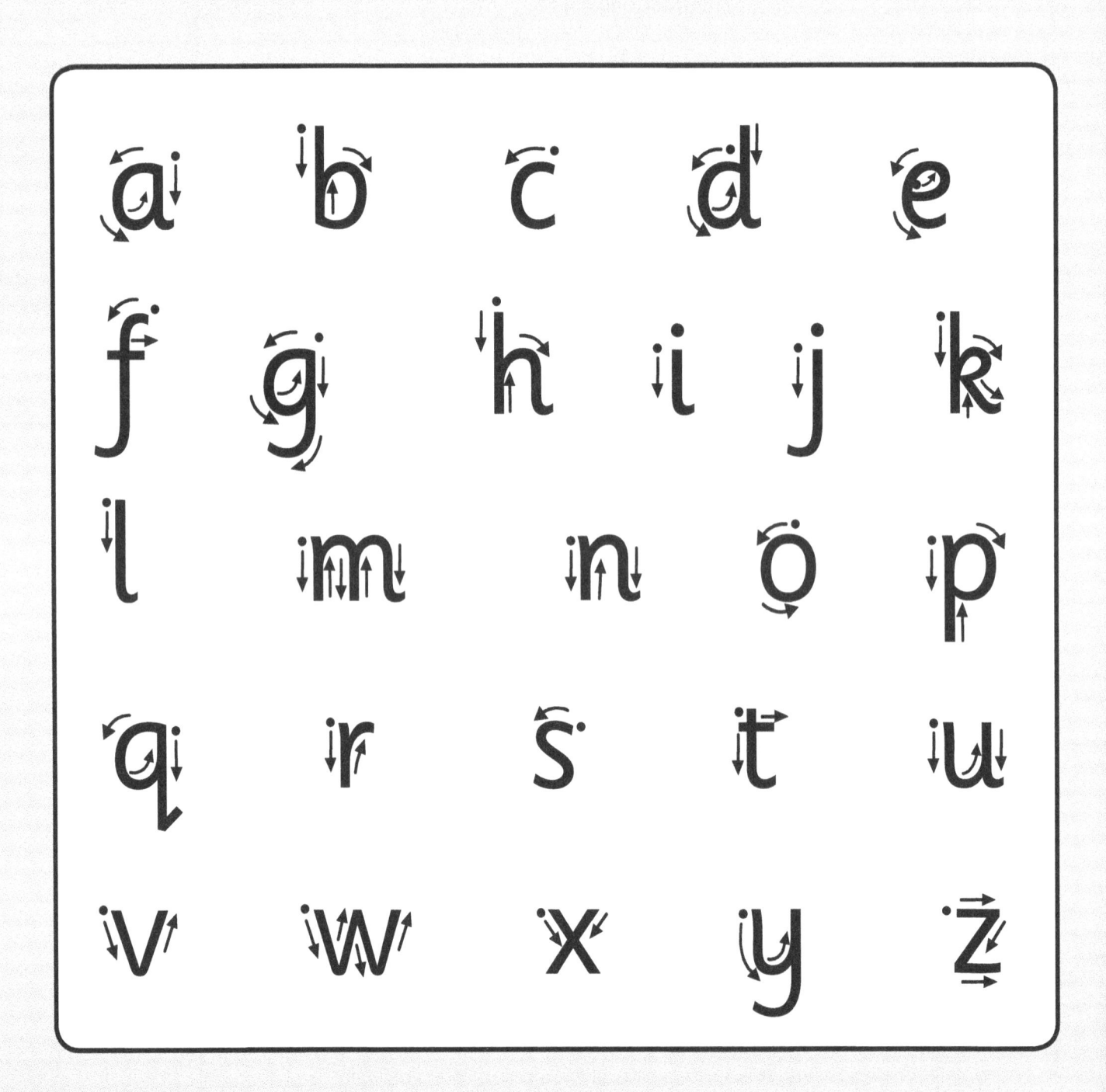

a b c d e
f g h i j k
l m n o p
q r s t u
v w x y z

About the programme

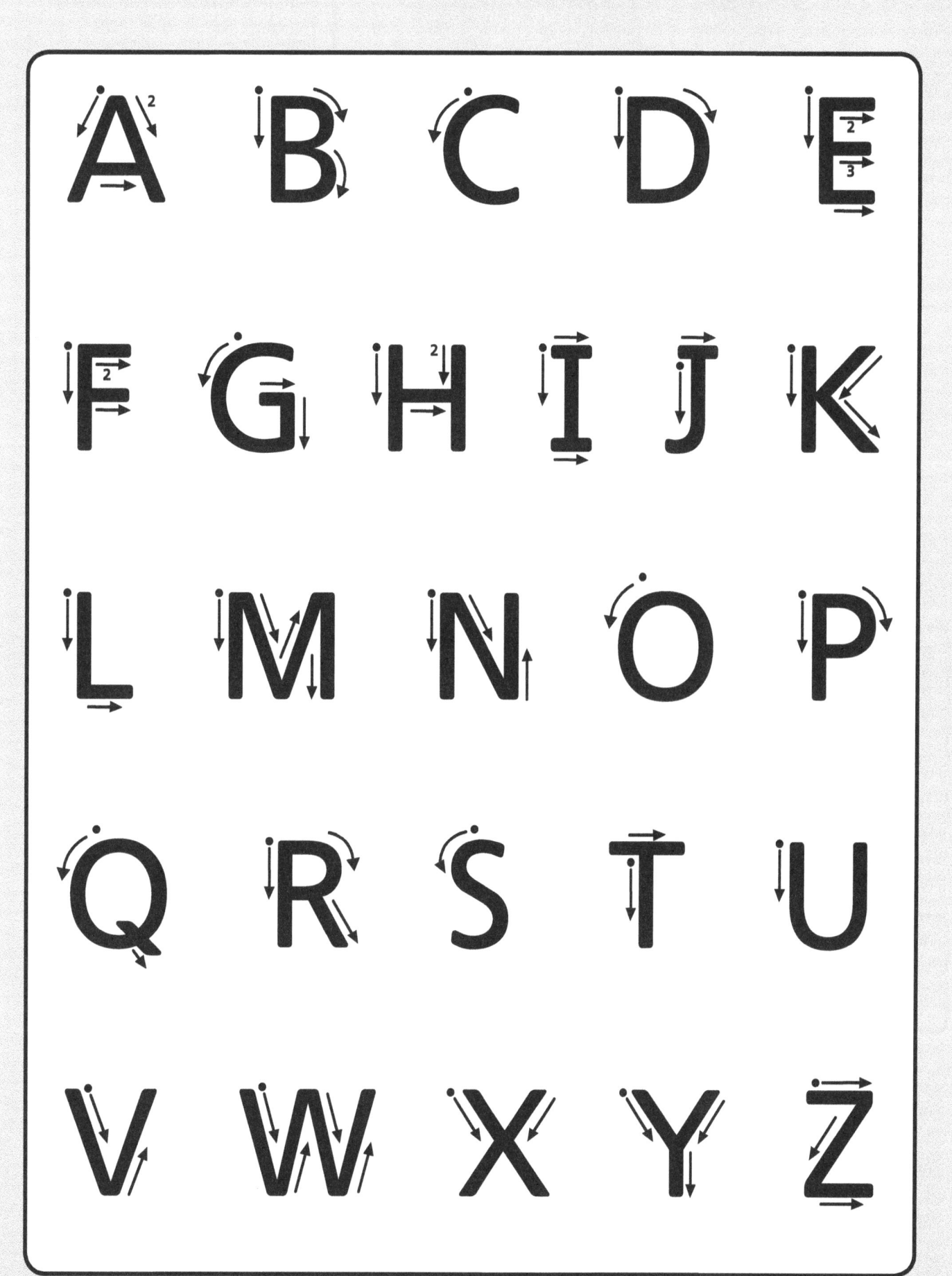

A B C D E
F G H I J K
L M N O P
Q R S T U
V W X Y Z

About the programme

Writing Logs: key features

Handwriting
An opportunity for pupils to practise key letters and letter joins.

High-interest stories and contexts
The pages cover a range of genres to develop children's awareness of different types of texts. The characters and contexts are chosen to appeal to older children, using humour and amazing facts to stimulate their own ideas. One double-page spread in the Writing Log provides the scaffold for two guided writing sessions.

Striking artwork and design
A ready-made context with a clear focus – helps children concentrate on what they want to say, and is guaranteed to appeal to the older struggling writer.

Text boxes
Small boxes of text prevent the writing task from seeming daunting.

Self-assessment 'thumbs'
The 'thumbs' at the bottom of each Writing Log page are designed for children to show at a glance how confident they felt in completing the writing activities.

Handwriting   Spelling   Phonics

BANG!   Have a go

Q. What dog has no tail?   A. A hot dog!

About the programme

Spelling / Phonics
Short activities that practise the key words used in the main writing session.

Handwriting Spelling Phonics

Have a go

Q What do sheep do on sunny days?
A Have a Baa-baa-cue!

Joke
The joke at the bottom of each page is a fun way to round off a successful writing session!

9

About the programme

Guided writing sessions: key features

All the elements of the writing process
In each 30-minute session, children are taught the skills of handwriting and spelling, constructing and punctuating sentences, and ensuring that their sentences link.

Writing Log page
The relevant Writing Log page is shown on every set of session notes, so you can quickly locate the page that you need.

At-a-glance information
A summary gives the desired outcome, the writing targets and the resources you'll need.

Warm Up
Short, fun activities get children 'tuned in' to the idea of writing, and provide an opportunity to practise the letters and spellings needed in the rest of the session.

Guiding the Writing
The main part of the session includes plenty of speaking and listening; demonstration writing; and short, supported independent writing tasks

Talk for Writing
Plenty of opportunities for group discussion and partner work help children to share ideas.

UNIT 1
BANG! SESSION 1

Outcome:
- Speech bubbles

Writing Targets:
- Handwriting: 'y' and 'p'
- Target words: 'help', 'you'
- Sentences: a question and an answer

You will need:
- Writing Logs page 1
- Whiteboards and pens
- Cards to cover spellings

Warm Up

Handwriting: 'y' and 'p' — 3 minutes
- Ask the children what the following words have in common: yes, you, your, yellow.
- Ensure that all children can hear the 'y' phoneme and say its letter name.
- Demonstrate how to form the letter 'y' correctly positioned on the line. (See page 6.)
- Ask the children to trace the letter with their finger on their whiteboards. Then ask them to write the letter five times in the Handwriting box.
- Repeat the sequence with the letter 'p'. Start by asking the children what the following words have in common: pen, pet, paper, purple.

Observe how the children hold their pens. Correct any awkward grips.

Spelling: 'you' — 3 minutes
- Explain that 'you' is an irregular word so they will learn to spell it using letter names.
- Demonstrate spelling the word 'you', saying the letter names as you write.
- Wipe the board clean and ask the children to trace the word with their finger on their whiteboard, saying the letter names as they do so.
- Ask the children to write the word on their whiteboards three times.
- Tell the children to wipe their boards clean and to write 'you' in the Spelling box three times.

Check that the children know the letter names for 'y-o-u'.

Ensure that the children write the whole word from memory.

Phonics: 'help' — 3 minutes
- Robot-speak the word 'h/e/l/p'. Then ask the children to blend the sounds to make the word.
- Listen as they robot-speak and then blend the whole word.
- As they robot-speak 'help' again, write the letters on the board.
- Wipe your board clean, then ask the children to write the word on their whiteboards and add phoneme buttons.
- Tell the children to wipe their boards clean and to write 'help' in the phoneme frame in the Phonics box, cover it and write it again twice underneath.

Guiding the Writing

Talk for Writing — 3 minutes
- Look together at the first picture. Set the scene by reading the following story starter to the group:
- *Rusty is a robot. He is old and rusty but he likes to help people. One day, Rusty saw a man with a motorbike.*
- Ask the children to discuss what is happening in the picture. What is the problem for the man? What might he be asking Rusty? What is Rusty going to do? Share the children's ideas.

About the programme

In-depth notes
Each double-page offers guidance for a 30-minute session and relates to one Writing Log page. The guidance is in detailed yet easy-to-follow notes. The written outcomes are highlighted in bold.

Brisk, well-paced lessons
Guidance on timings helps to ensure each session is well-paced so that children work in a brisk and focussed way.

Check points
Alert you to common pitfalls for children who struggle with writing.

Rounding off
Reading back with expression plays a vital role in helping children to hear and refine their writing too.

Software activity reference
Each session has linked software activities, providing the opportunity for consolidation and practice of the skills rehearsed in the group session.

Review
An opportunity for children to reflect on their own writing and evaluate their performance.

Demonstration Writing — 4 minutes
- I think the man is asking Rusty to help him and so in the speech bubble I am going to write: **Can you help?** I will start my sentence with a capital letter and finish it with a question mark, because it is a question.
- First demonstrate writing the word 'Can', with a capital letter, and ask the children to write it in the Have a go box, reminding them about the capital letter. Then, as you finish writing the sentence, ask the children to write 'you' and 'help' in the Have a go box.
- Demonstrate how to write a question mark and get the children to practise it in the Have a go box.
- Read the sentence together.

Independent Writing — 2 minutes
- Allow the children to look at your sentence for 10 seconds, and then wipe your board clean.
- Tell the children to cover their practised words.
- Ask the children to turn to a partner and to repeat the whole question and then write it in the first speech bubble.
- Check the children's work.

Remind the children that they practised the words 'you' and 'help' earlier in the session.

Talk for Writing — 2 minutes
- Look at the second picture on the page. What is Rusty doing? What do you think Rusty is saying to the man? Turn to a partner and think of a sentence that starts: 'I can ...'.
- Share the children's ideas.

Demonstration Writing — 4 minutes
- I think Rusty is saying that he can help the man. So in the speech bubble I am going to write: **I can help you.**
- Demonstrate how to write the sentence on the board.
- Ask the group if you need to put a question mark at the end. Explain that because it is not a question, you don't need a question mark, but you do need a full stop.
- Read the sentence together.

Independent Writing — 2 minutes
- Allow the children to look at your sentence for 10 seconds, and then wipe your board clean.
- Tell the children to cover their practised words.
- Ask the children to turn to a partner and repeat the sentence, and then write it in the second speech bubble. Remind them about the full stop.
- Check the children's work.

Praise children who remember the whole sentence without prompting.

Rounding Off — 2 minutes
- Invite two children to take the parts of the man and Rusty. They should read the conversation they have written with expression.
- Do they think the man is pleased that is Rusty is helping?

Review — 2 minutes
- Ask the children to tell you the difference in the punctuation between the first sentence and the second sentence? (One is a question with a question mark.)
- Challenge the children to pick one of the words from the start of the session ('you', 'help') to spell from memory on a whiteboard.
- How well do the children think they did? Ask them to colour in one of the thumbs.
- Share the joke!

1.1

About the programme

Using the *Rapid Writing* Pupil Software

Rapid Writing Pupil Software is perfect for helping children to practise the essential skills they need for writing. Using software is a fun way to practise the same skills in a different medium; it also provides an opportunity for children to work independently.

When to use the software

Each *Rapid Writing* Pupil Software session is designed to take approximately 10 to 15 minutes to complete. For children to get the most out of the experience, we suggest that the software sessions are completed after the guided writing sessions, as they revisit the same spelling, vocabulary and grammar skills. The software provides an extra chance for children to practise the skills that they have just been working on in a fun and motivating way.

What the activities involve

The activities in the *Rapid Writing* Pupil Software are short, fun and targeted at specific skills. Children may be asked to drag letter tiles to form a word, to punctuate a sentence correctly and to test their understanding of sentence structure by rearranging a jumbled sentence. Throughout the programme, two cartoon characters provide clear instructions and feedback on children's performance.

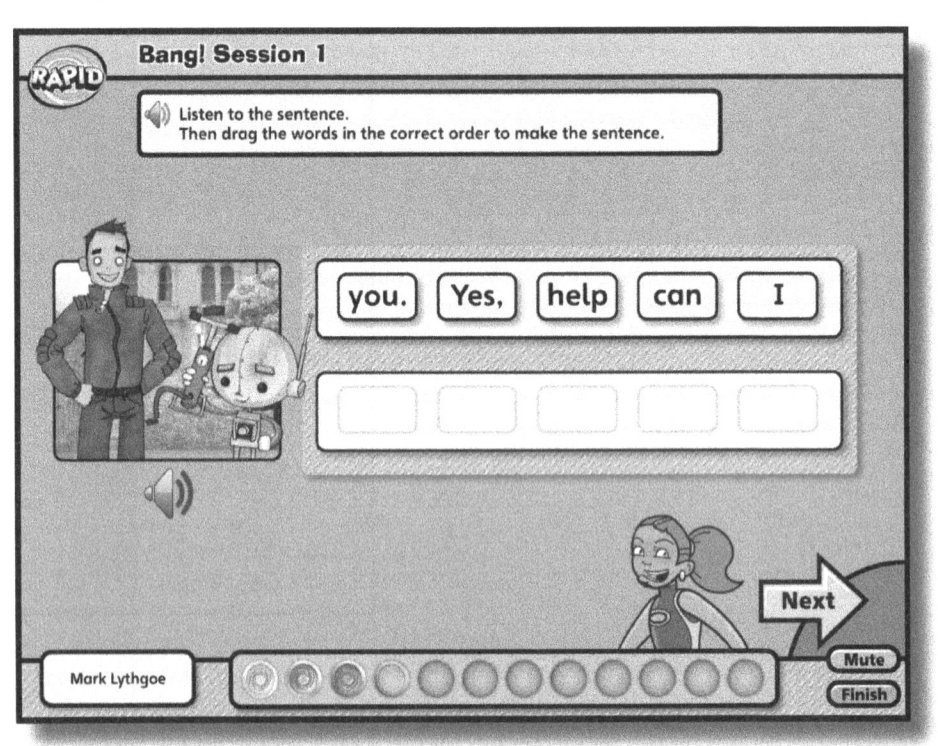

There are typically seven or eight activities in each *Rapid Writing* Pupil Software session; for each activity, the child has three attempts before the answer is shown. Children will love collecting the medals that appear at the bottom of the screen, and trying to beat their last score. A gold medal is awarded when the correct answer is entered on the first attempt; silver on the second attempt and bronze on the third attempt. The tasks are carefully levelled so that children have the best chance at success – keeping their motivation and confidence high.

About the programme

Text-to-speech technology

Selected activities employ text-to-speech technology, which allows children to hear the computer read back their own work to them. This means that children can independently practise the skills of sentence construction that they have rehearsed in the group session. In this way the text-to-speech activities make the perfect link between the scaffolded writing in the guided writing sessions and the independent writing task back in the classroom. Children will find the text-to-speech activities highly motivational, as well as reinforcing the concept of sentence construction.

In a text-to-speech activity, children see a picture or pictures on screen, with a suggestion of what they might like to write about. Clicking on the dictionary icon will give them a selection of vocabulary prompts; these are words which they may want to use in their writing but might find too difficult to spell independently. These words can either be copied using the keyboard, or can be inserted into the sentence when clicked.

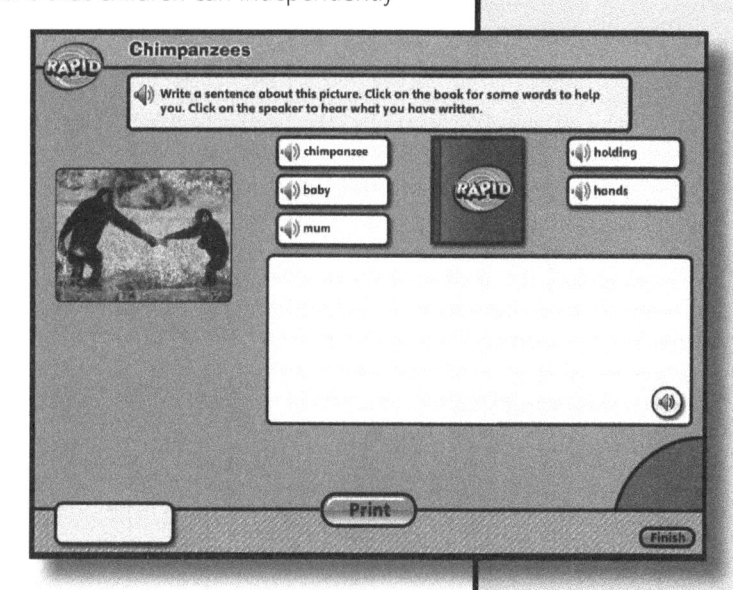

Once children have typed some text into the text box, clicking the speaker icon will play the text back to them, allowing them to hear, reflect on, and perhaps decide to improve, their own work. The text can be edited as many times as needed. The finished text can be printed off, and is saved automatically when the session has finished.

Because the computer will read back anything that is typed into it, if you have any concerns that the software might be misused you may wish to have an adult on hand to monitor what children are entering. The activities are accessed through the Teacher log-in, so can be used at your discretion.

Tracking and assessment

The *Rapid Writing* Pupil Software has an easy-to-use management system, which allows you to add pupils, allocate activities to them and monitor their progress through the programme. The software user guide contains a fuller description of how to use it; the following is an overview.

Entering pupils and allocating sessions

The 'pupil admin' function allows you to add pupil details; to arrange them in groups if you wish, and to change some activity settings for their individual needs. You can also remove pupils from the system if they have left the programme.

By default, all sessions are allocated to any child entered on the system; they are set to start at the first session of the first book. However, because we know that children may join the *Rapid Writing* programme at different times and at different stages, a simple click allows you to allocate different sessions for different children should you wish.

Monitoring progress

Once a child has completed a software session, their results are stored in the system for you to refer back to. A detailed breakdown of their performance allows you to pick up any areas of weakness and to target these at another time, if necessary. You can also decide to reallocate a session to a child if you wish to; these results are also recorded so that you can monitor children's progress over time.

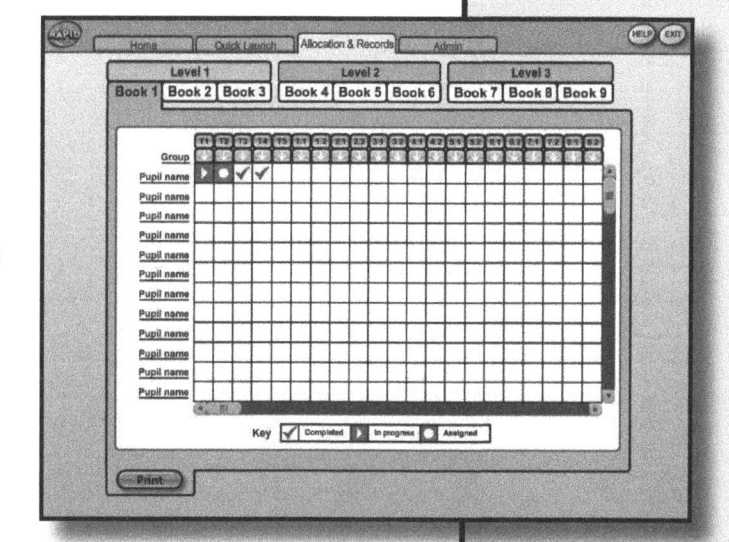

Scope and Sequence: Writing Log 7 (Units 1–10)

The number of words that children write in any session in this book is between 23 and 29.

Unit	Session	Fiction/Non-fiction	Unit title	Phonics	Spelling	Revision words	Outcome	Text type	Cross-curricular link	Rapid reading book link
1	1	Fiction	Bad Hair Day	bigger	wash, their	people	A report	Report		Series 1 Stage 5 Set A: Scary Hair
1	2	Fiction	Bad Hair Day	hairdryers, dry	doesn't		A report	Report		Series 1 Stage 5 Set A: Scary Hair
2	1	Non-fiction	Extreme Hair	important	wore, thought		A report	Report	History	Series 1 Stage 5 Set A: Scary Hair
2	2	Non-fiction	Extreme Hair	permed	colour	thought, wacky	A report	Report	History	Series 1 Stage 5 Set A: Scary Hair
3	1	Fiction	School Trouble	arms	human, four		A cartoon	Comic book		Series 1 Stage 5 Set A: Space School
3	2	Fiction	School Trouble	hand, say, mouths		something	A cartoon	Comic book		Series 1 Stage 5 Set A: Space School
4	1	Non-fiction	Ride the Twister	brave	enough	scary	A brochure for a theme park	Persuasive text		Series 1 Stage 5 Set A: Fun or Fear?
4	2	Non-fiction	Ride the Twister	slowly, upside	first	twists	A brochure for a theme park	Persuasive text		Series 1 Stage 5 Set A: Fun or Fear?
5	1	Fiction	In the Arena	grabbed	sword, toe		A diary entry	Recount	History	Series 2 Stage 5 Set A: Romans Rule!
5	2	Fiction	In the Arena	shouting	waving, scared	because	A diary entry	Recount	History	Series 2 Stage 5 Set A: Romans Rule!

Scope and Sequence: Writing Log 7 (Units 1–10)

Unit	Session	Fiction/Non-fiction	Unit title	Phonics	Spelling	Revision words	Outcome	Text type	Cross-curricular link	Rapid reading book link
6	1	Non-fiction	Gladiators		exciting, towards, everyone		Live commentary on a gladiator fight	Recount	History	Series 2 Stage 5 Set A: Romans Rule!
6	2	Non-fiction	Gladiators	dies, means	thumb		Live commentary on a gladiator fight	Recount	History	Series 2 Stage 5 Set A: Romans Rule!
7	1	Fiction	Drum Beat	row, drum, beat		though	A diary entry	Story with a historical setting	History	Series 2 Stage 5 Set A: Viking Raiders!
7	2	Fiction	Drum Beat	stopped, which, cheer		something	A diary entry	Story with a historical setting	History	Series 2 Stage 5 Set A: Viking Raiders!
8	1	Non-fiction	Vile Vikings	rowed, longship	Vikings		An audio commentary in a Viking museum	Information text	History	Series 2 Stage 5 Set A: Viking Raiders!
8	2	Non-fiction	Vile Vikings	still, rotten, smelly		sometimes	An audio commentary in a Viking museum	Information text	History	Series 2 Stage 5 Set A: Viking Raiders!
9	1	Fiction	Call 999	lights	wondered, putting		A police statement	Report	Citizenship	Series 2 Stage 5 Set B: Power Pack
9	2	Fiction	Call 999	began, notes	instead		A police statement	Report	Citizenship	Series 2 Stage 5 Set B: Power Pack
10	1	Non-fiction	Stop the Smuggling!	belt	caught	wearing	A poster	Persuasive text	Citizenship	Series 2 Stage 5 Set B: Secrets and Sounds
10	2	Assessment	Write It!	Revision of all skills covered in Writing Log 7						Series 1 Stage 5 Set A: Fun or Fear; Series 2 Stage 5 Set A: Romans Rule; Series 2 Stage 5 Set A: Viking Raiders

Scope and Sequence: Writing Log 8 (Units 11–20)

The number of words that children write in any session in this book is between 23 and 32.

Unit	Session	Fiction/Non-fiction	Unit title	Phonics	Spelling	Revision words	Outcome	Text type	Cross-curricular link	Rapid reading book link
11	1	Fiction	Cheat!	cheat	children, water		A newspaper report	Report	Citizenship	Series 2 Stage 5 Set B: Heat Wave
11	2	Fiction	Cheat!	sprayed, arrested, gave		bravery	A newspaper report	Report	Citizenship	Series 2 Stage 5 Set B: Heat Wave
12	1	Non-fiction	Get the Message!	letter, sending	message		An online encyclopaedia entry	Information text	Design and Technology	Series 2 Stage 5 Set B: Over and Out
12	2	Non-fiction	Get the Message!	quick	anywhere, million	text	An online encyclopaedia entry	Information text	Design and Technology	Series 2 Stage 5 Set B: Over and Out
13	1	Fiction	Mole Man	speed	trouble, school		A fact file	Information text		Series 1 Stage 5 Set B: Mountain Madness
13	2	Fiction	Mole Man	mole, track		twisting	A superhero adventure	Adventure story		Series 1 Stage 5 Set B: Mountain Madness
14	1	Non-fiction	Climbing Everest	crack, deep	climb		Argument against climbing Mount Everest	Persuasive text	Geography	Series 1 Stage 5 Set B: Mountain Madness
14	2	Non-fiction	Climbing Everest	stand	hero	world	Argument for climbing Mount Everest	Persuasive text	Geography	Series 1 Stage 5 Set B: Mountain Madness
15	1	Fiction	Save the Pole!	melting, under	pizza	because	A superhero comic	Adventure story		Series 1 Stage 5 Set B: Antarctic Adventures
15	2	Fiction	Save the Pole!	hole, freezes	oven	faster	A superhero comic	Adventure story		Series 1 Stage 5 Set B: Antarctic Adventures

Scope and Sequence: Writing Log 8 (Units 11–20)

Unit	Session	Fiction/Non-fiction	Unit title	Phonics	Spelling	Revision words	Outcome	Text type	Cross-curricular link	Rapid reading book link
16	1	Non-fiction	Race to the Pole		sledges, ourselves, believe		A diary entry	Recount	Geography	Series 1 Stage 5 Set B: Antarctic Adventures
16	2	Non-fiction	Race to the Pole	hope	nothing	our	A diary entry	Recount	Geography	Series 1 Stage 5 Set B: Antarctic Adventures
17	1	Fiction	Unsolved Mystery	started, smoke	scared		An article for a magazine about unsolved mysteries	Report		Series 1 Stage 6 Set A: Ghostly
17	2	Fiction	Unsolved Mystery	suddenly, thank	appeared		An article for a magazine about unsolved mysteries	Report		Series 1 Stage 6 Set A: Ghostly
18	1	Non-fiction	The Loch Ness Monster	monster	guess		Email correspondence	Recount		Series 1 Stage 6 Set A: Dangers of the Deep
18	2	Non-fiction	The Loch Ness Monster	wait, photo, date			Email correspondence	Recount		Series 1 Stage 6 Set A: Dangers of the Deep
19	1	Fiction	A Real Alien?	lied, about	alien		A report	Report		Series 1 Stage 6 Set A: Mystery in the Skies
19	2	Fiction	A Real Alien?	clever	only, sure	everyone	A report	Report		Series 1 Stage 6 Set A: Mystery in the Skies
20	1	Non-fiction	UFOs	contact	disappeared, before		A questionnaire	Information text	Science	Series 1 Stage 6 Set A: Mystery in the Skies
20	2	Composite	Write It!	Revision of all skills covered in Writing Log 8						Series 2 Stage 5 Set B: Heat Wave; Series 1 Stage 6 Set A: Ghostly; Series 1 Stage 6 Set A: Dangers of the Deep

Scope and Sequence: Writing Log 9 (Units 21–30)

The number of words that children write in any session in this book is between 26 and 38.

Unit	Session	Fiction/Non-fiction	Unit title	Phonics	Spelling	Revision words	Outcome	Text type	Cross-curricular link	Rapid reading book link
21	1	Fiction	Merlin Mystery	trainer	voice, whispered		Two dramatic paragraphs	Story with a familiar setting	History	Series 2 Stage 6 Set A: Legends of Stonehenge
21	2	Fiction	Merlin Mystery	darker, stones	front	getting	Two dramatic paragraphs	Story with a familiar setting	History	Series 2 Stage 6 Set A: Legends of Stonehenge
22	1	Non-fiction	Stonehenge	roads	built, machines		An explanation	Explanation text	History	Series 2 Stage 6 Set A: Legends of Stonehenge
22	2	Non-fiction	Stonehenge	hundreds, dragged	rollers		An explanation	Explanation text	History	Series 2 Stage 6 Set A: Legends of Stonehenge
23	1	Fiction	Danger at Sea	crashes, knocked, filling			A plan of a dramatic plot	Adventure story		Series 1 Stage 6 Set B: Trapped!
23	2	Fiction	Danger at Sea	last	won't, manages		A plan of a dramatic plot	Adventure story		Series 1 Stage 6 Set B: Trapped!
24	1	Non-fiction	Fire!	door, open, crawl			A bulleted list of instructions	Instructions	Science / Citizenship	Series 1 Stage 6 Set B: Trapped!
24	2	Non-fiction	Fire!	window, clothes	handle		A bulleted list of instructions	Instructions	Science / Citizenship	Series 1 Stage 6 Set B: Trapped!
25	1	Fiction	Robbers!		later, evening, I'll		Writing dialogue to move action forward	Adventure story		Series 1 Stage 6 Set B: Animal Heroes
25	2	Fiction	Robbers!	phone	heard, noise	through	Writing dialogue to move action forward	Adventure story		Series 1 Stage 6 Set B: Animal Heroes

Scope and Sequence: Writing Log 9 (Units 21–30)

Unit	Session	Fiction/Non-fiction	Unit title	Phonics	Spelling	Revision words	Outcome	Text type	Cross-curricular link	Rapid reading book link
26	1	Non-fiction	Man's Best Friend	safe	blind, guide		A personal account	Recount	Citizenship	Series 1 Stage 6 Set B: Animal Heroes
26	2	Non-fiction	Man's Best Friend	stuck, floor	hours		A personal account	Recount	Citizenship	Series 1 Stage 6 Set B: Animal Heroes
27	1	Fiction	The Clean Team	those, maggots, disgusting		crawling	Dialogue in a reality TV show	Playscript		Series 2 Stage 6 Set B: The Yuk Factor
27	2	Fiction	The Clean Team	clean, room	untidy		Dialogue in a reality TV show	Playscript		Series 2 Stage 6 Set B: The Yuk Factor
28	1	Non-fiction	Sneezes Spread Diseases!	matter	cover, sneeze		A leaflet to persuade people not to spread diseases	Persuasive text	Science	Series 2 Stage 6 Set B: The Yuk Factor
28	2	Non-fiction	Sneezes Spread Diseases!		breathe, spread, yourself		A leaflet to persuade people not to spread diseases	Persuasive text	Science	Series 2 Stage 6 Set B: The Yuk Factor
29	1	Fiction	Have You Got Talent?	groaned	judges	across	The climax of a story	Story with a familiar setting		Series 2 Stage 6 Set B: Music Makers
29	2	Fiction	Have You Got Talent?		shook, another	last	The climax of a story	Story with a familiar setting		Series 2 Stage 6 Set B: Music Makers
30	1	Non-fiction	Football Facts	agreed, England	rules		A time line	Information text	History	Series 2 Stage 6 Set B: On The Ball
30	2	Revision	Write It!	Revision of all skills covered in Writing Log 9						Series 2 Stage 6 Set A: Legends of Stonehenge; Series 2 Stage 6 Set B: The Yuk Factor; Series 2 Stage 6 Set B: Music Makers

UNIT 1

BAD HAIR DAY: *SESSION 1*

Outcome:
- A report

Writing targets:
- Target words: 'wash', 'their', 'bigger'
- Revision word: 'people'
- Sentences: three bullet points, a summary sentence

You will need:
- Writing Logs page 1
- Whiteboards and pens
- Card for covering spellings

Warm Up

Spelling: 'wash' — 2 minutes
- Explain that 'wash' is an irregular word so they will learn to spell it using letter names.
- Demonstrate how to spell the word 'wash', saying the letter names as you write.
- Wipe your board clean and ask the children to trace the word with their finger on their whiteboard, saying the letter names as they do so. Then ask them to write 'wash' on their whiteboards.
- Tell the children to wipe their boards clean, then write the word three times in the Spelling box.

The word 'wash' is irregular as the letter 'a' is making an 'o' sound.

Spelling: 'their' — 2 minutes
- Explain that 'their' is an irregular word so they will learn to spell it using letter names.
- Demonstrate how to spell the word 'their', saying the letter names as you write. Tell the children that this spelling of 'their' always refers to something belonging to someone or something.
- Wipe your board clean and ask the children to trace the word with their finger on their whiteboard, saying the letter names as they do so. Then ask them to write 'their' on their whiteboards.
- Tell the children to wipe their boards clean, then write the word three times in the Spelling box.

Children might find it useful to remember the spelling of 'their' by thinking of 'the' + 'ir'.

Phonics: 'bigger' — 2 minutes
- Robot-speak the word 'b/i/gg/er' then ask the children to blend the phonemes to make the word.
- Listen as they robot-speak and then blend the whole word.
- As they robot-speak 'bigger' again, write the letters on the board.
- Wipe your board clean, then ask the children to write the word on their whiteboards and add phoneme buttons.
- Tell the children to wipe their boards clean and to write 'bigger' three times in the Phonics box.

Point out that the letters 'gg' represent one phoneme, and the letters 'er' represent one phoneme.

Guiding the Writing

Talk for Writing — 3 minutes
- *Look at the picture. It shows the aliens Ziggy and Pod who have been sent to Earth to find out how humans live, but they always misunderstand what is going on. Ziggy and Pod are going to send a Mission Report back to their planet explaining what happens in a hairdresser's. Ziggy and Pod think that hairdressers are where you go to get your brain washed! They also think that it hurts when your hair is cut!*
- Tell the children they will be writing as if they were Ziggy and Pod so they will be using 'We'. Explain that the report will start: 'We think that:'.

20

- *Turn to a partner and think about what Ziggy and Pod might write. Start the first bullet point: 'people wash …'. Start the second bullet point: 'they let people cut …'.*
- Share the children's ideas.

Demonstration Writing   4 minutes
- *For the first bullet point I am going to write:* **people wash their brains**. *Watch as I write the word 'people'. As I write it, say the letter names. I have not put a full stop because it is not the end of a sentence.*
- *For the second bullet point I am going to write:* **they let people cut their hair**. *As I write 'people' I want you to practise it in the Have a go box. I need to show how wrong Ziggy and Pod are. They think it hurts when your hair is cut, so I am going to add in brackets:* **(that must hurt!)**.
- Read your writing together. Point out that you have put an exclamation mark after 'that must hurt' to show how awful the aliens think it must be to have your hair cut.

> Ask the children if they know a way to remember how to spell 'people'. (Pronounce it 'pe-ople'.)

Independent Writing   3 minutes
- Allow the children 20 seconds to study your writing then wipe your board clean, leaving the word 'brains' for them to copy.
- Ask the children to turn to a partner and read the two bullet points on the board.
- Tell them to cover their practised words and then write the bullet points.
- Check the children's work.

Talk for Writing   3 minutes
- *Now we are going to sum up what Ziggy and Pod think about people.*
- *What did we know about Ziggy and Pod? (They always get things wrong.) When they see the hairdryers they think they are machines that make your brain bigger!*
- *Turn to a partner and think of a bullet point that will describe what Ziggy and Pod think the hairdryers are used for. Start the bullet point: 'they use hairdryers …'.*
- *Then think of a sentence that sums up what Ziggy and Pod think about people. Start your sentence: 'People are …'.*
- Share the children's ideas.

Demonstration Writing   3 minutes
- *I am going to write:* **they use hairdryers to make their brains bigger**. *As I write, I want you to practise 'use' in the Have a go box.*
- *I am going to write:* **People are very silly**. *This time I will start 'People' with a capital letter. Why? (because it's at the start of a sentence)*
- Read the sentence together.

> Remind the children that they practised 'used' in a previous session. The word 'use' is just 'used' without the 'd'.

Independent Writing   2 minutes
- Allow the children 20 seconds to study your sentence, then wipe your board clean, leaving the word 'hairdryers' for them to copy.
- Ask the children to turn to a partner and repeat what they are going to write.
- Tell them to cover their practised words and then to write the final bullet point and the summing up sentence on the final line.
- Check the children's work.

Rounding Off   3 minutes
- What did Ziggy and Pod get wrong? (people wash their brains; it hurts to have your hair cut; hairdryers make your brains bigger)
- What might Ziggy and Pod think a car wash is? (where cars are taken for a shower)

Review   3 minutes
- Write the word 'big' on your board. Then write 'bigger'. Ask the children what has changed. (double the 'g' before adding 'er') Ask the children to tell you how to spell 'biggest'. Wipe your board clean and challenge children to write 'big', 'bigger' and 'biggest' on their whiteboards.
- Ask the children why we did not start the bullet points with capital letters. (It was not the start of a sentence.)
- How well do the children think they did? Ask them to colour in one of the thumbs.
- Share the joke!

1.1

UNIT 1

BAD HAIR DAY: *SESSION 2*

Outcome:
- A report

Writing targets:
- Target words: 'doesn't', 'hairdryers', 'dry'
- Sentences: three bullet points, a summary sentence

You will need:
- Writing Logs page 2
- Whiteboards and pens
- Card for covering spellings

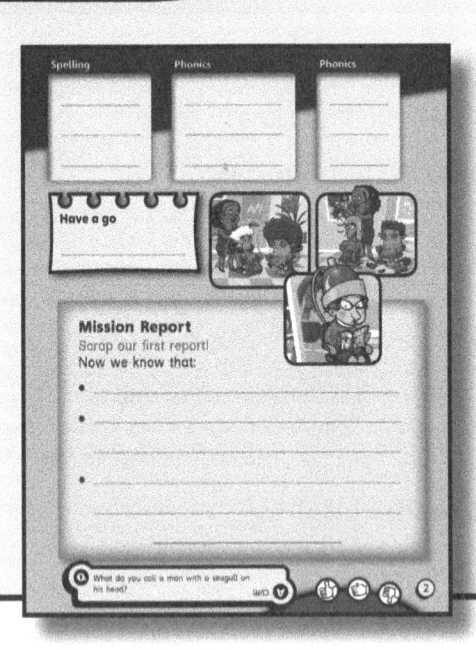

Warm Up

Spelling: 'doesn't' — 2 minutes
- Explain that 'doesn't' is an irregular word so they will learn to spell it using letter names.
- Demonstrate how to spell the word 'doesn't', saying the letter names as you write. Draw attention to the apostrophe and ask the children why it is needed. (To show that the letter 'o' is missing.)
- Wipe your board clean and ask the children to trace the word with their finger on their whiteboard, saying the letter names as they do so. Then ask them to write 'doesn't' on their whiteboards.
- Tell the children to wipe their boards clean, then write the word three times in the Spelling box.

> Ensure that children put the apostrophe in the right place.

Phonics: 'hairdryers' — 2 minutes
- Break the word 'hairdryers' into two smaller words: 'hair/dryers'.
- Robot-speak the word 'h/air/d/r/y/ers' then ask the children to blend the phonemes to make the word.
- Listen as they robot-speak and then blend the whole word.
- As they robot-speak 'hairdryers' again, write the letters on the board.
- Wipe your board clean, then ask the children to write the word on their whiteboards and add phoneme buttons.
- Tell the children to wipe their boards clean and to write 'hairdryers' three times in the Phonics box.

> Ensure that the children understand that 'air' makes one sound.

Phonics: 'dry' — 2 minutes
- Ask the children to find the word 'dry' in the word 'hairdryers'.
- Robot-speak the word 'd/r/igh' then ask the children to blend the phonemes to make the word.
- Listen as they robot-speak and then blend the whole word.
- As they robot-speak 'dry' again, write the letters on the board.
- Wipe your board clean, then ask the children to write the word on their whiteboards and add phoneme buttons (d/r/y).
- Tell the children to wipe their boards clean and to write 'dry' three times in the Phonics box.

> Ensure that children understand that the letter 'y' is making the long vowel 'i' sound.

Guiding the Writing

Talk for Writing — 3 minutes
- *Reread the report that Ziggy and Pod sent to their home planet last time. Now they are going to send a second report. They have realised that they got things wrong in their first report so now they're going to explain what really happens in a hairdresser's on Earth.*

22

- Tell the children that they will be writing as if they were Ziggy and Pod so they will be using 'We'. Explain that they are going to write another list with bulleted points after the opening of the report, which is: 'Now we know that:'.
- *Turn to a partner and think about what Ziggy and Pod might write. Start the first point: 'people wash ...'. Start the second point: 'it doesn't hurt ...'.*
- Share the children's ideas.

Demonstration Writing   4 minutes
- *I am going to write:* **people wash their hair**. *As I write 'their' I want you to write it in the Have a go box. Why have I not put a full stop? (because it is not the end of a sentence)*
- *Next I am going to write:* **it doesn't hurt to have your hair cut**. *Why do I need an apostrophe in the word 'doesn't'?*
- Read the start of the report together.

> Ensure that children use the right 'their' (not 'there').

Independent Writing   2 minutes
- Allow the children 20 seconds to study your writing then wipe your board clean.
- Ask the children to turn to a partner and repeat the start of the report.
- Tell them to cover their practised words and then to write the start of the report.
- Check the children's work.

Talk for Writing   4 minutes
- *Now we are going to write a third bullet point and sum up what Ziggy and Pod think about people.*
- *What are they going to say about hairdryers? (They dry hair.)*
- *Turn to a partner and think of a bullet point starting: 'people use hairdryers to ...'.*
- *Then think of a sentence that sums up Ziggy and Pod's thoughts about people. What did they say in their first report? ('People are silly.') Start your sentence: 'People are not ...'.*
- Share the children's ideas.

Demonstration Writing   3 minutes
- *I am going to write:* **people use hairdryers to dry their hair.** *As I write, I want you to write 'hair' in the Have a go box.*
- *Finally I am going to write:* **People are not so silly.** *This time I will start 'People' with a capital letter. Why? (because it is at the start of a sentence)*
- Read the sentences together.

> Point out that you have put a full stop because it is now the end of the sentence you started before the colon ('Now we know that').

Independent Writing   2 minutes
- Allow the children 20 seconds to study your writing then wipe your board clean.
- Ask the children to turn to a partner and repeat what they are going to write.
- Tell them to cover their practised words and then to write the final bullet point and the summing up sentence.
- Check the children's work.

Rounding Off   3 minutes
- Ask the children what they think the aliens back on Ziggy and Pod's home planet will think about them changing their minds. (They might think that Ziggy and Pod are the silly ones.)
- Are Ziggy and Pod good at their job of finding out how humans live? Why or why not?

Review   3 minutes
- Write the words 'drying' and 'dries' on the board. Ask the children what is different between 'dry', and 'dries'. ('Dries' only has one syllable so we drop the 'y' before adding 'es'.) Wipe your board and challenge the children to write 'dry' and 'dries'.
- Ask the children to tell you what punctuation we used after the heading. (a colon) Why? (to show something was coming next)
- How well do the children think they did? Ask them to colour in one of the thumbs.
- Share the joke!

1.2

UNIT 2

EXTREME HAIR: *SESSION 1*

Outcome:
- A report

Writing targets:
- Target words: 'wore', 'important', 'thought'
- Sentences: three simple sentences, one complex sentence starting with 'If'

You will need:
- Writing Logs page 3
- Whiteboards and pens
- Card for covering spellings

Warm Up

Spelling: 'wore' — *2 minutes*
- Explain that 'wore' is an irregular word so they will learn to spell it using letter names.
- Demonstrate how to spell the word 'wore', saying the letter names as you write.
- Wipe your board clean and ask the children to trace the word with their finger on their whiteboard, saying the letter names as they do so. Then ask them to write 'wore' on their whiteboards.
- Tell the children to wipe their boards clean, then write the word three times in the Spelling box.

Phonics: 'important' — *2 minutes*
- Say the word 'important', breaking it up into three syllables. Ask the children how many syllables they can hear in the word (three).
- Robot-speak the word 'i/m/p/or/t/a/n/t' then ask the children to blend the phonemes to make the word.
- Listen as they robot-speak and then blend the whole word.
- As they robot-speak 'important' again, write the letters on the board.
- Wipe your board clean, then ask the children to write the word on their whiteboards and add phoneme buttons.
- Tell the children to wipe their boards clean and write 'important' three times in the Phonics box.

Spelling: 'thought' — *2 minutes*

> If children are familiar with the letters 'ough' representing the sound 'or', then this could be taught using phonics.

- Explain that 'thought' is an irregular word so they will learn to spell it using letter names.
- Demonstrate how to spell the word 'thought', saying the letter names as you write.
- Wipe your board clean and ask the children to trace the word with their finger on their whiteboard, saying the letter names as they do so. Then ask them to write 'thought' on their whiteboards.
- Tell the children to wipe their boards clean, then write the word three times in the Spelling box.

Guiding the Writing

Talk for Writing — *3 minutes*
- Look at the title: '18th Century'. Ask the children if they know what this means. Explain that we are now in the 21st century, so the 18th century was 300 years ago.
- Look at the picture. Explain that 300 years ago people wore wigs made from horsehair to cover up their dirty, smelly hair because in those days people did not wash their hair.
- *Turn to a partner and think of a sentence that tells the reader what the wigs were made from. Start the sentence: 'People wore wigs ...'.*
- Share the children's ideas.

Demonstration Writing · 2 minutes
- *I am going to write:* **People wore wigs made from horsehair.** *As I write 'wigs', I want you to sound out the four phonemes w/i/g/s. Then write the word in the Have a go box.*
- Read the sentence together.

Independent Writing · 2 minutes
- Allow the children 10 seconds to study your sentence, then wipe your board clean, leaving the word 'horsehair' for them to copy.
- Ask the children to turn to a partner and repeat what they are going to write.
- Tell them to cover their practised words and then to write the sentence.
- Check the children's work.

Talk for Writing · 2 minutes
- *In those days, the bigger your wig the more important you were.*
- *Turn to a partner and think of a sentence starting: 'If you were very important …'.*
- Share the children's ideas.

Demonstration Writing · 2 minutes
- *I am going to write:* **If you were very important you wore a very big wig.** *As I write, I want you to write 'were' in the Have a go box.*
- Read the sentence together.

Independent Writing · 2 minutes
- Allow the children 10 seconds to study your sentence, then wipe your board clean.
- Ask the children to turn to a partner and repeat what they are going to write.
- Tell them to cover their practised words and then to write the sentence.
- Check the children's work.

Talk for Writing · 2 minutes
- *Now we are going write two sentences. Another reason why people wore wigs was that they thought that the wigs looked cool! Finally we will ask the reader if they think the wigs made people look cool.*
- *Turn to a partner and think of a sentence starting: 'They thought …'. Then think of a question starting: 'What do …'.*
- Share the children's ideas.

Demonstration Writing · 2 minutes
- *First I am going to write:* **They thought they looked cool.**
- *I will finish by writing the question:* **What do you think?**
- Read the sentences together.

Independent Writing · 2 minutes
- Allow the children 20 seconds to study your sentences, then wipe your board clean.
- Ask the children to turn to a partner and repeat what they are going to write.
- Tell them to cover their practised words and to write the sentences, making sure they write the final sentence in the box next to the picture.
- Check the children's work.

Rounding Off · 3 minutes
- Ask the children if they can remember three reasons why people wore wigs in the 18th century. (To cover up their smelly hair, to look important, to look cool.)
- Ask the children what hairstyles they think do look cool today.

Review · 2 minutes
- Write the word 'important' on your whiteboard and invite children to break it up into syllables. Why it is a good idea to break words into syllables when you come to write them? (It is easier to think about how to spell each syllable in turn.)
- How well do the children think they did? Ask them to colour in one of the thumbs.
- Share the joke!

UNIT 2

EXTREME HAIR: *SESSION 2*

Outcome:
- A report

Writing targets:
- Target words: 'colour', 'permed'
- Revision words: 'thought', 'wacky'
- Sentences: four simple sentences, one question

You will need:
- Writing Logs page 4
- Whiteboards and pens
- Card for covering spellings

Warm Up

Spelling: 'colour' *2 minutes*
- Explain that 'colour' is an irregular word so they will learn to spell it using letter names.
- Demonstrate how to spell the word 'colour', saying the letter names as you write.
- Wipe your board clean and ask the children to trace the word with their finger on their whiteboard, saying the letter names as they do so. Then ask them to write 'colour' on their whiteboards.
- Tell the children to wipe their boards clean, then write the word three times in the Spelling box.

Phonics: 'permed' *2 minutes*
- Robot-speak the word 'p/er/m/d' then ask the children to blend the phonemes to make the word.
- Listen as they robot-speak and then blend the whole word.
- As they robot-speak 'permed' again, write the letters on the board.
- Wipe your board clean, then ask the children to write the word on their whiteboards and add phoneme buttons (p/er/m/ed).
- Tell the children to wipe their boards clean and to write 'permed' three times in the Phonics box.

> Ensure that children understand that the sound 'd' at the end of the word is made with the letters 'ed'.

Revision: 'thought' *1 minute*
- Remind the children that they learned to spell 'thought' in an earlier session. Write it on your board as you say the letter names. Point at each letter and ask the children to say the letter names.
- Tell the children to study the word for five seconds. Wipe your board clean, then ask them to write the word in the Have a go box.

Guiding the Writing

Talk for Writing *4 minutes*
- Look at the title: '20th Century'. Explain that we are now in the 21st century so the end of the 20th century was only a few years ago.
- *Look at the first photograph. This is a very wacky hairstyle that some people had about 30 years ago. People who did this were called 'punks'. They had to use hair gel to make their hair stand up. Some people liked to dye their hair different colours and some people shaved their heads and just kept a bit of hair.*
- *Turn to a partner and think of a sentence that tells the reader that some people had wacky hairstyles, starting: 'Some people had …'.*
- *Then tell the reader that they put lots of colour in their hair. Start this sentence: 'They put lots …'.*
- Share the children's ideas.

26

Demonstration Writing 3 minutes
- *I am going to write:* **Some people had wacky hair.** *As I write the word 'wacky', I want you to study it. Write 'wacky' in the Have a go box.*
- *Now I am going to write:* **They put lots of colour in their hair.**
- Read the sentences together.

> Remind the children that 'ck' is one sound and the 'ee' sound is made with the letter 'y'.

Independent Writing 2 minutes
- Allow the children 20 seconds to study your sentences, then wipe your board clean.
- Ask the children to turn to a partner and repeat what they are going to write.
- Tell them to cover their practised words and then to write the sentences next to the photo of the punk.
- Check the children's work.

> Remind the children to write 'They' with a capital letter because it is at the start of a sentence.

Talk for Writing 3 minutes
- *Look at the second picture. Thirty years ago, some famous footballers started to perm their hair. They thought this made them look very cool.*
- *Turn to a partner and think of two sentences. The first sentence should start: 'Some men even …'. The second sentence should start: 'They thought they looked …'.*
- Share the children's ideas.

Demonstration Writing 3 minutes
- *I am going to write:* **Some men even permed their hair.** *As I write, I want you to practise 'even' in the Have a go box. Then I am going to write:* **They thought they looked cool!** *I have finished with an exclamation mark because not everyone thought they looked cool.*
- Read the sentences together.

Independent Writing 2 minutes
- Allow the children 20 seconds to study your sentences then wipe your board clean.
- Ask the children to turn to a partner and repeat what they are going to write.
- Tell them to cover their practised words and then to write the sentences next to the photo of the footballer with permed hair.
- Check the children's work.

Demonstration Writing 2 minutes
- *Now we are going to finish by asking the reader if they think these people look cool. I am going to write the question:* **What do you think?** *As I write, I want you to practise 'What' in the Have a go box.*
- Read the sentence together.

Independent Writing 2 minutes
- Allow the children 10 seconds to study your sentence, then wipe your board clean.
- Ask the children to turn to a partner and repeat what they are going to write.
- Tell them to cover their practised words and to write the question in the box.
- Check the children's work.

Rounding Off 2 minutes
- Ask the children if they would like to have any of the hairstyles in the photos. Do they think the people looked cool?
- What hairstyle do they think is the wackiest out of the two sessions? Why?

Review 2 minutes
- Challenge the children to spell 'colour' on their whiteboards.
- Why did they end each session with a question? (to engage the reader)
- How well do the children think they did? Ask them to colour in one of the thumbs.
- Share the joke!

2.2

UNIT 3

SCHOOL TROUBLE: *SESSION 1*

Outcome:
- A cartoon

Writing targets:
- Target words: 'human', 'arms', 'four'
- Sentences: two statements, a question, a two-word sentence

You will need:
- Writing Logs page 5
- Whiteboards and pens
- Card for covering spellings

Warm Up

Spelling: 'human' — 2 minutes

- Explain that 'human' is an irregular word so they will learn to spell it using letter names.
- Demonstrate how to spell the word 'human', saying the letter names as you write.
- Wipe your board clean and ask the children to trace the word with their finger on their whiteboard, saying the letter names as they do so. Then ask them to write 'human' on their whiteboards.
- Tell the children to wipe their boards clean, then write the word three times in the Spelling box.

> The word 'human' is irregular as the letter 'u' makes the sound 'you'.

Phonics: 'arms' — 2 minutes

- Robot-speak the word 'ar/m/s' then ask the children to blend the phonemes to make the word.
- Listen as they robot-speak and then blend the whole word.
- As they robot-speak 'arms' again, write the letters on the board.
- Wipe your board clean, then ask the children to write the word on their whiteboards and add phoneme buttons.
- Tell the children to wipe their boards clean and to write 'arms' three times in the Phonics box.

> Ensure that children understand that the letters 'ar' are one phoneme.

Spelling: 'four' — 2 minutes

- Explain that 'four' is an irregular word so they will learn to spell it using letter names.
- Demonstrate how to spell the word 'four', saying the letter names as you write.
- Wipe your board clean and ask the children to trace the word with their finger on their whiteboard, saying the letter names as they do so. Then ask them to write 'four' on their whiteboards.
- Tell the children to wipe their boards clean, then write the word three times in the Spelling box.

Guiding the Writing

Talk for Writing — 3 minutes

- Remind the children that they met the aliens Ziggy and Pod in an earlier session. Can they remember why Ziggy and Pod have been sent to Earth? (To find out about humans.) But what always happens to their plans? (They always misunderstand what is going on.)
- In this cartoon Ziggy and Pod are going into a human school. They don't want anyone to realise that they are aliens so they have to wear a disguise. Pod sometimes forgets what humans look like so the first thing he is going to ask Ziggy is if his disguise is OK. Look closely at the picture. What part of his human disguise has Pod, the alien on the left, got wrong? (He has four legs.)

28

- *Turn to a partner and think of a question that Pod will ask Ziggy, starting: 'Do I look …'. Then think of a sentence that Pod will say to describe what his disguise is like, starting: 'I have one head …'.*
- Share the children's ideas.

Demonstration Writing   4 minutes
- *In the first speech bubble I am going to write:* **Do I look like a human?** *What punctuation will I put after 'human'?* (a question mark)
- *Then I am going to write:* **I have one head, two arms and four legs.** *As I write the words 'one' and 'head' I want you to write them in the Have a go box. I have put a comma after the word 'head' because we separate items in a list with a comma.*
- Read the sentences together.

> Remind the children that they have met 'leg' in a previous session. The word 'legs' is just 'leg' with an 's' at the end.

Independent Writing   3 minutes
- Allow the children 20 seconds to study your sentences, then wipe your board clean.
- Ask the children to turn to a partner and repeat what they are going to write.
- Tell them to cover their practised words and then write the sentences in Pod's speech bubble.
- Check the children's work.

Talk for Writing   3 minutes
- *Now we are going to write Ziggy's reply. He likes to think that he is much better at pretending to be human than Pod, so first of all he's going to say 'You fool!', then he is going to correct what Pod says. So what will Ziggy say Pod should have?* (one head, two arms and two legs)
- *Turn to a partner and think of a sentence starting: 'Humans have …'.*
- Share the children's ideas.

> Remind the children that they have met 'foolish' in a previous session. The word 'fool' is just 'foolish' without the 'ish' at the end.

Demonstration Writing   3 minutes
- *I am going to write:* **You fool!** *As I write, I want you to write 'fool' in the Have a go box. Because it is quite a rude thing to say, will add an exclamation mark.*
- *Next I am going to write:* **Humans have one head, two arms and two legs.** *Why have I put a comma after 'head'?* (because it is a list) *As I write the word 'two', I want you to write it in your Have a go box. How can I show a reader that Ziggy would say the word 'two' with emphasis?* (underline the word)
- Read the sentences together.

> As you write 'humans', point out that they have written the singular 'human' already in this session.

Independent Writing   3 minutes
- Allow the children 20 seconds to study your sentences, then wipe your board clean.
- Ask the children to turn to a partner and repeat what they are going to write.
- Tell them to cover their practised words and then to write the two sentences in Ziggy's speech bubble.
- Check the children's work.

Rounding Off   3 minutes
- Ask the children why Ziggy and Pod want to look like school children. (They want to go inside a human school to find out what goes on without being noticed.)
- Ask the children to think of some things in a school that Ziggy and Pod might misunderstand. What might they think the school bell would mean? (a music lesson, a warning about a fire)

Review   2 minutes
- Ask the children how to spell the word 'four'. Write it on the board. Challenge the children to write 'your' and 'pour'.
- Ask the children why we put an exclamation mark after 'You fool!'. (To show the reader that it is quite a rude thing to say.)
- How well do the children think they did? Ask them to colour in one of the thumbs.
- Share the joke!

3.1

UNIT 3

SCHOOL TROUBLE: *SESSION 2*

Outcome:
- A cartoon

Writing targets:
- Target words: 'hand', 'say', 'mouths'
- Revision word: 'something'
- Sentences: two complex sentences, a simple sentence

You will need:
- Writing Logs page 6
- Whiteboards and pens
- Card for covering spellings

Warm Up

Phonics: 'hand' *2 minutes*
- Robot-speak the word 'h/a/n/d' then ask the children to blend the phonemes to make the word.
- Listen as they robot-speak and then blend the whole word.
- As they robot-speak 'hand' again, write the letters on the board.
- Wipe your board clean, then ask the children to write the word on their whiteboards and add phoneme buttons.
- Tell the children to wipe their boards clean and to write 'hand' three times in the Phonics box.

Phonics: 'say' *2 minutes*
- Robot-speak the word 's/ay' then ask the children to blend the phonemes to make the word.
- Listen as they robot-speak and then blend the whole word.
- As they robot-speak 'say' again, write the letters on the board.
- Wipe your board clean, then ask the children to write the word on their whiteboards and add phoneme buttons.
- Tell the children to wipe their boards clean and to write 'say' three times in the Phonics box.

> Ensure that children understand that 'ay' is one phoneme.

Phonics: 'mouths' *2 minutes*
- Robot-speak the word 'm/ow/th/s' then ask the children to blend the phonemes to make the word.
- Listen as they robot-speak and then blend the whole word.
- As they robot-speak 'mouths' again, write the letters on the board.
- Wipe your board clean, then ask the children to write the word on their whiteboards and add phoneme buttons (m/ou/th/s).
- Tell the children to wipe their boards clean and to write 'mouths' three times in the Phonics box.

> Ensure that children understand that the letters 'ou' and 'th' each represent one phoneme.

Guiding the Writing

Talk for Writing *4 minutes*
- *Reread the speech bubbles from the previous session. What did Pod get wrong? (His disguise had four legs.) Now Ziggy and Pod are inside the classroom. What do teachers like you to do if you want to ask something or answer a question? (Put up your hand.)*
- *Turn to a partner and think of what the teacher, Miss West will say to Pod when he calls out. Start your sentence: 'Put up your hand when …'.*
- *Share the children's ideas.*

Demonstration Writing
3 minutes
- *In Miss West's speech bubble I am going to write:* **Put up your hand when you want to say something.** *When I get to the word 'when', I want you to tell me how to spell it and then write it in your Have a go box. When I get to the word 'something', I want you to tell me which two words make up the word ('some' and 'thing'). Watch as I spell it, then write it in your Have a go box.*
- Read the sentence together.

> Point out that one way remember how to spell 'some' is to think of it as 'so' and 'me'.

Independent Writing
2 minutes
- Allow the children 10 seconds to study your writing then wipe your board clean.
- Ask the children to turn to a partner and repeat what they are going to write.
- Tell them to cover their practised words and then to write the sentence in Miss West's speech bubble.
- Check the children's work.

Talk for Writing
3 minutes
- *Now we are going to write about why Pod thinks human children have to put up their hands before they speak. Remember, the aliens always get things wrong. Pod thinks that humans' mouths only work when they put their hands up.*
- *Turn to a partner and think of a sentence starting: 'Humans have to put up …'.*
- Share the children's ideas.

Demonstration Writing
3 minutes
- *I am going to write:* **Humans have to put up their hands to make their mouths work.** *As I write the sentence, I want you to write the word 'work' in the Have a go box.*
- Read the sentence together.
- *Finally, I need to write something in Ziggy's speech bubble. Remember, he always thinks that he is cleverer than Pod, so I'm going to write:* **I knew that!**

Independent Writing
3 minutes
- Allow the children 20 seconds to study your sentences then wipe your board clean.
- Ask the children to turn to a partner and repeat what they are going to write.
- Tell them to cover their practised words and then to write the first sentence in Pod's speech bubble and the second sentence in Ziggy's speech bubble.
- Check the children's work.

Rounding Off
3 minutes
- Ask the children what mistake Ziggy and Pod made this time. (They thought that putting up your hand in class was the only way human children could speak.)
- How can the children tell that Ziggy thinks he is better than Pod? (He says 'I knew that!'). Do they think Ziggy really knew, or does he just want to seem cleverer than Pod?
- Ask the children if they would like to have two aliens visiting their class. Would they be able to recognise them if they had human disguises?

Review
3 minutes
- Write the letters 'b', 'l' and 's' on the board. Challenge the children to write on their whiteboards three words that rhyme with 'hand' using the letters on the board ('band', 'land', 'sand').
- Why did they add exclamation marks after Ziggy's words? (To show the reader how to say the words; to show that Ziggy does not want to be thought of as foolish.)
- How well do the children think they did? Ask them to colour in one of the thumbs.
- Share the joke!

3.2

UNIT 4

RIDE THE TWISTER: *SESSION 1*

Outcome:
- A brochure for a theme park

Writing targets:
- Target words: 'brave', 'enough'
- Revision word: 'scary'
- Sentences: two questions, a simple sentence

You will need:
- Writing Logs page 7
- Whiteboards and pens
- Card for covering spellings

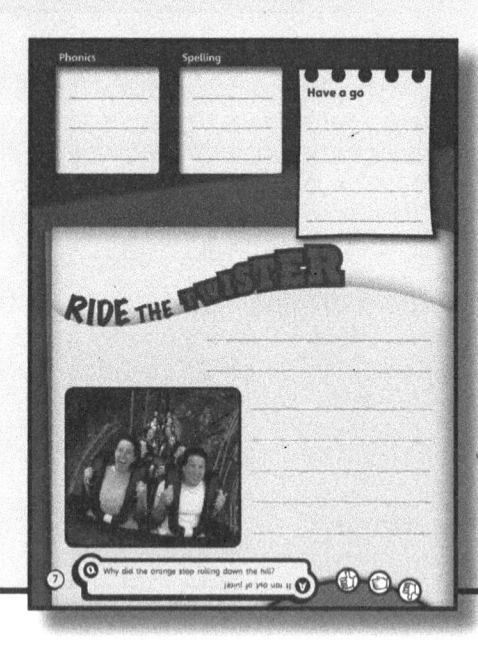

> Explain that 'enough' is irregular because 'ough' makes the sound 'uf'.

Warm Up

Phonics: 'brave' — 2 minutes
- Robot-speak the word 'b/r/ay/v' then ask the children to blend the phonemes to make the word.
- Listen as they robot-speak and then blend the whole word.
- As they robot-speak 'brave' again, write the letters on the board. Ask the children to identify which letters are making the long vowel 'ay' sound. Tell the children to link the 'a' and 'e'.
- Wipe your board clean, then ask the children to write the word on their whiteboards.
- Tell the children to wipe their boards clean and to write 'brave' three times in the Phonics box.

Spelling: 'enough' — 2 minutes
- Explain that 'enough' is an irregular word so they will learn to spell it using letter names.
- Demonstrate how to spell the word 'enough', saying the letter names as you write.
- Wipe your board clean and ask the children to trace the word with their finger on their whiteboard, saying the letter names as they do so. Then ask them to write 'enough' on their whiteboards three times.
- Tell the children to wipe their boards clean, then write the word three times in the Spelling box.

Revision: 'scary' — 1 minute
- Write the word 'scary' on your board and say it. Point at each letter in turn and say the letter name.
- Tell the children to close their eyes and picture the word as they repeat the letters.
- Wipe your board clean, then ask them to write 'scary' in the Have a go box.

Guiding the Writing

Talk for Writing — 3 minutes
- Explain to the children that they are going to write a brochure for a theme park. Look at the title: 'Ride the Twister'. Ask them if the title makes it sound as if the rides in the park could be scary.
- *What scary rides have you been on? What made the ride scary? In the brochure we need to try to entice people to come to the theme park, so we will start by asking the readers whether they like doing really scary things.*
- *Turn to a partner and think of a question starting: 'Do you like to …'.*
- Share the children's ideas.

Demonstration Writing *3 minutes*
- *I am going to write:* **Do you like to do things that are really scary?** *As I write this sentence, I want you to study the word 'really', then write it in the Have a go box.*
- Read the sentence together.

> Remind the children that they have practised 'really' in a previous session. The word 'really' is 'real' plus 'ly', so there are two 'l's in the word.

Independent Writing *3 minutes*
- Allow the children 10 seconds to study your question, then wipe your board clean.
- Ask the children to turn to a partner and repeat what they are going to write.
- Tell them to cover their practised words and then to write the question.
- Check the children's work.

Talk for Writing *3 minutes*
- *Now we are going to ask the reader whether they are brave enough to go on the huge roller-coaster and then tell them that it is the fastest in the world. That should make them want to come to the theme park.*
- *Turn to a partner and think of a question and a statement. The question should start: 'Are you brave enough …' and the next sentence should start: 'It is the fastest …'.*
- Share the children's ideas.

Demonstration Writing *4 minutes*
- *I am going to write:* **Are you brave enough to go on our huge roller-coaster?** *As I write, I want you to write 'huge' in the Have a go box.*
- *Then I am going to write:* **It is the fastest in the world.** *As I write my sentence, I want you to write 'fastest' in the Have a go box*
- *I want to make sure that the readers notice that it is the fastest roller-coaster in the world. What could I do to make the word 'fastest' stand out from the other words? (underline it, make it bold, use capital letters)*
- Read the sentences together.

> Remind the children that they have practised 'fast' in a previous session. The word 'fastest' is just 'fast' with 'est' on the end.

Independent Writing *3 minutes*
- Allow the children 20 seconds to study your sentences then wipe your board clean, leaving the word 'roller-coaster' for them to copy.
- Ask the children to turn to a partner and repeat what they are going to write.
- Tell them to cover their practised words and then to write each sentence on a new line. Doing this draws the reader's attention to the questions and answers and makes it more eye-catching.
- Check the children's work.

Rounding Off *3 minutes*
- Ask the children if they like to be a little bit scared when they go on a ride at a theme park.
- Tell the children to get into pairs and to take turns reading the sentences. Would the brochure make them want to go to the theme park? What sentence makes them want to go to this theme park the most?

Review *3 minutes*
- Ask the children to write the word 'brave' from memory on their whiteboards. Then tell them to write 'cave', 'gave' and 'save'. What letters do these words have in common? ('ave') What letters make the long vowel 'ay' sound? (the 'a' and the 'e')
- Why did they make the word 'fastest' stand out from the other words? (to make it sound more exciting)
- How well do the children think they did? Ask them to colour in one of the thumbs.
- Share the joke!

4.1

UNIT 4

RIDE THE TWISTER: *SESSION 2*

Outcome:
- A brochure for a theme park

Writing targets:
- Target words: 'slowly', 'upside', 'first'
- Revision word: 'twists'
- Sentences: two simple sentences, one compound sentence with ellipsis, one question

You will need:
- Writing Logs page 8
- Whiteboards and pens
- Card for covering spellings

Warm Up

Phonics: 'slowly' — 2 minutes
- Robot-speak the word 's/l/oh/l/y' then ask the children to blend the phonemes to make the word.
- Listen as they robot-speak and then blend the whole word.
- As they robot-speak 'slowly' again, write the letters on the board.
- Wipe your board clean, then ask the children to write the word on their whiteboards and add phoneme buttons (s/l/ow/l/y).
- Tell the children to wipe their boards clean and to write 'slowly' three times in the Phonics box.

Phonics: 'upside' — 2 minutes
- Ask the children how many syllables they can hear in the word 'upside'. Tell them to think of the two syllables in their head when they write the word.
- Robot-speak the word 'u/p/s/igh/d' then ask the children to blend the phonemes to make the word.
- Listen as they robot-speak and then blend the whole word.
- As they robot-speak 'upside' again, write the letters on the board. Ask the children to identify which letters are making the long vowel 'igh' sound. Tell the children to link the 'i' and 'e'.
- Wipe your board clean, then ask the children to write the word on their whiteboards.
- Tell the children to wipe their boards clean and to write 'upside' three times in the Phonics box.

Spelling: 'first' — 2 minutes
- Explain that 'first' is an irregular word so they will learn to spell it using letter names.
- Demonstrate how to spell the word 'first', saying the letter names as you write.
- Wipe your board clean and ask the children to trace the word with their finger on their whiteboard, saying the letter names as they do so. Then ask them to write 'first' on their whiteboards.
- Tell the children to wipe their boards clean, then write the word three times in the Spelling box.

> The word 'first' is irregular because the 'ur' sound is made with the letters 'ir'. If children are familiar with the phoneme 'ir', then this word could be taught using phonics.

Guiding the Writing

Talk for Writing — 3 minutes
- Explain to the children that they are going to finish writing the brochure from a theme park that they started in the previous session.
- *Have you ever been on a roller-coaster? What happens? (It goes up slowly, then down very, very fast.)*

34

- *Turn to a partner and think of two sentences. The first one should start: 'First you go …'. The second sentence should start: 'Then you go …'.*
- Share the children's ideas.

Demonstration Writing   3 minutes
- *I am going to write:* **First you go up very slowly.** *As I write this sentence, I want you to write 'very' in the Have a go box.*
- *Next I am going to write:* **Then you go down very, very fast.**
- Point out that you have started the first sentence with 'First', and the second sentence with 'Then' because it tells the reader the order of events.
- Read the sentences together.

Independent Writing   2 minutes
- Allow the children 20 seconds to study your sentences, then wipe your board clean.
- Ask the children to turn to a partner and repeat what they are going to write.
- Tell them to cover their practised words and then write the sentences.
- Check the children's work.

Talk for Writing   3 minutes
- *Now I am going to tell the reader that the roller-coaster twists and turns, and that you actually go upside down!*
- Turn to a partner and think of a sentence starting: 'It twists and turns…'.
- Share the children's ideas.

Demonstration Writing   4 minutes
- *I am going to write:* **It twists and turns … then you go upside down.** *As I write 'twists', sound out the phonemes and count them. (There are six – t/w/i/s/t/s.) I want you to study the word and then write it in the Have a go box.*
- *I have put dots between the first and second part of my sentence to show the reader that they should pause before reading the second part of the sentence.*
- *Finally, I am going to ask the reader if they would go on the roller-coaster. So I am going to write:* **Will you ride the twister?**
- Read the sentences together.

> Remind the children that they have practised 'turned' in a previous session. Explain that 'turns' is the word 'turn' with an 's' added.

Independent Writing   4 minutes
- Allow the children 20 seconds to study your sentences then wipe your board clean.
- Ask the children to turn to a partner and repeat what they are going to write.
- Tell them to cover their practised words and then to write the sentences.
- Check the children's work.

Rounding Off   2 minutes
- Tell the children to work with a partner and to decide how to read the brochure. How would they read the questions and how would they read the facts? They should then swap over and listen to how their partner reads.

Review   3 minutes
- Ask the children to write the words 'upside down' from memory on their whiteboards. How will they break the words up to help them? (Think of the two smaller words in 'upside' before you write.) Challenge them to write 'inside out'. What will they do to help them to write 'inside'? (Think of the two smaller words.)
- Why did they put dots in the sentence: 'It twists and turns … and then you go upside down'? (To build suspense about what will happen next.)
- How well do the children think they did? Ask them to colour in one of the thumbs.
- Share the joke!

4.2

UNIT 5

IN THE ARENA: *SESSION 1*

Outcome:
- A diary entry

Writing targets:
- Target words: 'grabbed', 'sword', 'toe'
- Sentences: one simple sentence, one compound sentence

You will need:
- Writing Logs page 9
- Whiteboards and pens
- Card for covering spellings

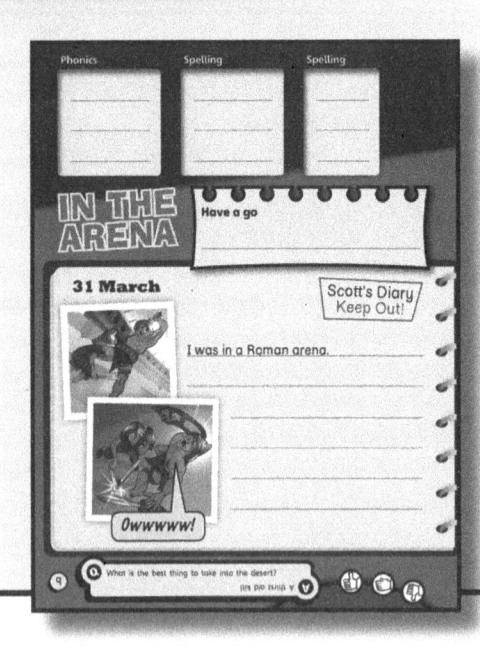

Warm Up
Phonics: 'grabbed' — 2 minutes
- Robot-speak the word 'g/r/a/bb/d' then ask the children to blend the phonemes to make the word.
- Listen as they robot-speak and then blend the whole word.
- As they robot-speak 'grabbed' again, write the letters on the board.
- Wipe your board clean, then ask the children to write the word on their whiteboards and add phoneme buttons (g/r/a/bb/ed).
- Tell the children to wipe their boards clean and to write 'grabbed' three times in the Phonics box.

> Point out that the 'd' sound at the end of 'grabbed' is made with the letters 'ed'.

Spelling: 'sword' — 2 minutes
- Explain that 'sword' is an irregular word so they will learn to spell it using letter names.
- Demonstrate how to spell the word 'sword', saying the letter names as you write.
- Wipe your board clean and ask the children to trace the word with their finger on their whiteboard, saying the letter names as they do so. Then ask them to write 'sword' on their whiteboards.
- Tell the children to wipe their boards clean, then write the word three times in the Spelling box.

Spelling: 'toe' — 2 minutes
- Explain that 'toe' is an irregular word so they will learn to spell it using letter names.
- Demonstrate how to spell the word 'toe', saying the letter names as you write.
- Wipe your board clean and ask the children to trace the word with their finger on their whiteboard, saying the letter names as they do so. Then ask them to write 'toe' on their whiteboards.
- Tell the children to wipe their boards clean, then write the word three times in the Spelling box.

> If the children are familiar with the letters 'oe' making the long vowel 'oh' sound, this word could be taught using phonics.

Guiding the Writing
Talk for Writing — 4 minutes
- Tell the children to look at the pictures. Explain that the boy is Scott and he has slipped back in time to the age of the gladiators. He has found himself in a Roman arena and he has to fight a huge gladiator. Ask the children what they think the gladiator wants to do. (He wants to kill Scott.) Who do they think will win the fight?
- Explain that they are going to pretend to be Scott writing in his diary when he gets back to his real time. Point out that, because it is a diary, there is a date at the top of the page. They will write in the first person (using 'I'). Look together at what Scott has written first in his diary: 'I was in a Roman Arena'.

- *Turn to a partner and think about what Scott will write next in his diary. He needs to explain exactly what happened, but he also wants to make it sound dramatic. Think of a sentence starting: 'A huge gladiator tried ...'.*
- *Share the children's ideas.*

Demonstration Writing   3 minutes
- *I am going to start the diary entry by writing:* **A huge gladiator tried to kill me.**
- *Watch as I write 'huge'. I want you to say the letter names.*
- *As I write 'tried', I want you to write it in the Have a go box.*
- *Read the sentence together.*

> Look at the word 'gladiator'. Help the children to break it up into syllables: 'glad/i/a/tor'.

Independent Writing   2 minutes
- Allow the children 10 seconds to study your sentence then wipe your board clean, leaving the word 'gladiator' for them to copy.
- Ask the children to turn to a partner and repeat what they are going to write.
- Tell them to cover their practised words and then write the sentence.
- Check the children's work.

Talk for Writing   3 minutes
- *Now we need Scott to describe what he did to defend himself. Look at the pictures. Scott grabbed his sword but it was so heavy that he dropped it. What happened next? (It landed on the gladiator's toe.)*
- *Turn to a partner and think of a long sentence starting: 'I grabbed my sword to ...' and then join the next part of your sentence with 'but it fell ...'. Finally, finish the sentence: 'and landed on ...'.*
- *Share the children's ideas.*

> Ask the children to think about how they could use the word 'toe' that they practised earlier.

Demonstration Writing   3 minutes
- *I am going to write the sentence:* **I grabbed my sword to stop him, but it fell out of my hand and landed on his toe.**
- *Write the words 'fell' and 'landed' in your Have a go box.*
- *Read the sentence together.*
- *What did the gladiator say when the sword landed on his toe? ('Owwwwww!')*

Independent Writing   3 minutes
- Allow the children 20 seconds to study your sentence then wipe your board clean.
- Ask the children to turn to a partner and repeat what they are going to write.
- Tell them to cover their practised words and then to write the sentence.
- Check the children's work.

Rounding Off   3 minutes
- Ask the children which word describes the gladiator ('huge'). Challenge them to think of more describing words for the gladiator ('scary', 'angry', 'strong').
- Ask the children: If they slipped back to the time of the gladiators, would they try to fight one or would they run away?

Review   3 minutes
- Write the words 'grab', 'grabbed' and 'grabbing' on the board. Ask the children what changes when an ending is added (the 'b' is doubled). Wipe your board and ask the children to write the words.
- There are two linking words in the second sentence ('but', 'and'). Ask the children what we call those kinds of word (a conjunction or a joining word).
- How well do the children think they did? Ask them to colour in one of the thumbs.
- Share the joke!

5.1

UNIT 5

IN THE ARENA: *SESSION 2*

Outcome:
- A diary entry

Writing targets:
- Target words: 'shouting', 'waving', 'scared'
- Revision word: 'because'
- Sentences: one simple sentence, two complex sentences

You will need:
- Writing Logs page 10
- Whiteboards and pens
- Card for covering spellings

Warm Up

Phonics: 'shouting' — *2 minutes*
- Robot-speak the word 'sh/ow/t/i/ng' then ask the children to blend the phonemes to make the word.
- Listen as they robot-speak and then blend the whole word.
- As they robot-speak 'shouting' again, write the letters on the board.
- Wipe your board clean, then ask the children to write the word on their whiteboards and add phoneme buttons (sh/ou/t/i/ng).
- Tell the children to wipe their boards clean and to write 'shouting' three times in the Phonics box.

> Ensure that children understand that the letters 'ou' make an 'ow' sound.

Spelling: 'waving' — *2 minutes*
- Explain that 'waving' is an irregular word so they will learn to spell it using letter names.
- Demonstrate how to spell the word 'waving', saying the letter names as you write.
- Wipe your board clean and ask the children to trace the word with their finger on their whiteboard saying the letter names as they do so. Then ask them to write 'waving' on their whiteboards.
- Tell the children to wipe their boards clean, then write the word three times in the Spelling box.

Spelling: 'scared' — *2 minutes*
- Explain that 'scared' is an irregular word so they will learn to spell it using letter names.
- Demonstrate how to spell the word 'scared', saying the letter names as you write.
- Wipe your board clean and ask the children to trace the word with their finger on their whiteboard, saying the letter names as they do so. Then ask them to write 'scared' on their whiteboards.
- Tell the children to wipe their boards clean, then write the word three times in the Spelling box.

> The word 'scared' is treated as irregular because the letters 'ar' make the sound 'air'.

Guiding the Writing

Talk for Writing — *4 minutes*
- Remind the children that Scott can slip back in time. What time had he gone back to? (the time of the gladiators in Rome) Ask the children if they have ever seen any films or TV programmes with gladiators fighting.
- Reread the diary entry from Session 1. Explain to the children that they are going to write the next two sentences in the diary.
- *Look at the first picture. What is about to attack Scott now? (a lion) Sometimes gladiators would fight lions in the arena. What does the lion look as though it is about to do? (attack Scott)*

38

- *In his first sentence, Scott needs to explain what the lion was going to do. Now look at the second picture. In his second sentence, Scott needs to say what he did. Start your first sentence: 'Next, a lion was …'. Start your second sentence: 'I ran at it …'. Use the words 'shouting' and 'waving' in your second sentence.*
- Share the children's ideas.

Demonstration Writing   4 minutes
- *First I am going to write in the diary:* **Next, a lion was going to attack me.** *As I write 'Next', I want you to practise it in the Have a go box. As I write 'lion', I want you to tell me how to spell it saying the letter names.*
- *In the second sentence, I am going to write:* **I ran at it, shouting and waving my sword.** *When I come to the word 'sword', I want you to write it in the Have a go box. I have put a comma after 'it' to break up the sentence slightly.*
- Read the sentences together.

> Ensure that the children can hear the four phonemes in 'attack' (a/tt/a/ck).

Independent Writing   3 minutes
- Allow the children 20 seconds to study your sentences, then wipe your board clean.
- Ask the children to turn to a partner and repeat what they are going to write.
- Tell them to cover their practised words and then write the sentences in the diary.
- Check the children's work.

> Praise children who remember the comma after the word 'Next'.

Talk for Writing   3 minutes
- *What is the lion doing in the second picture? (running away) Why? (It was scared when it saw Scott running at him waving a sword and shouting.)*
- *Turn to a partner and think of a sentence that describes what the lion did and why Scott thinks it did this. Start your sentnce: 'I must have scared it because …'.*
- Share the children's ideas.

Demonstration Writing   3 minutes
- *I am going to write the sentence:* **I must have scared it because it turned and ran away.** *As I write the word 'because', I want you to tell me how to spell it and then to write it in the Have a go box.*
- Read the sentence together.

Independent Writing   2 minutes
- Allow the children 20 seconds to study your sentence, then wipe your board clean.
- Ask the children to turn to a partner and repeat what they are going to write.
- Tell them to cover their practised words and then to write the sentence in the diary.
- Check the children's work.

Rounding Off   3 minutes
- Ask the children if they would have charged at the lion, like Scott.
- Ask the children whether they would rather fight a lion or a gladiator in the arena.
- Do they think Scott has really gone back in time or was it just a dream?

Review   2 minutes
- Write the word 'shout' on the board. Challenge the children to think of as many words as they can that use this word as their root ('shouts', 'shouted', 'shouting').
- How can we tell that the writing is in a diary? (It is written in the first person; it explains what Scott did; it has a date at the top of the page.)
- How well do the children think they did? Ask them to colour in one of the thumbs.
- Share the joke!

> Go to the orange box on page 21 in the Writing Log for an unaided writing activity.
> See page 142 of this Teachin Guide for guidance notes.

5.2

UNIT 6

GLADIATORS: *SESSION 1*

Outcome:
- Live commentary on a gladiator fight

Writing targets:
- Target words: 'exciting', 'towards', 'everyone'
- Sentences: one expanded compound sentence using 'and', a one-word sentence, two simple sentences

You will need:
- Writing Logs page 11
- Whiteboards and pens
- Card for covering spellings

Warm Up
Spelling: 'exciting' — 2 minutes
- Explain that 'exciting' is an irregular word so they will learn to spell it using letter names.
- Demonstrate how to spell the word 'exciting', saying the letter names as you write.
- Wipe your board clean, then ask the children to trace the word with their finger on their whiteboard, saying the letter names as they do so. Then ask them to write 'exciting' on their whiteboards.
- Tell the children to wipe their boards clean, then write the word three times in the Spelling box.

Spelling: 'towards' — 2 minutes
- Explain that 'towards' is an irregular word so they will learn to spell it using letter names.
- Demonstrate how to spell the word 'towards', saying the letter names as you write.
- Wipe your board clean and ask the children to trace the word with their finger on their whiteboard, saying the letter names as they do so. Then ask them to write 'towards' on their whiteboards.
- Tell the children to wipe their boards clean, then write the word three times in the Spelling box.

Spelling: 'everyone' — 2 minutes

> The word 'everyone' is treated as irregular because the letters 'one' represent the sound 'wun'.

- Explain that 'everyone' is an irregular word so they will learn to spell it using letter names.
- Demonstrate how to spell the word 'everyone', saying the letter names as you write.
- Wipe your board clean and ask the children to trace the word with their finger on their whiteboard, saying the letter names as they do so. Then ask them to write 'everyone' on their whiteboards.
- Tell the children to wipe their boards clean, then write the word three times in the Spelling box.

Guiding the Writing
Talk for Writing — 4 minutes
- Explain to the children that they are going to write a live commentary of a gladiator fight. Check that they know what a gladiator is and when they lived. (They were fighters in Roman times. They were often slaves or criminals who were made to fight one another.)
- Ask them if they have ever listened to a live commentary, for example of a football match. Explain that in Roman times people didn't have microphones like the ones football commentators use, but that they are going to write as if they are speaking into a microphone, describing what they see in front of them.

- *Look at the picture. One gladiator has a sword and the other has a net. To start with, the commentator will tell the audience what each gladiator is armed with. Turn to a partner and think of a sentence starting: 'In this very exciting fight ...'.*
- Share the children's ideas.

Demonstration Writing 3 minutes
- *I am going to write:* **In this very exciting fight, one gladiator has a sword and the other has a net.** *As I write this sentence, I want you to write 'fight' in the Have a go box.*
- Read the sentence together.

Independent Writing 2 minutes
- Allow the children 20 seconds to study your sentence then wipe your board clean, leaving the word 'gladiator' for them to copy.
- Ask the children to turn to a partner and repeat what they are going to write.
- Tell them to cover their practised words and then write the sentence.
- Check the children's work.

Talk for Writing 2 minutes
- Now we are going to tell the audience that one of the gladiators has fallen. The other gladiator is the victor.
- Turn to a partner and think of how to describe what has happened. Start with: 'Look! One man ...'.
- Share the children's ideas.

Demonstration Writing 4 minutes
- *I am going to write:* **Look! One man has fallen.** *I have put an exclamation mark to show how the commentator will have shouted 'Look!' He wants to make sure that the audience has seen the man on the ground.*
- *As I write the word 'fallen' on the board, look closely at it. You have practised the word 'fall' in a previous session. Which letters have been added to 'fall' to make 'fallen'? ('en') Now write 'fallen' in the Have a go box.*
- *Now I want to point out that everyone is looking towards the Emperor's box, so I am going to write:* **Everyone is looking towards the Emperor's box.** *As I write, I want you to practise the word 'looking' in the Have a go box.*
- Read the sentences together.

> Explain that 'Look!' is a one-word sentence because it is an instruction.

Independent Writing 3 minutes
- Allow the children 20 seconds to study your sentences then wipe your board clean, leaving the word 'Emperor's' for them to copy.
- Ask the children to turn to a partner and repeat what they are going to write.
- Tell them to cover their practised words and then to write the sentences.
- Check the children's work.

> Tell the children to look very carefully at where you put the apostrophe between the 'r' and the 's' in 'Emperor's'.

Rounding Off 3 minutes
- Ask the children if they know why everyone is looking towards the Emperor's box. What do they think might happen next?
- Can they think of a sport today where two people fight? (boxing, judo)
- Invite children to read the commentary so far to the group. Encourage them to use expression and intonation when they read.

Review 3 minutes
- Remind the children that they wrote 'Look!' as a one-word sentence. Can they think of other instruction words that could be a one-word sentence? ('Go', 'Stop', 'Help') Challenge them to write the words on their whiteboards.
- Ask them what they need to remember when writing a commentary (to describe what they see; to try to make it exciting).
- How well do the children think they did? Ask them to colour in one of the thumbs.
- Share the joke!

6.1

UNIT 6

GLADIATIORS: *SESSION 2*

Outcome:
- Live commentary on a gladiator fight

Writing targets:
- Target words: 'thumb', 'dies', 'means'
- Sentences: one complex sentence, three simple sentences

You will need:
- Writing Logs page 12
- Whiteboards and pens
- Card for covering spellings

If the children are familiar with 'mb' as a phonic letter combination, then this word could be taught using phonics.

Ensure that children understand that the letters 'ie' are making the long vowel sound 'igh'.

Ensure that children understand that the letters 'ea' are making the long vowel sound 'ee'.

Warm Up

Spelling: 'thumb' *2 minutes*
- Explain that 'thumb' is an irregular word so they will learn to spell it using letter names.
- Demonstrate how to spell the word 'thumb', saying the letter names as you write.
- Wipe your board clean and ask the children to trace the word with their finger on their whiteboard, saying the letter names as they do so. Then ask them to write 'thumb' on their whiteboards.
- Tell the children to wipe their boards clean, then write the word three times in the Spelling box.

Phonics: 'dies' *2 minutes*
- Robot-speak the word 'd/igh/s' then ask the children to blend the phonemes to make the word.
- Listen as they robot-speak and then blend the whole word.
- As they robot-speak 'dies' again, write the letters on the board.
- Wipe your board clean, then ask the children to write the word on their whiteboards and add phoneme buttons (d/ie/s).
- Tell the children to wipe their boards clean and to write 'dies' three times in the Phonics box.

Phonics: 'means' *2 minutes*
- Robot-speak the word 'm/ee/n/s' then ask the children to blend the phonemes to make the word.
- Listen as they robot-speak and then blend the whole word.
- As they robot-speak 'means' again, write the letters on the board.
- Wipe your board clean, then ask the children to write the word on their whiteboards and add phoneme buttons (m/ea/n/s).
- Tell the children to wipe their boards clean and to write 'means' three times in the Phonics box.

Guiding the Writing

Talk for Writing *4 minutes*
- Explain to the children that they are going to continue the live commentary on the gladiator fight. Ask them to reread what they wrote in Session 1.
- Explain that it was the custom for the Emperor to decide whether the gladiator should live or die. If the Emperor put his thumb up the gladiator lived, but if he put it down the gladiator would be killed.
- *As we are writing a commentary, we are going to write as if we are talking. Everyone watching the fight will be wondering what the Emperor is going to do, so the commentator will ask the question that is on everyone's minds.*

- *Turn to a partner and think of two sentences. The first should be a question starting: 'What will ...'. The second should remind the viewers how the Emperor will decide the gladiator's fate, and start with: 'As you know, thumb up means ...'.*
- Share the children's ideas.

Demonstration Writing   4 minutes
- *I am going to write:* **What will the Emperor do?** *As I write this sentence, I want you to write 'What' in the Have a go box.*
- *Then I am going to write:* **As you know, thumb up means the gladiator lives but thumb down means he dies.** *As I write my sentence, I want you to write 'know' and 'lives' in the Have a go box. The commentator has started his sentence with: 'As you know ...' because it is important that he speaks directly to his audience.*
- Read the sentences together.

> Remind the children to write 'What' with a capital letter.

Independent Writing   4 minutes
- Allow the children 20 seconds to study your sentences, then wipe your board clean, leaving the words 'Emperor' and 'gladiator' for them to copy.
- Ask the children to turn to a partner and repeat what they are going to write.
- Tell them to cover their practised words and then to write the question in the first box and the second in the second box.
- Check the children's work.

Talk for Writing   2 minutes
- *Look at the picture. What has the Emperor decided? Now we are going to tell the audience that the Emperor has given the thumb down sign so the gladiator will die.*
- *Turn to a partner and think of two sentences to describe what has happened. Your first sentence should start: 'The thumb ...' and your second sentence: 'The gladiator ...'.*
- Share the children's ideas.

Demonstration Writing   2 minutes
- *I am going to write:* **The thumb is down. The gladiator will die.** *As I write my sentences, I want you to write 'down' in the Have a go box.*
- *I have written two short sentences because this makes the reader pause after each sentence, so the decision that the gladiator will die seems even more dramatic.*
- Read the sentences together.

Independent Writing   2 minutes
- Allow the children 10 seconds to study your sentences then wipe your board clean, leaving the word 'gladiator' for them to copy.
- Ask the children to turn to a partner and repeat what they are going to write.
- Tell them to cover their practised words and then to write the sentences.
- Check the children's work.

Rounding Off   3 minutes
- Ask the children to turn to a partner and to take turns rereading the whole commentary with expression. Remind them to pause between the final two short sentences.
- What else might the commentator say to his audience about the fight? (Did he agree with the Emperor's decision? Did he think it was a good fight, or was it over too quickly? What will the victor get as his prize?)

Review   3 minutes
- Ask the children what two letters make the long vowel 'igh' phoneme in 'dies'? ('ie') Invite them to write 'cries', 'lies' and 'tries' on their whiteboards.
- Ask them what they need to remember when writing a commentary. (Talk directly to the audience; tell people what is going on; describe the scene.)
- How well do the children think they did? Ask them to colour in one of the thumbs.
- Share the joke!

6.2

UNIT 7

DRUM BEAT: *SESSION 1*

Outcome:
- A diary entry

Writing targets:
- Target words: 'row', 'drum', 'beat'
- Revision word: 'thought'
- Sentences: two simple sentences, two complex sentences

You will need:
- Writing Logs page 13
- Whiteboards and pens
- Card for covering spellings

Warm Up
Phonics: 'row' — 2 minutes
- Robot-speak the word 'r/ow' (to rhyme with 'grow') then ask the children to blend the phonemes to make the word.
- Listen as they robot-speak and then blend the whole word.
- As they robot-speak 'row' again, write the letters on the board.
- Wipe your board clean, then ask the children to write the word on their whiteboards and add phoneme buttons.
- Tell the children to wipe their boards clean and to write 'row' three times in the Phonics box.

> Ensure that children understand that the letters 'ow' represent one phoneme.

Phonics: 'drum' — 2 minutes
- Robot-speak the word 'd/r/u/m' then ask the children to blend the phonemes to make the word.
- Listen as they robot-speak and then blend the whole word.
- As they robot-speak 'drum' again, write the letters on the board.
- Wipe your board clean, then ask the children to write the word on their whiteboards and add phoneme buttons.
- Tell the children to wipe their boards clean and to write 'drum' three times in the Phonics box.

Phonics: 'beat' — 2 minutes
- Robot-speak the word 'b/ee/t' then ask the children to blend the phonemes to make the word.
- Listen as they robot-speak and then blend the whole word.
- As they robot-speak 'beat' again, write the letters on the board.
- Wipe your board clean, then ask the children to write the word on their whiteboards and add phoneme buttons (b/ea/t).
- Tell the children to wipe their boards clean and to write 'beat' three times in the Phonics box.

> Ensure that children understand that 'ea' makes the sound 'ee'.

Guiding the Writing
Talk for Writing — 4 minutes
- Ask the children to look at the picture on the right. It shows Scott, who has slipped back in time to the age of the Vikings.
- *Scott is on board a Viking longship on its way to attack England. What is Scott doing? (rowing) What is the man at the back of the picture doing? (He is beating a drum.) His name is Big Olaf. Why might Big Olaf be beating a drum? (so the rowers keep time) Does the rowing look like hard work?*
- Explain to the group that they are going to pretend to be Scott writing in his diary when he gets back to his real time. Because it is a diary they will write it in the first person (using 'I').

- *Turn to a partner and think of two sentences to start off Scott's journal entry. He needs to explain exactly where he is and what he has to do. Start the first sentence: 'I was on a ...' and the second sentence: 'We had to row fast ...'.*
- Share the children's ideas.

Demonstration Writing   3 minutes
- *First I am going to write:* **I was on a Viking ship.** *As I write the word 'ship', I want you to write it in the Have a go box.*
- *Next I am going to write:* **We had to row fast in time to Big Olaf's drum.** *As I write 'fast', I want you to write it in the Have a go box.*
- Read the sentences together.
- *Why have I used capitals for Big Olaf? (because that is the name he is known by)*

> Point out that 'Viking' uses a capital 'V' because it is the name of a group of people.

Independent Writing   3 minutes
- Allow the children 20 seconds to study your sentences, then wipe your board clean, leaving the words 'Viking' and 'Olaf's' for them to copy.
- Ask the children to turn to a partner and repeat what they are going to write.
- Tell them to cover their practised words and then to write the sentences.
- Check the children's work.

Talk for Writing   3 minutes
- *Now we need to describe what would happen if the rowers didn't row fast enough. Look at the second picture. What has Big Olaf got in his hand? (a whip) He would beat them if their rowing was too slow. How would you feel if you had to pull a big, heavy oar faster and faster?*
- *Turn to a partner and think of a sentence starting: 'He beat us if ...'.*
- *Then think of a second sentence that describes how Scott felt that starts with: 'I thought I ...'.*
- Share the children's ideas.

Demonstration Writing   3 minutes
- *I am going to write:* **He beat us if we were too slow.**
- *Say the letter names for 'were' as I write it. Then, as I write the word 'slow', I want you to write it in your Have a go box.*
- *Now I am going to write:* **I thought I would die.** *As I write the word 'thought', say the letter names with me, then write it in the Have a go box.*
- Read the sentences together.

> Remind the children that they have practised the word 'slowly' in a previous session. The word 'slow' is just 'slowly' without the 'ly'.

Independent Writing   3 minutes
- Allow the children 20 seconds to study the sentences, then wipe your board clean.
- Ask the children to turn to a partner and repeat what they are going to write.
- Tell them to cover their practised words and then to write the sentences.
- Check the children's work.

Rounding Off   2 minutes
- Ask the children how they can tell that Scott found the work very hard. (He says he thought he would die.)
- Ask the children what they would do to get away from Big Olaf if they slipped back to the time of the Vikings. (Creep up behind and push him overboard; distract him by pointing out an albatross!)

Review   3 minutes
- Write the letters 'h', 'n' and 's' on your board. Challenge the children to make three 'eat' words using the letters ('heat', 'neat', 'seat').
- Reread both sentences and work out who each pronoun refers to ('I' = Scott; 'We' = all the rowers; 'He' = Big Olaf; 'we' = all the rowers; 'I' = Scott; 'I' = Scott).
- How well do the children think they did? Ask them to colour in one of the thumbs.
- Share the joke!

7.1

UNIT 7

DRUM BEAT: *SESSION 2*

Outcome:
- A diary entry

Writing targets:
- Target words: 'stopped', 'which', 'cheer'
- Revision word: 'something'
- Sentences: two simple sentences, one complex sentence

You will need:
- Writing Logs page 14
- Whiteboards and pens
- Card for covering spellings

Warm Up

Phonics: 'stopped' — *2 minutes*
- Robot-speak the word 's/t/o/p/t' then ask the children to blend the phonemes to make the word.
- Listen as they robot-speak and then blend the word.
- As they robot-speak 'stopped' again, write the letters on the board.
- Wipe your board clean and ask the children to write the word on their whiteboards and add phoneme buttons (s/t/o/pp/ed).
- Tell the children to wipe their boards clean and to write 'stopped' three times in the Phonics box.

> Point out that the 't' sound at the end of the word is made with the letters 'ed'.

Phonics: 'which' — *2 minutes*
- Robot-speak the word 'wh/i/ch' then ask the children to blend the phonemes to make the word.
- Listen as they robot-speak and then blend the whole word.
- As they robot-speak 'which' again, write the letters on the board.
- Wipe your board clean, then ask the children to write the word on their whiteboards and add phoneme buttons.
- Tell the children to wipe their boards clean and to write 'which' three times in the Phonics box.

Phonics: 'cheer' — *2 minutes*
- Robot-speak the word 'ch/eer' then ask the children to blend the phonemes to make the word.
- Listen as they robot-speak and then blend the whole word.
- As they robot-speak 'cheer' again, write the letters on the board.
- Wipe your board clean, then ask the children to write the word on their whiteboards and add phoneme buttons.
- Tell the children to wipe their boards clean and to write 'cheer' three times in the Phonics box.

> Ensure that children know that the letters 'eer' are one phoneme.

Guiding the Writing

Talk for Writing — *4 minutes*
- Reread Scott's journal so far. How can we tell it's a diary? (We are using 'I'; there is a date at the top of the page.)
- *Now we need to write the 'action' part of the diary to explain what Scott does to stop Big Olaf. Scott feels he must do something. Why? (Big Olaf is making them row so fast they feel like they might die.) Scott stopped rowing. When one rower stops his oar, all the other oars will hit each other and jam. Then the ship will stop suddenly. Look at the pictures. What has happened to Big Olaf? (He has fallen into the sea because the ship stopped so suddenly.)*

46

- *Turn to a partner and think of two sentences. First Scott is going to describe how he felt about the situation, so start the first sentence: 'I had to do ...'. Then he is going to describe what happened, so start the second sentence: 'I stopped rowing which made ...'.*
- Share the children's ideas.

Demonstration Writing   4 minutes
- *First I am going to write a short, dramatic sentence:* **I had to do something.** *What two words is 'something' made up of? ('some' + 'thing') Practise spelling it in the Have a go box.*
- *Next I am going to write the long sentence:* **I stopped rowing which made all the oars jam and then Big Olaf fell into the sea.** *You practised 'row' last time, so practise 'rowing' in the Have a go box. When I come to the word 'sea' I want you to tell me how to spell it.*
- Read the sentence together.

> Remind the children that 'rowing' is just 'row' and 'ing'.

Independent Writing   3 minutes
- Allow the children 20 seconds to study your sentences, then wipe your board clean, leaving the words 'oars' and 'Olaf' for them to copy..
- Ask the children to turn to a partner and repeat what they are going to write.
- Tell them to cover their practised words and then write the sentences.
- Check the children's work.

Talk for Writing   3 minutes
- *Look again at the second picture. What is everyone on the ship doing? (cheering) Now we need to finish the journal entry by saying what everyone did once they had got rid of Big Olaf.*
- *Turn to a partner and think of a sentence starting 'We all gave ...'. Think about how you can use the word 'cheer' that you practised earlier.*
- Share the children's ideas.

Demonstration Writing   2 minutes
- *I am going to write the sentence:* **We all gave a big cheer.** *As I write the word 'gave', I want you to write it in your Have a go box.*
- Read the sentence together.

Independent Writing   2 minutes
- Allow the children 10 seconds to study your sentence, then wipe your board clean.
- Ask the children to turn to a partner and repeat what they are going to write.
- Tell them to cover their practised words and then to write the sentence.
- Check the children's work.

Rounding Off   3 minutes
- How did Scott help everyone? (He stopped rowing; the boat stopped suddenly and Big Olaf fell into the sea.)
- Do they think the rowers will go back to pick up Big Olaf? Should they?
- Do they think Scott's plan was clever? (Yes, because it all happened so quickly that there was no time for Big Olaf to use his whip on Scott.)

Review   3 minutes
- Write the letters 'wh' on your board. Challenge children to make four 'question' words starting with 'wh' ('when', 'what', 'why', 'where', 'who') and to write them on their whiteboards.
- Tell the children to work with a partner and reread the whole journal entry. Challenge them to make the reading as dramatic as they can.
- How well do the children think they did? Ask them to colour in one of the thumbs.
- Share the joke!

7.2

UNIT 8

VILE VIKINGS: *SESSION 1*

Outcome:
- An audio commentary in a Viking museum

Writing targets:
- Target words: 'rowed', 'longship', 'Vikings'
- Sentences: one complex sentence, two simple sentences

You will need:
- Writing Logs page 15
- Whiteboards and pens
- Card for covering spellings

Warm Up

Phonics: 'rowed' *2 minutes*

- Robot-speak the word 'r/oh/d' then ask the children to blend the phonemes to make the word.
- Listen as they robot-speak and then blend the whole word.
- As they robot-speak 'rowed' again, write the letters on the board.
- Wipe your board clean, then ask the children to write the word on their whiteboards and add phoneme buttons (r/ow/ed).
- Tell the children to wipe their boards clean and to write 'rowed' three times in the Phonics box.

> Ensure that children understand the 'oh' sound is represented by the letters 'ow', and the 'd' sound is represented by the letters 'ed'.

Phonics: 'longship' *2 minutes*

- Ask the children what two words they can hear in 'longship' ('long' + 'ship'). Explain that this was a type of ship that the Vikings built.
- Robot-speak the word 'l/o/ng/sh/i/p' then ask the children to blend the phonemes to make the word.
- Listen as they robot-speak and then blend the whole word.
- As they robot-speak 'longship' again, write the letters on the board.
- Wipe your board clean, then ask the children to write the word on their whiteboard and add phoneme buttons.
- Tell the children to wipe their boards clean and to write 'longship' three times in the Phonics box.

> Ensure that children understand that the two letters 'ng' make one phoneme, and that 'sh' is also one phoneme.

Spelling: 'Vikings' *2 minutes*

- Explain that 'Vikings' is an irregular word so they will learn to spell it using letter names.
- Demonstrate how to spell the word 'Vikings', saying the letter names as you write. Remind the children that it has a capital letter because it is the name of a group of people.
- Wipe your board clean and ask the children to trace the word with their finger on their whiteboard, saying the letter names as they do so. Then ask them to write 'Vikings' on their whiteboards.
- Tell the children to wipe their boards clean, then write the word three times in the Spelling box.

> The word 'Vikings' is treated as irregular because the letter 'i' makes the long vowel sound 'igh'.

Guiding the Writing

Talk for Writing *3 minutes*

- Explain to the children that they are going to write an audio commentary for visitors to a Viking museum. Visitors will listen to this as they go around the exhibition. The commentary will tell the listener about how the Vikings lived and what they did.

48

- The children should imagine that the visitors are standing near a model of a Viking longship. The commentary needs to say that Vikings used boats like these to row across the sea and attack their enemies.
- *Turn to a partner and think of a sentence staring with: 'Vikings rowed across the …'. Try to use one of the words you've just practised in your sentence.*
- Share the children's ideas.

Demonstration Writing   3 minutes
- *I am going to write:* **Vikings rowed across the sea in longships to attack their enemies.** *As I write my sentence, I want you to study the word 'enemies' and then write it in the Have a go box.*
- Read the sentence together.

> Remind the children to write 'Viking' with a capital letter because it is the name of a group of people.

Independent Writing   3 minutes
- Allow the children 20 seconds to study your sentence, then wipe your board clean.
- Ask the children to turn to a partner and repeat what they are going to write.
- Tell them to cover their practised words and then to write the sentence under the picture of the longship.
- Check the children's work.

Talk for Writing   3 minutes
- *Now we are going to tell the visitors some more about life on a Viking longship. The rowers had to row to the beat of a drum in order to keep the rowing in time. This was very hard work and the rowers had to be very strong.*
- *Turn to a partner and think of a sentence to describe how the rowers kept in time. Start your sentence: 'They had to row …'. Then think of a second sentence starting 'It was very …'.*
- Share the children's ideas.

Demonstration Writing   3 minutes
- *I am going to write:* **They had to row in time to a drum. It was very hard work.**
- *As I write my sentences, I want you to write the word 'time' in the Have a go box.*
- Read the sentences together.

Independent Writing   3 minutes
- Allow the children 20 seconds to study your sentences, then wipe your board clean.
- Ask the children to turn to a partner and repeat what they are going to write.
- Tell them to cover their practised words and then to write the sentences.
- Check the children's work.

Rounding Off   3 minutes
- Ask the children if they have ever listened to an audio commentary in a museum. Why do they think museums provide audio commentaries? (To give information; to make it more interesting.)
- Have they learned anything new about the Vikings that they did not know before?
- Look together at the illustration. Does it give them any more information about Viking longships? (There is a dragon at the front of the ship to make it look more frightening; there are lots of rowers; they put their shields along the side of the ship.)

Review   3 minutes
- Ask the children which two words make the word 'longship' ('long' + 'ship'). Do they know any other words that are made from two smaller words? ('snowman', 'someone', 'into')
- Why did they use a capital letter when they wrote 'Viking'?
- How well do the children think they did? Ask them to colour in one of the thumbs.
- Share the joke!

8.1

UNIT 8

VILE VIKINGS: *SESSION 2*

Outcome:
- An audio commentary in a Viking museum

Writing targets:
- Target words: 'still', 'rotten', 'smelly'
- Revision word: 'sometimes'
- Sentences: one simple sentence, a compound sentence using 'and' and 'but'

You will need:
- Writing Logs page 16
- Whiteboards and pens
- Card for covering spellings

Warm Up

Phonics: 'still' — 2 minutes
- Robot-speak the word 's/t/i/ll' then ask the children to blend the phonemes to make the word.
- Listen as they robot-speak and then blend the whole word.
- As they robot-speak 'still' again, write the letters on the board.
- Wipe your board clean, then ask the children to write the word on their whiteboards and add phoneme buttons.
- Tell the children to wipe their boards clean and to write 'still' three times in the Phonics box.

Phonics: 'rotten' — 2 minutes
- Robot-speak the word 'r/o/tt/e/n' then ask the children to blend the phonemes to make the word.
- Listen as they robot-speak and then blend the whole word.
- As they robot-speak 'rotten' again, write the letters on the board.
- Wipe your board clean, then ask the children to write the word on their whiteboard and add phoneme buttons.
- Tell the children to wipe their boards clean and to write 'rotten' three times in the Phonics box.

> Ensure that children understand that in order to keep the 'o' as a short vowel they need to double the consonant 't'.

Phonics: 'smelly' — 2 minutes
- Robot-speak the word 's/m/e/ll/y' then ask the children to blend the phonemes to make the word.
- Listen as they robot-speak and then blend the whole word.
- As they robot-speak 'smelly' again, write the letters on the board.
- Wipe your board clean, then ask the children to write the word on their whiteboard and add phoneme buttons.
- Tell the children to wipe their boards clean and to write 'smelly' three times in the Phonics box.

Guiding the Writing

Talk for Writing — 4 minutes
- Explain to the children that they are going to write some more information about life on a Viking ship for the audio commentary.
- *The journeys took many days, and the Vikings had to take all their food and water with them. They used to put meat and fish into barrels and pack them in salt to stop them from going rotten.*
- *Turn to a partner and think of a sentence that will tell the listeners about how the Vikings took all their food with them, starting: 'They had to …'.*
- Share the children's ideas.

Demonstration Writing 2 minutes
- *I am going to write:* **They had to take all their food with them.** *As I write this sentence, I want you to write the word 'their' in the Have a go box.*
- Read the sentence together.

> Remind the children that a way to remember how to spell 'their' is 'the' + 'ir'.

Independent Writing 2 minutes
- Allow the children 10 seconds to study your sentence, then wipe your board clean.
- Ask the children to turn to a partner and repeat what they are going to write.
- Tell them to cover their practised words and then write the sentence.
- Check the children's work.

Talk for Writing 3 minutes
- *Now we are going to tell the visitors some more about the food. What food do you think they took with them? Sometimes the food would go rotten and it was very smelly, but they still had to eat it!*
- *Turn to partner and think of a sentence starting: 'Sometimes the food went ...' and then continue it with: 'but ...' to explain what happened to this food.*
- Share the children's ideas.

Demonstration Writing 3 minutes
- *I am going to write:* **Sometimes the food went rotten and it was very smelly but they still had to eat it!**
- *Which words can you hear in the word 'sometimes'? Study the word as I write it, then think of the two smaller words as you write 'sometimes' in the Have a go box.*
- Read the sentence together.

> Point out that the two joining words 'and' and 'but' help to give all the information in one long sentence.

Independent Writing 3 minutes
- Allow the children 20 seconds to study your sentence, then wipe your board clean.
- Ask the children to turn to a partner and repeat what they are going to write.
- Tell them to cover their practised words and then to write the sentence.
- Check the children's work.

Rounding Off 3 minutes
- Ask the children to read back the commentary they have written over the last two sessions. What have they learned about the Vikings? (The boats were called longships; they had drummers on board to keep the rowers in time; they had to take all their food and drink with them; sometimes the food went bad.)
- What else would they like to know about life on a longship? (What happened if a man did not keep up with the drum? Did women and children also go in the boats?)

Review 4 minutes
- Write the words 'rot' and 'rotten' on the board. Point out that when a suffix is added, the consonant is doubled to keep the vowel short. Challenge the children to write the words on their whiteboards.
- The last sentence could be divided into three short sentences. What are they? ('Sometimes the food went rotten.'; 'It was very smelly.'; 'They still had to eat it.') What words did they use to join the sentences? ('and', 'but')
- How well do the children think they did? Ask them to colour in one of the thumbs.
- Share the joke!

8.2

UNIT 9

CALL 999: *SESSION 1*

Outcome:
- A police statement

Writing targets:
- Target words: 'lights', 'wondered', 'putting'
- Sentences: two compound sentences

You will need:
- Writing Logs page 17
- Whiteboards and pens
- Card for covering spellings

Warm Up

Phonics: 'lights' — 2 minutes
- Robot-speak the word 'l/igh/t/s' then ask the children to blend the phonemes to make the word.
- Listen as they robot-speak and then blend the whole word.
- As they robot-speak 'lights' again, write the letters on the board.
- Wipe your board clean, then ask the children to write the word on their whiteboards and add phoneme buttons.
- Tell the children to wipe their boards clean and to write 'lights' three times in the Phonics box.

Ensure that children understand that the letters 'igh' are one phoneme.

Spelling: 'wondered' — 2 minutes
- Explain that 'wondered' is an irregular word so they will learn to spell it using letter names.
- Demonstrate how to spell the word 'wondered', saying the letter names as you write.
- Wipe your board clean and ask the children to trace the word with their finger on their whiteboard, saying the letter names as they do so. Then ask them to write 'wondered' on their whiteboards.
- Tell the children to wipe their boards clean, then write the word three times in the Spelling box.

Ensure that children understand the meaning of the word 'wondered': to ask yourself about something.

Spelling: 'putting' — 2 minutes
- Explain that 'putting' is an irregular word so they will learn to spell it using letter names.
- Demonstrate how to spell the word 'putting', saying the letter names as you write.
- Wipe your board clean and ask the children to trace the word with their finger on their whiteboard, saying the letter names as they do so. Then ask them to write 'putting' on their whiteboards.
- Tell the children to wipe their boards clean, then write the word three times in the Spelling box.

Guiding the Writing

Talk for Writing — 4 minutes
- Tell the children to look at the picture of Alex and Sarah looking in at a window. They can see a man using a copier to print bank notes.
- *Imagine that Alex and Sarah are at the police station. The police want to convict the man, but first they need to hear from the children what they saw the man doing and what they did. This is called a police statement. Alex is going to talk to the police first.*
- *Alex and Sarah were curious about the house because they had seen the lights on for two whole days, so they wondered what was going on.*

- *Turn to a partner and think of what Alex will say to the police. Start your sentence: 'We saw that the lights …', and then join the second part of your sentence with: 'and we wondered …'.*
- Share the children's ideas.

Demonstration Writing   3 minutes
- *I am going to write:* **We saw that the lights were on all day and we wondered what was going on.** *As I write the word 'were', I want you to write it in the Have a go box. When I come to the word 'wondered' I want you to tell me how to spell it.*
- Read the sentence together.

Independent Writing   3 minutes
- Allow the children 20 seconds to study your sentence then wipe your board clean.
- Ask the children to turn to a partner and repeat what they are going to write.
- Tell them to cover their practised words and then to write the sentence.
- Check the children's work.

Talk for Writing   3 minutes
- *Now Alex wants to tell the police what they saw. What did they see when they looked in the window? (the man putting bank notes into a copier) Why was he doing this? (To make lots of money for himself.)*
- *Turn to a partner and think of a sentence starting: 'We looked in and saw …'. Think about how you can use the word 'putting' that you practised earlier.*
- Share the children's ideas.

Demonstration Writing   3 minutes
- *I am going to write the sentence:* **We looked in and saw a man putting bank notes in a copier.**
- *As I write, I want you to tell me how to spell 'looked' and 'saw'. Then I want you to write them in your Have a go box.*
- Read the sentence together.

> Remind the children that they have practised 'looking' in a previous session. Explain that 'looked' has 'ed' in place of the 'ing'.

Independent Writing   2 minutes
- Allow the children 20 seconds to study your sentence, then wipe your board clean, leaving 'bank notes' and 'copier' for them to copy.
- Ask the children to turn to a partner and repeat what they are going to write.
- Tell them to cover their practised words and then to write the sentence.
- Check the children's work.

Rounding Off   3 minutes
- Ask the class if, based on the picture, they think Alex is making an accurate statement to the police. Why is it important for him to be accurate? (The police will use it as evidence to convict the man.)
- Do the group think Sarah and Alex were sensible to look in the window? What might happen next?

Review   3 minutes
- Write the letters 'f', 'm', 'n', 'r' and 's' on your board. Challenge the children to make five 'ight' words using the letters ('fight', 'might', 'night', 'right', 'sight') and to write these on their whiteboards.
- What questions might the police have asked Sarah and Alex? (Why did you go near the house? What did you see when you looked in?)
- How well do the children think they did? Ask them to colour in one of the thumbs.
- Share the joke!

9.1

UNIT 9

CALL 999: *SESSION 2*

Outcome:
- A police statement

Writing targets:
- Target words: 'instead', 'began', 'notes'
- Sentences: two compound sentences, a short sentence

You will need:
- Writing Logs page 18
- Whiteboards and pens
- Card for covering spellings

If the children are familiar with the letters 'ea' making the short 'e' sound, this word could be taught using phonics.

Warm Up

Spelling: 'instead' — 2 minutes
- Explain that 'instead' is an irregular word so they will learn to spell it using letter names.
- Demonstrate how to spell the word 'instead', saying the letter names as you write.
- Wipe your board clean and ask the children to trace the word with their finger on their whiteboard, saying the letter names as they do so. Then ask them to write 'instead' on their whiteboards.
- Tell the children to wipe their boards clean, then write the word three times in the Spelling box.

Phonics: 'began' — 2 minutes
- Robot-speak the word 'b/e/g/a/n' then ask the children to blend the phonemes to make the word.
- Listen as they robot-speak and then blend the whole word.
- As they robot-speak 'began' again, write the letters on the board.
- Wipe your board clean, then ask the children to write the word on their whiteboards and add phoneme buttons.
- Tell the children to wipe their boards clean and to write 'began' three times in the Phonics box.

Phonics: 'notes' — 2 minutes
- Robot-speak the word 'n/oh/t/s' then ask the children to blend the phonemes to make the word.
- Listen as they robot-speak and then blend the whole word.
- As they robot-speak 'notes' again, write the letters on the board. Ask the children to identify which letters are making the long vowel 'oh' sound. Tell the children to link the 'o' and 'e'.
- Wipe your board clean, then ask the children to write the word on their boards.
- Tell the children to wipe their boards clean and to write 'notes' three times in the Phonics box.

Guiding the Writing

Talk for Writing — 3 minutes
- Reread the first part of the police statement from the previous session. Explain that Sarah now has to describe what happened next.
- *Look at the first picture. Sarah tripped over. The man heard the noise and came out to see what was going on. What might the man have been thinking of doing? (hurting or at least frightening the children) Turn to a partner and think of what Sarah will say to the police. Start your sentence: 'I tripped over and …'.*
- Share the children's ideas.

Demonstration Writing 2 minutes
- *I am going to write:* **I tripped over and the man saw us.** *Watch carefully as I write the word 'tripped'. Tell me the letter names as I write them. Then write it in your Have a go box.*

  > Point out the double 'p' in 'tripped'.
- Read the sentence together.

Independent Writing 2 minutes
- Allow the children 10 seconds to study your sentence, then wipe your board clean.
- Ask the children to turn to a partner and repeat what they are going to write.
- Tell them to cover their practised words and then write the sentence.
- Check the children's work.

Talk for Writing 4 minutes
- *Look at the second picture. The man suspected that Alex and Sarah had already phoned the police, so he decided to put the bank notes in a bag and try to get away before the police arrive.*
- *First Sarah is going to tell the police what happened after the man saw them. What did Sarah think when she saw the man?* (that he was going to hurt them) *What did the man do instead?* (put the bank notes in his bag and tried to get away)
- *Turn to a partner and think of a long sentence starting: 'We thought he was …'. Join the second part of your sentence with the words: 'but instead he began …'.*
- Share the children's ideas.

Demonstration Writing 3 minutes
- *I am going to write the sentence:* **We thought he was going to hurt us but instead he began putting the bank notes in a bag.**
- *As I write, I want you to tell me how to spell 'thought' and 'hurt'. Then I want you to write them in your Have a go box.*
- Read the sentence together.

Independent Writing 3 minutes
- Allow the children 20 seconds to study your sentence, then wipe your board clean.
- Ask the children to turn to a partner and repeat what they are going to write.
- Tell them to cover their practised words and then to write the sentence.
- Check the children's work.

Demonstration Writing 1 minute
- *To finish off, Sarah tells the police that she called them. So I am going to write:* **I called 999.** *Write that now on your police statement.*

Rounding Off 3 minutes
- Ask the group if they think Alex and Sarah were brave. What might have happened to them?
- Will the police be pleased with Alex and Sarah? Might they get a reward?
- What might happen to the man?

Review 3 minutes
- Ask the children to look again at the word 'instead'. How will they remember how to spell it? (listen to the sounds; remember that the 'e' sound is made with the letters 'ea') Challenge them to write 'head', 'dead' and 'bread' on their whiteboards.
- Tell the children to look at the pronouns in the statement. Work out who each pronoun refers to ('I' = Sarah; 'us' = Sarah and Alex; 'We' = Sarah and Alex; 'he' = the man forging the money; 'us' = Sarah and Alex; 'he' = the man; 'I' = Sarah).
- How well do the children think they did? Ask them to colour in one of the thumbs.
- Share the joke!

9.2

UNIT 10

STOP THE SMUGGLING!

Outcome:
- A poster

Writing targets:
- Target words: 'belt', 'caught'
- Revision word: 'wearing'
- Sentences: one expanded simple sentence, two simple sentences

You will need:
- Writing Logs page 19
- Whiteboards and pens
- Card for covering spellings

> The word 'caught' is treated as irregular because the letters 'augh' represent the sound 'or'.

Warm Up

Phonics: 'belt' *2 minutes*
- Robot-speak the word 'b/e/l/t' then ask the children to blend the phonemes to make the word.
- Listen as they robot-speak and then blend the whole word.
- As they robot-speak 'belt' again, write the letters on the board.
- Wipe your board clean, then ask the children to write the word on their whiteboard, adding phoneme buttons.
- Tell the children to wipe their boards clean and to write 'belt' three times in the Phonics box.

Spelling: 'caught' *2 minutes*
- Explain that 'caught' is an irregular word so they will learn to spell it using letter names.
- Demonstrate how to spell the word 'caught', saying the letter names as you write.
- Wipe your board clean and ask the children to trace the word with their finger on their whiteboard, saying the letter names as they do so. Then ask them to write 'caught' on their whiteboards.
- Tell the children to wipe their boards clean, then write the word three times in the Spelling box.

Revision: 'wearing' *1 minute*
- Remind the children that they have practised the word 'wear' in an earlier session. The word 'wearing' is just the same but with 'ing' added onto the end.
- Write 'wearing' on your board, saying the letter names as you write it. Point at each letter and ask the children to say the letter names as you do so.
- Tell the children to study the word for five seconds, then wipe your board clean and ask them to write the word in the Have a go box.

Guiding the Writing

Talk for Writing *5 minutes*
- Explain to the children that they are going to write a poster that would be displayed at a Customs point. Explain that it is somewhere in an airport where Customs officers check whether anyone is bringing anything into the country illegally. The aim of the poster is to try to stop people smuggling animals into this country and to show people what happens if they get caught.
- *Look at the heading: 'Stop the smuggling!'. Why do you think people try to smuggle in animals? (because they can sell them for a lot of money) What animals do you think people might try to smuggle into this country?*

56

- *Look at the pictures. One shows a rare snake, and the other shows a man in handcuffs. The man tried to smuggle a snake into the country by pretending it was his belt, but the Customs officers caught him.*
- *Turn to a partner and think of two sentences that will describe what the man did. Start the first sentence: 'A man was caught …' and the second: 'He was wearing …'.*
- *Share the children's ideas.*

Demonstration Writing   4 minutes
- *I am going to write:* **A man was caught trying to hide a snake.** *As I write this sentence, I want you to write the word 'trying' in the Have a go box.*
- *Next I am going to write:* **He was wearing it as a belt!** *I have put an exclamation mark at the end of the sentence to emphasise how surprising this is.*
- *Read the sentences together.*

> Point out that you do not need to repeat 'A man' as the 'He' refers to the man.

Independent Writing   3 minutes
- *Allow the children 20 seconds to study your sentences, then wipe your board clean.*
- *Ask the children to turn to a partner and repeat what they are going to write.*
- *Tell them to cover their practised words and then to write the sentences.*
- *Check the children's work.*

Talk for Writing   3 minutes
- *Now we need to write what happened to the man. We want to make sure that everyone sees that smuggling is severely punished. What do you think his punishment should be?*
- *Turn to a partner and think of a sentence starting: 'He was sent to …'.*
- *Share the children's ideas.*

Demonstration Writing   2 minutes
- *To finish the poster I am going to write:* **He was sent to prison for two years.**
- *As I write my sentence, I want you to write 'went' in the Have a go box.*
- *Read the sentence together.*

Independent Writing   2 minutes
- *Allow the children 10 seconds to study your sentence, then wipe your board clean, leaving the word 'prison' for them to copy.*
- *Ask the children to turn to a partner and repeat what they are going to write.*
- *Tell them to cover their practised words and then to write the sentence.*
- *Check the children's work.*

Rounding Off   3 minutes
- *Ask the group whether they think that this poster would make a smuggler think twice about trying to bring in illegal animals.*
- *Ask the children: why shouldn't people be allowed to bring any animals into this country without declaring them? (Some of the animals are becoming extinct; many animals die because the journey is too long and the climate is not right for them; people could go to zoos to see the animals instead.)*

Review   3 minutes
- *Challenge the children to write 'caught' from memory on their whiteboards.*
- *What are the features in this poster? (a heading to draw the reader's attention; photographs to grab attention and to show that this is a true story; brief sentences to give information quickly)*
- *How well do the children think they did? Ask them to colour in one of the thumbs.*
- *Share the joke!*

10.1

UNIT 10
WRITE IT! *ASSESSMENT*

Outcome:
- Assessment of skills covered in Book 7

Writing targets:
- Handwriting: all letter formation
- Spelling: independent spelling of 31 key words
- Writing: accurately punctuating sentences

You will need:
- Writing Logs page 20
- Whiteboards and pens

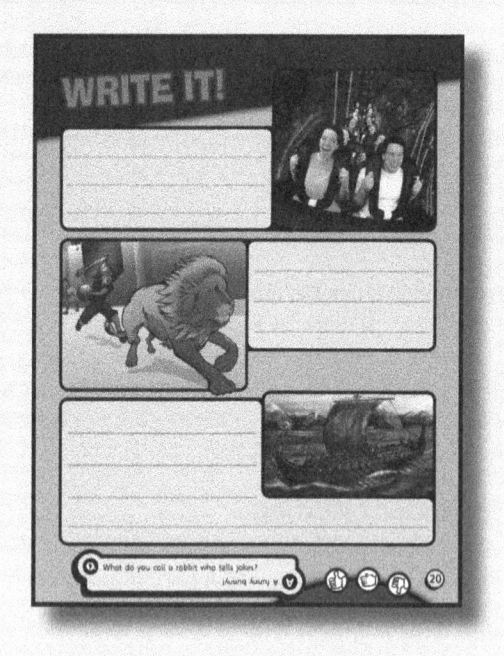

Writing Task

Revision: 'first' *1 minute*
- In a minute you are going spell the word 'first'. How are you going to remember how to spell that word? Have a go at writing 'first' on your whiteboard.

Assessment 1 *7 minutes*
- *Look at the first picture. It shows a roller-coaster going up the ramp. Remember writing a brochure enticing people to come to a theme park? The roller-coaster was the fastest in the world.*
- Tell the children that they are going to write two sentences: First you go up very slowly. Then you go down very, very fast.
- *What will you remember about starting a sentence and finishing it? What strategies can you use to help you with the spelling of the words? Say the sentences to yourself and then spell each word carefully. Also think about forming each letter accurately as you write it.*
- Warn the children that you will only say the sentences once.
- Dictate the sentences: **First you go up very slowly. Then you go down very, very fast.**

Check Points

- Encourage the children to picture the word 'f/ir/s/t'.

As the children write, observe:
- letter formation
- spelling strategies
- strategies to recall the sentence (rereading what they have written so far, saying the sentence to themselves).

After the children have written the sentences, ask them to check them and to decide if they have:
- remembered to write every word
- spelt each word correctly.

Revision: 'scared' *1 minute*
- *In a minute you are going to spell the word 'scared'. How are you going to remember how to spell that word? Have a go at writing the word on your whiteboard.*

- Encourage the children to picture the word 'scared'.

Assessment 2 *7 minutes*
- *Look at the second picture. Remember writing some diary entries for Scott who slipped back in time to find himself in an arena in Roman times? First he had to fight a gladiator, and then a lion entered the arena. Scott charged at the lion and it turned and ran away.*
- Tell the children that they are going to write the sentence: I must have scared it because it ran away.
- *How many words are there in that sentence? (9) What will you remember about starting a sentence and finishing it? What strategies can you use to help you with the spelling of the words? Say the sentences to yourself and then spell each word carefully. Also think about forming each letter accurately as you write it.*
- Warn the children you will only say the sentence once.
- Dictate the sentence: **I must have scared it because it ran away.**

As the children write, observe:
- letter formation
- spelling strategies
- strategies to recall the sentence (rereading what they have written so far, saying the sentence to themselves).

After the children have written the sentence, ask them to check it and to decide if they have:
- remembered to write every word
- spelt each word correctly.

Revision: 'sometimes' *1 minute*
- *In a minute you are going to spell the word 'sometimes'. How are you going to remember how to spell that word? What two words make the word 'sometimes'? ('some' + 'times') Have a go at writing the word on your whiteboard.*

- Encourage the children to picture the word 'sometimes'.

Assessment 3 *7 minutes*
- *Look at the third picture. Remember writing about life on a Viking longship? The sailors who rowed the boats across the seas had to take all their food and drink with them. They used to put meat and fish into barrels packed with salt to try to stop it going rotten, but often it went bad. It was the only food they had so they still had to eat it.*
- Tell the children they are going to write the sentence: Sometimes the food went rotten and it was very smelly but they still had to eat it!
- *How many words are there in that sentence? (17) What will you remember about starting a sentence and finishing it? What strategies can you use to help you with the spelling of the words? Say the sentence to yourself and then spell each word carefully. Also think about forming each letter accurately as you write it.*
- Warn the children that you will only say the sentence once.
- Dictate the sentence: **Sometimes the food went rotten and it was very smelly but they still had to eat it!**

As the children write observe:
- letter formation
- spelling strategies
- strategies to recall the sentence (rereading what they have written so far, saying the sentence to themselves).

After the children have written the sentence, ask them to check it and to decide if they have:
- remembered to write every word
- spelt each word correctly.

Review *6 minutes*
- Encourage the children to reread their writing. Are there any words that they think they might have got wrong? Tell them to put a little line under any letters they think might be wrong.
- Ask the children to look back through their book. Which writing activity did they like best? Which is their best writing?
- What have they learned? Encourage them to talk about: capital letters, full stops, question marks, spelling strategies, captions, labels, first-person writing.
- How well do the children think they did? Ask them to colour in one of the thumbs.
- Share the joke!

Go to the orange box on page 22 in the Writing Log for an unaided writing activity.
See page 143 of this Teaching Guide for guidance notes.

10.2

UNIT 11

CHEAT! SESSION 1

Outcome:
- A newspaper report

Writing targets:
- Target words: 'cheat', 'children', 'water'
- Sentences: one simple sentence, one compound sentence, one complex sentence

You will need:
- Writing Logs page 1
- Whiteboards and pens
- Card for covering spellings

Ensure that children understand that the 'ee' sound is made with the letters 'ea'.

Point out that 'children' is the word 'child' with 'ren' added to make the plural.

Warm Up

Phonics: 'cheat' — 2 minutes
- Robot-speak the word 'ch/ee/t' then ask the children to blend the phonemes to make the word.
- Listen as they robot-speak and then blend the whole word.
- As they robot-speak 'cheat' again, write the letters on the board.
- Wipe your board clean, then ask the children to write the word on their whiteboards and add phoneme buttons (ch/ea/t).
- Tell the children to wipe their boards clean and write 'cheat' three times in the Phonics box.

Spelling: 'children' — 2 minutes
- Explain that 'children' is an irregular word so they will learn to spell it using letter names.
- Demonstrate how to spell the word 'children', saying the letter names as you write.
- Wipe your board clean and ask the children to trace the word with their finger on their whiteboards, saying the letter names as they do so. Then ask them to write 'children' on their whiteboards.
- Tell the children to wipe their boards clean, then write the word three times in the Spelling box.

Spelling: 'water' — 2 minutes
- Explain that 'water' is an irregular word so they will learn to spell it using letter names.
- Demonstrate how to spell the word 'water', saying the letter names as you write.
- Wipe your board clean and ask the children to trace the word with their finger on their whiteboards, saying the letter names as they do so. Then ask them to write 'water' on their whiteboards.
- Tell the children to wipe their boards clean, then write the word three times in the Spelling box.

Guiding the Writing

Talk for Writing — 3 minutes
- Explain to the group that they are going to write a newspaper report about two children who discovered a man tricking people by selling water he has filled from the tap as 'spring water'.
- *Look at the picture and read the headline: 'Con Man Caught'. How is the man conning people? (He is selling bottles of water he has filled from the tap as 'spring water'.)*
- Explain that the newspaper wants its readers to know that this man is a cheat, so the first sentence will say just that. Then the second sentence will explain why he is a cheat.

- *Turn to a partner and think of a short and dramatic first sentence starting: This man …' . Start the second sentence: 'He fills bottles with …'.*
- Share the children's ideas.

Demonstration Writing   3 minutes
- *I am going to write:* **This man is a cheat!** *I have put an exclamation mark at the end to make the sentence more dramatic.*
- *For the second sentence I am going to write:* **He fills bottles with tap water and sells them.** *As I write the sentence, I want you to practise the words 'fills' and 'sells' in the Have a go box.*
- Read the sentences together.

Independent Writing   3 minutes
- Allow the children 20 seconds to study your sentences, then wipe your board clean, leaving the word 'bottles' for them to copy.
- Ask the children to turn to a partner and to repeat what they are going to write.
- Tell them to cover their practised words and then to write the sentences.
- Check the children's work.

Talk for Writing   3 minutes
- *Next we are going to explain what the two children, Alex and Sarah, did to stop the man.*
- *If you saw someone cheating in this way would you try to stop them? Would you be afraid that they might be very angry and attack you?*
- *The next sentence will be a longer sentence which links with the information we've written so far: 'When two children saw what he …'.*
- Share the children's ideas.

Demonstration Writing   3 minutes
- Write the following sentence, leaving the comma out for now: **When two children saw what he was doing, they told him to stop.**
- *As I write the word 'When' I want you to practise it in the Have a go box. When I come to the word 'doing', tell me the letter names to spell it.*
- Read the sentence together and explain that you will add a comma after 'doing' to help the reader follow the sense of the sentence.
- Read the sentence together.

> Point out that the word 'doing' in just 'do' + 'ing'.

Independent Writing   3 minutes
- Allow the children 20 seconds to study your sentence, then wipe your board clean.
- Ask the children to turn to a partner and repeat what they are going to write.
- Tell them to cover their practised words and then to write the sentence.
- Check the children's work.

Rounding Off   3 minutes
- Ask the children to say why they think the heading 'Con Man Caught' is good. (It is short and to the point.)
- Why does the newspaper call the man a cheat? (He was pretending that the water he was selling was special spring water, when in fact it was just tap water.)
- Is the newspaper sympathetic towards the man? (No, it is angry with him.)

Review   3 minutes
- Write the word 'cheat' on your board. Then write the letters: 'b', 'h', 'm', 'n', 's'. Challenge the children to write five words which rhyme with 'cheat' and use these letters on their whiteboards.
- Ask the group why they made the first sentence short and included an exclamation mark. (To grab the readers' attention and to be dramatic.)
- How well do the children think they did? Ask them to colour in one of the thumbs.
- Share the joke!

11.1

UNIT 11

CHEAT! *SESSION 2*

Outcome:
- A newspaper report

Writing targets:
- Target words: 'sprayed', 'arrested', 'gave'
- Revision word: 'bravery'
- Sentences: two compound sentences

You will need:
- Writing Logs page 2
- Whiteboards and pens
- Card for covering spellings

Warm Up

Phonics: 'sprayed' — 2 minutes
- Robot-speak the word 's/p/r/ay/d' then ask the children to blend the phonemes to make the word.
- Listen as they robot-speak and then blend the whole word.
- As they robot-speak 'sprayed' again, write the letters on the board.
- Wipe your board clean, then ask the children to write the word on their whiteboards and add phoneme buttons (s/p/r/ay/ed).
- Tell the children to wipe their boards clean and write 'sprayed' three times in the Phonics box.

> Ensure that children are aware that the letters 'ed' are making a 'd' sound.

Phonics: 'arrested' — 2 minutes
- Robot-speak the word 'a/rr/e/s/t/e/d' then ask the children to blend the phonemes to make the word.
- Listen as they robot-speak and then blend the whole word.
- As they robot-speak 'arrested' again, write the letters on the board.
- Wipe your board clean, then ask the children to write the word on their whiteboards and add phoneme buttons.
- Tell the children to wipe their boards clean and to write 'arrested' three times in the Phonics box.

> Ensure that children are aware that in this word the letters 'ed' are making the two sounds 'e' and 'd'.

Phonics: 'gave' — 2 minutes
- Robot-speak the word 'g/ay/v' then ask the children to blend the phonemes to make the word.
- Listen as they robot-speak and then blend the whole word.
- As they robot-speak 'gave' again, write the letters on the board. Ask the children to identify which letters are making the long vowel 'ay' sound. Tell the children to link the 'a' and 'e'.
- Wipe your board clean, then ask the children to write the word on their whiteboards.
- Tell the children to wipe their boards clean and to write 'gave' three times in the Phonics box.

Guiding the Writing

Talk for Writing — 4 minutes
- Reread the beginning of the newspaper report from Session 1. Explain to the group that we want to give the readers some more details about what happened when the children challenged the man.
- *Look at the first picture. How would the man be feeling when the children found him out? (angry) What does the picture show him doing? (spraying the children with water) What will the children do to get help? (call the police on 999)*

62

- *Turn to a partner and think of a long sentence that starts: 'The man was very angry and …'. Use the words 'sprayed' and 'water' in the first part of your sentence. Link the second part of the sentence with the words 'but they called …', and then explain what the children did.*
- Share the children's ideas.

Demonstration Writing   3 minutes
- *I am going to write:* **The man was very angry and he sprayed them with water but they called 999 just in time.** *As I write the word 'called', I want you to practise it in your Have a go box.*
- *I have used 'and' and 'but' to link together the parts of this long sentence.*
- *I have written 999 as numbers because it is a phone number.*
- Read the sentence together.

> Remind the children that they have learned the word 'angry' in a previous session.

Independent Writing   3 minutes
- Allow the children 20 seconds to study your sentence, then wipe your board clean.
- Ask the children to turn to a partner and repeat what they are going to write.
- Tell them to cover their practised words and then to write the sentence.
- Check the children's work.

Talk for Writing   3 minutes
- Explain to the group that they are now going to finish the newspaper report by telling the readers how the man was punished and the brave children were rewarded.
- *What would the police do when they saw what the man had been doing? (arrest him) Look at the pictures. The children have been given medals. Why have they been given medals? (because they reported a crime to the police)*
- *Turn to a partner and think of a sentence starting: 'The police arrested him and …'.*
- Share the children's ideas.

Demonstration Writing   2 minutes
- *I am going to write:* **The police arrested him and gave the children medals for their bravery.** *As I write, I want you to practise 'children' in the Have a go box.*
- Read the sentence together.

> Point out that they have learned the word 'brave' in a previous session. The word 'bravery' is just 'brave' with 'ry'.

Independent Writing   3 minutes
- Allow the children 10 seconds to study your sentence, then wipe your board clean, leaving the words 'police' and 'medals' for them to copy.
- Ask the children to turn to a partner and repeat what they are going to write.
- Tell them to cover their practised words and then to write the sentence.
- Check the children's work.

Rounding Off   3 minutes
- What do you think will happen to the man? (He will have to stop selling the water; he may have to pay a fine.)
- Why is it a good idea to have 'just in time' at the end of the first sentence? (It makes it sound more dramatic and more exciting for the reader.)
- Do you think the newspaper editor will be pleased with the story? Why would he or she want the story to be dramatic? (It will make more people buy the paper.)

Review   3 minutes
- Write the words 'brave', 'gave' and 'save' on the board and challenge the children to identify the pattern ('ave'). Ask them if 'ave' always rhymes with the word 'gave' (no, not in the word 'have').
- Ask the children which two words link the parts of the first sentence ('and', 'but'). What do we call these sorts of words? (conjunctions)
- How well do the children think they did? Ask them to colour in one of the thumbs.
- Share the joke!

11.2

UNIT 12

GET THE MESSAGE! *SESSION 1*

Outcome:
- An online encyclopaedia entry

Writing targets:
- Target words: 'message', 'letter', 'sending'
- Sentences: two complex sentences, one simple sentence

You will need:
- Writing Logs page 3
- Whiteboards and pens
- Card for covering spellings

Point out that there are two syllables in 'mess/age' and remind the children that breaking a word into syllables can help them to spell it.

Warm Up

Spelling: 'message' — 2 minutes
- Explain that 'message' is an irregular word so they will learn to spell it using letter names.
- Demonstrate how to spell the word 'message', saying the letter names as you write.
- Wipe your board clean and ask the children to trace the word with their finger on their whiteboards, saying the letter names as they do so. Then ask them to write 'message' on their whiteboards.
- Tell the children to wipe their boards clean, then write the word three times in the Spelling box.

Phonics: 'letter' — 2 minutes
- Robot-speak the word 'l/e/tt/er' then ask the children to blend the phonemes to make the word.
- Listen as they robot-speak and then blend the whole word.
- As they robot-speak 'letter' again, write the letters on the board.
- Wipe your board clean, then ask the children to write the word on their whiteboards and add phoneme buttons.
- Tell the children to wipe their boards clean and to write 'letter' three times in the Phonics box.

Phonics: 'sending' — 2 minutes
- Robot-speak the word 's/e/n/d/i/ng' then ask the children to blend the phonemes to make the word.
- Listen as they robot-speak and then blend the whole word.
- As they robot-speak 'sending' again, write the letters on the board.
- Wipe your board clean, then ask the children to write the word on their whiteboards and add phoneme buttons.
- Tell the children to wipe their boards clean and to write 'sending' three times in the Phonics box.

Remind children that the letters 'ng' represent one phoneme.

Guiding the Writing

Talk for Writing — 4 minutes
- Explain to the children that they are going to write an online encyclopaedia entry describing how people used to send messages to each other – using flags! Ask them if anyone knows what this is called (semaphore).
- *Look at the picture of the man using the flags. Why do you think there was someone using binoculars? (To be able to see the other people with flags responding.) Why do you think flags were used? (They were big enough to be seen; they were not too heavy to hold; they were brightly coloured.)*

64

- *Semaphore was used when people could see each other but couldn't hear each other. Turn to a partner and think of a sentence starting: 'People used flags to send …'.*
- Share the children's ideas.

Demonstration Writing   3 minutes
- *I am going to write:* **People used flags to send messages to people they could see but not hear.**
- *Study the word 'flags' as I write it and say the letter sounds to yourselves. How many phonemes are there in the word? (five – 'f/l/a/g/s') Now write it in the Have a go box.*
- Read the sentence together.

> Remind the children that one way to help with the spelling of 'people' is to say it as 'pe-ople'.

Independent Writing   2 minutes
- Allow the children 20 seconds to study your sentence, then wipe your board clean.
- Ask the children to turn to a partner and repeat what they are going to write.
- Tell them to cover their practised words and then to write the sentence.
- Check the children's work.

Talk for Writing   3 minutes
- *Now we are going to give the readers some more information about how flags were used to send a message. Look at the semaphore flags at the bottom of the page. What letters are they making? (A, B, C, D) Do you think semaphore is a fast or slow way of sending a message? Why?*
- *Turn to a partner and think of two sentences. The first sentence should describe how the flags were used, and start: 'A letter was made …'. The second sentence should say if this was a fast or slow way to send a message, and start: 'Sending a message was …'.*
- Share the children's ideas.

Demonstration Writing   3 minutes
- *I am going to write:* **A letter was made by the way you held the flags.** *As I write the sentence, I want you to write 'way' in the Have a go box.*
- *Then I am going to write:* **Sending a message was very slow.** *As I write the sentence, I want you to write 'slow' in the Have a go box.*
- Read the sentences together.

> Tell the children to think about how they spell 'say' and 'day' and to use the pattern to help them to spell 'way'.

Independent Writing   3 minutes
- Allow the children 20 seconds to study your sentences, then wipe your board clean.
- Ask the children to turn to a partner and repeat what they are going to write.
- Tell them to cover their practised words and then to write the sentences.
- Check the children's work.

Rounding Off   3 minutes
- Ask the children to think of situations when semaphore would be a useful way to send a message (between ships; across hills; where there is too much noise, for example directing aeroplanes at an airport).
- Why do they think that semaphore is not used very much today? (You can send emails, or you can use a mobile phone to speak or send text messages.)

Review   3 minutes
- Ask the children which two words they practised at the start of the session had double letters in them ('message', 'letters'). Challenge them to write these words on their whiteboards.
- Write the word 'sending' on the board and the letters 'b', 'l', 'm' and 'sp'. Challenge the children to write four words that rhyme with 'sending' on their whiteboards.
- How well do the children think they did? Ask them to colour in one of the thumbs.
- Share the joke!

12.1

UNIT 12

GET THE MESSAGE! *SESSION 2*

Outcome:
- An online encyclopaedia entry

Writing targets:
- Target words: 'anywhere', 'quick', 'million'
- Revision word: 'text'
- Sentences: four simple sentences

You will need:
- Writing Logs page 4
- Whiteboards and pens
- Card for covering spellings

Warm Up
Spelling: 'anywhere' — 2 minutes
- Ask the children what two words they can hear in 'anywhere' ('any' + 'where').
- Explain that 'anywhere' is an irregular word so they will learn to spell it using letter names.
- Demonstrate how to spell the word 'anywhere', saying the letter names as you write.
- Wipe your board clean and ask the children to trace the word with their finger on their whiteboards, saying the letter names as they do so. Then ask them to write 'anywhere' on their whiteboards.
- Tell the children to wipe their boards clean, then write the word three times in the Spelling box.

> Remind children that if they can break a long word into smaller words it makes it easier to spell.

Phonics: 'quick' — 2 minutes
- Robot-speak the word 'k/w/i/ck' then ask the children to blend the phonemes to make the word.
- Listen as they robot-speak and then blend the whole word.
- As they robot-speak 'quick' again, write the letters on the board.
- Wipe your board clean, then ask the children to write the word on their whiteboards and add phoneme buttons (qu/i/ck).
- Tell the children to wipe their boards clean and to write 'quick' three times in the Phonics box.

> Point out that a 'q' is followed by the letter 'u'.

Spelling: 'million' — 2 minutes
- Explain that 'million' is an irregular word so they will learn to spell it using letter names.
- Demonstrate how to spell the word 'million', saying the letter names as you write.
- Wipe your board clean and ask the children to trace the word with their finger on their whiteboards, saying the letter names as they do so. Then ask them to write 'million' on their whiteboards.
- Tell the children to wipe their boards clean, then to write the word three times in the Spelling box.

> The word 'million' is irregular in that the 'i' in 'ion' is sounded as 'ee'. If children are familiar with the letter 'i' making the 'ee' sound, this word could be taught using phonics.

Guiding the Writing
Talk for Writing — 3 minutes
- Explain to the children that they are going to write an online encyclopaedia entry describing how people send text messages today.
- *When you text, do you write in the same way that you write for school? What is different about your writing?*
- *Today you can text people anywhere in the world with a mobile phone. Turn to a partner and think of a sentence starting: 'People can text…'. Try to include one of the words you've just practised.*
- Share the children's ideas.

Demonstration Writing
2 minutes
- *I am going to write:* **People can text anywhere in the world.**
- *As I write this sentence I want you to study the word 'text'. How many phonemes are there in the word? Say the sounds 't/e/x/t' and then write the word in the Have a go box.*
- Read the sentence together.

Independent Writing
2 minutes
- Allow the children 10 seconds to study your sentence, then wipe your board clean
- Ask the children to turn to a partner and repeat what they are going to write.
- Tell them to cover their practised words and then to write the sentence.
- Check the children's work.

Talk for Writing
4 minutes
- *Next we want to make sure that everyone understands how quick it is to send a text. How many text messages do you think are sent every day in the UK? Over 200 million text messages are sent every day in the UK!*
- *Turn to a partner and think of two sentences. The first sentence should say that texting is very fast. What word did you learn at the start of the session that you could use instead of 'fast'? ('quick') Start your sentence: 'Sending a text is ...'.*
- *The second sentence should amaze people. Can you remember how many text messages are sent every day in the UK? Start your sentence: 'In the UK ...'.*
- Share the children's ideas.

Demonstration Writing
4 minutes
- *I am going to write:* **Sending a text is very quick.** *As I write that sentence I want you to write 'Sending' in the Have a go box.*
- Then I am going to write: **In the UK over 200 million texts are sent every day!** *As I write the sentence, I want you to write 'every' in the Have a go box.*
- *I am going to finish my sentence with an exclamation mark because that is such an amazing number of texts.*
- Read the sentences together.

> Remind the children to write 'Sending' with a capital letter because it is at the start of a sentence.

Independent Writing
3 minutes
- Allow the children 20 seconds to study your sentences then wipe your board clean.
- Ask the children to turn to a partner and repeat what they are going to write.
- Tell them to cover their practised words and then to write the sentences.
- Check the children's work.

Rounding Off
3 minutes
- Ask them to imagine they have a mobile phone and they want to send a message to a friend. Tell one child to suggest a message orally and the other to answer it.
- Do they know any of the ways they can make words shorter when sending a text? (For example 'Are you' can be shorted to 'RU'.) Write their suggestions on your board and share them with the group.
- Write the following texts on your board: CUl8ter (See You Later); LOL (Laughing Out Loud). Can the children work out what they mean?

Review
3 minutes
- Ask the children what two words make the word 'anywhere'. Can they think of other words that include the smaller word 'any'? ('anyone', 'anybody', 'anyhow', 'anything', 'anyway') Ask them to choose one of these words and to write it on their whiteboards.
- Why did you put an exclamation mark at the end of the sentence about the number of texts that are sent every day in the UK? (because it was such an amazing fact)
- How well do the children think they did? Ask them to colour in one of the thumbs.
- Share the joke!

12.2

UNIT 13

MOLE MAN: *SESSION 1*

Outcome:
- A fact file

Writing targets:
- Target words: 'trouble', 'speed', 'school'
- Sentences: five fact file entries

You will need:
- Writing Logs page 5
- Whiteboards and pens
- Card for covering spellings

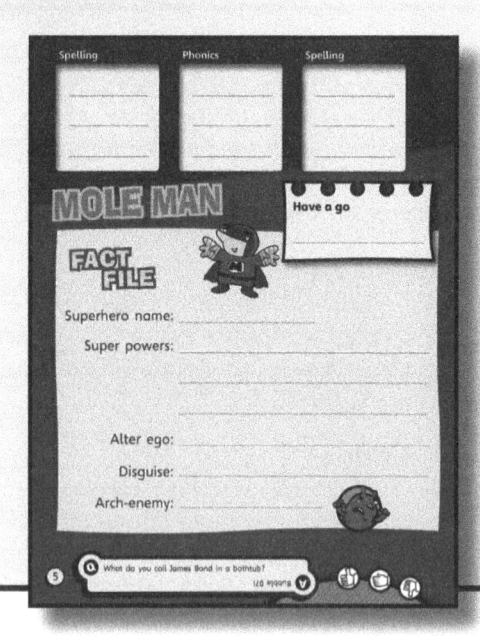

Warm Up

Spelling: 'trouble' — 2 minutes
- Explain that 'trouble' is an irregular word so they will learn to spell it using letter names.
- Demonstrate how to spell the word 'trouble', saying the letter names as you write.
- Wipe your board clean and ask the children to trace the word with their finger on their whiteboard, saying the letter names as they do so. Then ask them to write 'trouble' on their whiteboards.
- Tell the children to wipe their boards clean, then write the word three times in the Spelling box.

Phonics: 'speed' — 2 minutes
- Robot-speak the word 's/p/ee/d' then ask the children to blend the phonemes to make the word.
- Listen as they robot-speak and then blend the whole word.
- As they robot-speak 'speed' again, write the letters on the board.
- Wipe your board clean, then ask the children to write the word on their whiteboards and add phoneme buttons.
- Tell the children to wipe their boards clean and to write 'speed' three times in the Phonics box.

> Ensure that children understand that the letters 'ee' are one phoneme.

Spelling: 'school' — 2 minutes
- Explain that 'school' is an irregular word so they will learn to spell it using letter names.
- Demonstrate how to spell the word 'school', saying the letter names as you write.
- Wipe your board clean and ask the children to trace the word with their finger on their whiteboard, saying the letter names as they do so. Then ask them to write 'school' on their whiteboards.
- Tell the children to wipe their boards clean, then write the word three times in the Spelling box.

Guiding the Writing

Talk for Writing — 4 minutes
- Tell the children that they are going to complete a Fact File on the superhero Mole Man. Ask them if they know of any superpowers that other superheroes have. (Superman is super strong and can fly; Spider-Man can climb up buildings.)
- *Look at the picture of Mole Man. He is part boy, part mole. Moles are creatures that have very sensitive noses, and they can also dig very quickly. Can you guess what Mole Man's superpower might be? (His nose can smell trouble, and he can dig faster than the speed of light.)*

- *Explain that the colon shows the reader that what follows will give more detail about the headings.*
- *What will you write next to 'Superhero name'? (Mole Man) Turn to a partner and think about Mole Man's superpowers. Start the first sentence: 'His nose can ...' and the second sentence: 'He can dig faster than ...'.*
- *Share the children's ideas.*

Demonstration Writing   4 minutes
- *First, next to 'Superhero name' I am going to write:* **Mole Man**. *I have used capital letters because it's his name. I haven't used a full stop because it is not a complete sentence.*
- *Then, next to 'Super powers' I am going to write:* **His nose can smell trouble.** *As I write the sentence, I want you to practise 'smell' in the Have a go box.*
- *After that, I will write:* **He can dig faster than the speed of light.** *As I write the word 'light', I want you to practise it in the Have a go box.*
- *Read the entries together.*

> Remind the children that they have learned 'smelly' in an earlier session. The word 'smell' is just 'smelly' without the 'y'.

Independent Writing   3 minutes
- *Allow the children 20 seconds to study your writing, then wipe your board clean, leaving the words 'Mole' and 'nose' for them to copy.*
- *Ask the children to turn to a partner and repeat the entries.*
- *Tell them to cover their practised words and then write the entries.*
- *Check the children's work.*

Talk for Writing   3 minutes
- *Look at the Fact File. 'Alter ego' means the other personality that the superhero is known as. Mole Man is also known as Mo – an ordinary schoolboy.*
- *What is a disguise? How does Mole Man disguise himself? (as an ordinary schoolboy)*
- *Turn to a partner and think of two entries to go after each heading. The first one, should start: 'Everyone knows him as ...'. The second one should start: 'He looks like ...'.*
- *Share the children's ideas.*

Demonstration Writing   3 minutes
- *I am going to write:* **Everyone knows him as Mo.** *What two words are in 'everyone'? ('every' + 'one')*
- *Next to 'Disguise' I am going to write:* **He looks like a schoolboy.**
- *Every superhero has an arch-enemy. Mole Man's arch-enemy is the Big Slug, so I am going to write:* **Big Slug**.
- *Read the entries together.*

> Point out that 'schoolboy' is made up of the smaller words 'school' and 'boy'.

Independent Writing   3 minutes
- *Allow the children 20 seconds to study your writing, then wipe your board clean.*
- *Ask the children to turn to a partner and repeat what they are going to write.*
- *Tell them to cover their practised words and then to write the three entries.*
- *Check the children's work.*

Rounding Off   2 minutes
- *Ask the children: how did they make the reader realise how fast Mole Man can dig? (We used a metaphor – comparing his speed of digging with the speed of light.) What is the effect of doing that? (It makes Mole Man seem amazing; he can do things that ordinary humans could never do.)*
- *If they were a superhero what superpower would they like to have?*

Review   2 minutes
- *Write the words 'double' and 'trouble' on the board. Ask the children what the words have in common ('ouble'). Tell them to study the words, then wipe your board clean and challenge the children to spell both words on their whiteboards.*
- *What punctuation did we use after each heading? (a colon) Why? (To show that more information was coming.)*
- *How well do the children think they did? Ask them to colour in one of the thumbs.*
- *Share the joke!*

13.1

UNIT 13

MOLE MAN: *SESSION 2*

Outcome:
- A superhero adventure

Writing targets:
- Target words: 'mole', 'track'
- Revision word: 'twisting'
- Sentences: one simple sentence, one compound sentence

You will need:
- Writing Logs page 6
- Whiteboards and pens
- Card for covering spellings

Warm Up

Phonics: 'mole' — 2 minutes
- Robot-speak the word 'm/oh/l' then ask the children to blend the phonemes to make the word.
- Listen as they robot-speak and then blend the whole word.
- As they robot-speak 'mole' again, write the letters on the board. Ask the children to identify which letters are making the long vowel 'oh' sound. Tell the children to link the 'o' and 'e'.
- Wipe your board clean, then ask the children to write the word on their whiteboards.
- Tell the children to wipe their boards clean and to write 'mole' three times in the Phonics box.

Phonics: 'track' — 2 minutes
- Robot-speak the word 't/r/a/ck' then ask the children to blend the phonemes to make the word.
- Listen as they robot-speak and then blend the whole word.
- As they robot-speak 'track' again, write the letters on the board.
- Wipe your board clean, then ask the children to write the word on their whiteboards.
- Tell the children to wipe their boards clean and to write 'track' three times in the Phonics box.

> Ensure that children understand that the letters 'ck' are one phoneme.

Revision: 'twisting' — 2 minutes
- Remind the children that they learned to spell the word 'twisting' in a previous session. Ask them to count the phonemes in 'twisting' on their fingers (There are seven: t/w/i/s/t/i/ng.)
- Write the word on your board and invite a child to add phoneme buttons.
- Wipe your board clean and tell the children to work with a partner. One child should sound out the phonemes while the other child writes the word in their Have a go box.
- Check the children's work then ask them to swap roles.

> Ensure that children can hear that the letters 'ng' are one phoneme.

Guiding the Writing

Talk for Writing — 3 minutes
- Read together the heading on the page: 'Superhero saves the day'. Explain to the children that they are going to write one of Mole Man's adventures. Look at the pictures. Explain that the Big Slug is spoiling Mount Everest by turning it into a huge roller-coaster. Ask the group if they have ever been on a roller-coaster. What might happen if there was a roller-coaster on Everest? (It might cause an avalanche.)
- *Turn to a partner and think of the challenge facing Mole Man. What does the Big Slug want to do? Think of a sentence starting: 'The Big Slug wanted ...'.*
- Share the children's ideas.

70

Demonstration Writing 3 minutes
- *I am going to write:* **The Big Slug wanted to turn Mount Everest into a huge roller-coaster**. *As I write the word 'wanted', I want you to practise it in the Have a go box.*
- *Why have I used capital letters for Big Slug? (It is his name.)*
- Read the sentence together.

Independent Writing 2 minutes
- Allow the children 10 seconds to study your sentence, then wipe your board clean, leaving the words 'Mount Everest' and 'roller-coaster' for them to copy.
- Ask the children to turn to a partner and repeat what they are going to write.
- Tell them to cover their practised words and then to write the sentence.
- Check the children's work.

Talk for Writing 3 minutes
- *Now we are going to write how Mole Man saves the day. Look at the second picture. It shows that Mole Man and the yaks have twisted the track of the roller-coaster. What has happened to the Big Slug? (He has gone flying up into the air.)*
- *Turn to a partner and think of a sentence that starts: 'Mole Man stopped him by ...' and then continues: 'and sending Big Slug ...'.*
- Share the children's ideas.

Demonstration Writing 5 minutes
- *I am going to write:* **Mole Man stopped him by twisting the track and sending the Big Slug flying!** *Why have I used capitals for Mole Man and Big Slug? (They are names.)*
- *Look carefully at the word 'flying'. You have learned the word 'fly' before. Practise spelling it in the Have a go box.*
- *What punctuation have I put at the end of the sentence (an exclamation mark). Why? (It shows the reader that something amazing has happened.)*
- *Now I want to congratulate Mole Man, so I am going to write:* **Well done, Mole Man!** *I have put a comma after 'done' and an exclamation mark after 'Man'.*
- Read the sentences together.

> Point out that they have learned the word 'fly' in an earlier session. The word 'flying' is 'fly' with 'ing' at the end.

Independent Writing 3 minutes
- Allow the children 20 seconds to study the sentences then wipe your board clean.
- Ask the children to turn to a partner and repeat what they are going to write.
- Tell them to cover their practised words and then to write the sentences in the second box.
- Check the children's work.

Rounding Off 2 minutes
- Ask the children why they described the roller-coaster as 'huge'. (To let the reader know how big it is, and also to avoid repeating the word 'big' – Big Slug; big roller-coaster.)
- Challenge the children to find the verbs and verb chains in the sentences ('wanted to turn', 'stopped', 'twisting', 'sending', 'flying'). What do verbs add to a sentence? (action and movement)

Review 3 minutes
- Write the verbs 'twist', 'send' and 'fly' on the board. Tell the children to study the verbs then wipe your board clean and challenge the children to write all three verbs with an 'ing' ending.
- Ask the children which words join the sections of the second sentence ('by', 'and'). Explain that conjunctions are linking words which make longer sentences flow well so the reader can understand what is happening.
- How well do the children think they did? Ask them to colour in one of the thumbs.
- Share the joke!

13.2

UNIT 14
CLIMBING EVEREST: *SESSION 1*

Outcome:
- Argument against climbing Mount Everest

Writing targets:
- Target words: 'climb', 'crack', 'deep'
- Sentences: four simple sentences

You will need:
- Writing Logs page 7
- Whiteboards and pens
- Card for covering spellings

If children are familiar with the letters 'mb' sounding 'm' this word could be taught using phonics.

Ensure that children understand that the letters 'ck' represent one phoneme.

Warm Up
Spelling: 'climb' — *2 minutes*
- Explain that 'climb' is an irregular word so they will learn to spell it using letter names.
- Demonstrate how to spell the word 'climb', saying the letter names as you write. Point out that the 'b' is not sounded when the word is spoken.
- Wipe your board clean and ask the children to trace the word with their finger on their whiteboard, saying the letter names as they do so. Then ask them to write 'climb' on their whiteboards.
- Tell the children to wipe their boards clean, then write the word three times in the Spelling box.

Phonics: 'crack' — *2 minutes*
- Robot-speak the word 'c/r/a/ck' then ask the children to blend the phonemes to make the word.
- Listen as they robot-speak and then blend the whole word.
- As they robot-speak 'crack' again, write the letters on the board.
- Wipe your board clean, then ask the children to write the word on their whiteboards and add phoneme buttons.
- Tell the children to wipe their boards clean and write 'crack' three times in the Phonics box.

Phonics: 'deep' — *2 minutes*
- Robot-speak the word 'd/ee/p' then ask the children to blend the phonemes to make the word.
- Listen as they robot-speak and then blend the whole word.
- As they robot-speak 'deep' again, write the letters on the board.
- Wipe your board clean, then ask the children to write the word on their whiteboard and add phoneme buttons.
- Tell the children to wipe their boards clean and to write 'deep' three times in the Phonics box.

Guiding the Writing
Talk for Writing — *5 minutes*
- Explain to the children that they are going to pretend they are taking part in a debate about whether or not people should climb Mount Everest, the highest mountain in the world. They are going to write down notes for and against the argument. First they are going to write notes for the argument against people climbing Mount Everest.
- *This side of the argument will say how dangerous it is to climb Everest. Many people have died trying to get to the top. Do you think people are mad to try something so dangerous?*

- *In a debate you need to persuade people to agree with you so you need to put over your point of view very strongly. You need to grab the audience's attention with a dramatic opening statement.*
- *Turn to a partner and think of two sentences. The first one should start: 'You would have to be ...'. The second sentence should warn people about the dangers of climbing Mount Everest, and start: 'Over 200 people have ...'.*
- Share the children's ideas.

Demonstration Writing 3 minutes
- *I am going to write:* **You would have to be mad to climb Everest.**
- *For my second sentence, I am going to write:* **Over 200 people have died trying to get to the top.** *As I write the sentence, I want you to practise 'died' in the Have a go box.*
- Read the sentences together.

> Point out that they learned 'try' in a previous session. To make 'trying' they just need to add 'ing'.

Independent Writing 3 minutes
- Allow the children 20 seconds to study your sentences, then wipe your board clean, leaving the word 'Everest' for them to copy.
- Ask the children to turn to a partner and repeat what they are going to write.
- Tell them to cover their practised words and then to write the sentences.
- Check the children's work.

Talk for Writing 3 minutes
- *Now we are going to write more points in our notes to explain how dangerous climbing Everest is. What do you think might be a problem to the climbers? The mountain is covered in deep cracks that are difficult to cross but are easy to fall into. Also, in the deep snow it is easy to get lost.*
- *Turn to a partner and think of two sentences to describe these dangers. Start your first sentence: 'You might fall ...'. Try to use some of the words you learned at the start of the session. Start your second sentence: 'You might get ...'.*
- Share the children's ideas.

Demonstration Writing 3 minutes
- *For my first sentence I am going to write:* **You might fall down a deep crack.** *As I write that sentence I want you to write 'fall' in the Have a go box.*
- *For my second sentence I am going to write:* **You might get lost in the snow.** *As I write the sentence I want you to write 'lost' in the Have a go box.*
- Read the sentences together.

> Tell the children to think about how they spell 'all' and 'ball' and how they use the same pattern to spell 'fall'.

Independent Writing 2 minutes
- Allow the children 20 seconds to study your sentences, then wipe your board clean.
- Ask the children to turn to a partner and repeat what they are going to write.
- Tell them to cover their practised words and then to write the sentences.
- Check the children's work.

Rounding Off 2 minutes
- Ask the children if they can think of any other dangers they might meet (falling rocks, strong winds, frostbite).
- Have they ever seen anything on TV about climbers on Everest? Why do they think people risk their lives to climb a mountain?

Review 3 minutes
- Challenge the children to write 'deep', 'weep', 'sleep' and 'creep' on their whiteboards. What do all the words have in common? ('eep')
- Tell the children to reread this side of the debate. Do they think they will have persuaded people not to climb Everest?
- How well do the children think they did? Ask them to colour in one of the thumbs.
- Share the joke!

14.1

UNIT 14

CLIMBING EVEREST: *SESSION 2*

Outcome:
- Argument for climbing Mount Everest

Writing targets:
- Target words: 'stand', 'hero'
- Revision word: 'world'
- Sentences: four simple sentences

You will need:
- Writing Logs page 8
- Whiteboards and pens
- Card for covering spellings

Warm Up
Phonics: 'stand' — 2 minutes
- Robot-speak the word 's/t/a/n/d' then ask the children to blend the phonemes to make the word.
- Listen as they robot-speak and then blend the whole word.
- As they robot-speak 'stand' again, write the letters on the board.
- Wipe your board clean, then ask the children to write the word on their whiteboards and add phoneme buttons.
- Tell the children to wipe their boards clean and to write 'stand' three times in the Phonics box.

Spelling: 'hero' — 2 minutes
- Explain that 'hero' is an irregular word so they will learn to spell it using letter names.
- Demonstrate how to spell the word 'hero', saying the letter names as you write.
- Wipe your board clean and ask the children to trace the word with their finger on their whiteboard, saying the letter names as they do so. Then ask them to write 'hero' on their whiteboards.
- Tell the children to wipe their boards clean, then write the word three times in the Spelling box.

Revision: 'world' — 1 minute

Point out that 'world' is irregular in that the letters 'or' make the sound 'er'. Tell the children to emphasise the letter names 'o' and 'r' as they spell the word.

- Remind the children that they practised the word 'world' in an earlier session. Write it on your board, saying the letter names as you do so. Point at each letter and ask the children to say the letter names.
- Tell the children to study the word for five seconds, then wipe your board clean and ask them to write the word in the Have a go box.

Guiding the Writing
Talk for Writing — 3 minutes
- Remind the children that in the previous session they wrote notes for one side of a debate: arguing against people climbing Mount Everest. They told people about the dangers of climbing Everest. Explain that now they are going to write notes for the other side of the debate and argue for the good things about climbing Everest. Tell them to reread their writing from last time.
- *What characteristics do you think the person would need to take up this challenge? (bravery, strength, determination)*
- *Turn to a partner and think of a sentence starting: 'You would have to be … '.*
- Share the children's ideas.

74

Demonstration Writing *2 minutes*
- *I am going to write:* **You would have to be brave to climb Everest.** *As I write my sentence, I want you to write 'brave' in the Have a go box.*
- Read the sentence together.

Independent Writing *2 minutes*
- Allow the children 10 seconds to study the sentence then wipe your board clean, leaving the word 'Everest' for them to copy.
- Ask the children to turn to a partner and repeat what they are going to write.
- Tell them to cover their practised words and then to write the sentence.
- Check the children's work.

Talk for Writing *3 minutes*
- *Now we are going to write some more reasons that might persuade people that it is a good idea to try to climb Everest. If they reached the top they would have stood on the top of the world – you would be one in a million!*
- *Turn to a partner and think of two sentences. Start your first sentence: 'You would stand …' and your second sentence: 'You would be …'.*
- Share the children's ideas.

> Check that the children understand the expression 'one in a million'.

Demonstration Writing *3 minutes*
- *I am going to write:* **You would stand on the top of the world.** *As I write that sentence, I want you to practise 'would' in the Have a go box.*
- *Then I am going to write:* **You would be one in a million.**
- Read the sentences together.

Independent Writing *3 minutes*
- Allow the children 20 seconds to study your sentences, then wipe your board clean.
- Ask the children to turn to a partner and repeat what they are going to write.
- Tell them to cover their practised words and then to write the sentences.
- Check the children's work.

> Remind the children that there are two 'l's in 'million'.

Demonstration Writing *2 minutes*
- *I am going to finish the argument by writing:* **Everyone would think you were a hero.** *As I write my sentence I want you to write 'Everyone' in the Have a go box.*

Independent Writing *2 minutes*
- Allow the children 20 seconds to study your sentence, then wipe your board clean.
- Ask the children to turn to a partner and repeat what you are going to write.
- Tell them to cover their practised words and then to write the sentence.
- Check the children's work.

> Tell the children to break the word 'Everyone' into the two smaller words: 'every' and 'one'.

Rounding Off *2 minutes*
- What characteristics would someone who had climbed Everest have shown? (bravery, strength, determination)
- Choose two children to read out each argument. Then take a group vote with a show of hands.

Review *3 minutes*
- Give the children one minute to write on their whiteboards as many words as they can that end with 'and'.
- Ask the children what words in the debate might persuade some people to climb Everest. ('brave'; 'hero'; 'one in a million')
- How well do the children think they did? Ask them to colour in one of the thumbs.
- Share the joke!

14.2

UNIT 15

SAVE THE POLE! *SESSION 1*

Outcome:
- A superhero comic

Writing Targets:
- Target words: 'melting', 'pizza', 'under'
- Revision word: 'because'
- Sentences: one complex sentence, one simple sentence

You will need:
- Writing Logs page 9
- Whiteboards and pens
- Card for covering spellings

Warm Up

Phonics: 'melting' — 2 minutes
- Robot-speak the word 'm/e/l/t/i/ng' then ask the children to blend the phonemes to make the word.
- Listen as they robot-speak and then blend the whole word.
- As they robot-speak 'melting' again, write the letters on the board.
- Wipe your board clean, then ask the children to write the word on their whiteboards and add phoneme buttons.
- Tell the children to wipe their boards clean and to write 'melting' three times in the Phonics box.

> Ensure that children know the letters 'ng' represent one phoneme.

Spelling: 'pizza' — 2 minutes
- Explain that 'pizza' is an irregular word so they will learn to spell it using letter names.
- Demonstrate how to spell the word 'pizza', saying the letter names as you write.
- Wipe your board clean and ask the children to trace the word with their finger on their whiteboard, saying the letter names as they do so. Then ask them to write 'pizza' on their whiteboards.
- Tell the children to wipe their boards clean, then write the word three times in the Spelling box.

> Explain that 'pizza' is an Italian word. The letter 'i' makes an 'ee' sound and the letters 'zz' make a 'ts' sound.

Phonics: 'under' — 2 minutes
- Robot-speak the word 'u/n/d/er' then ask the children to blend the phonemes to make the word.
- Listen as they robot-speak and then blend the whole word.
- As they robot-speak 'under' again, write the letters on the board.
- Wipe your board clean, then ask the children to write the word on their whiteboards and add phoneme buttons.
- Tell the children to wipe their boards clean and to write 'under' three times in the Phonics box.

> Ensure that children know the letters 'er' represent one phoneme.

Guiding the Writing

Talk for Writing — 4 minutes
- Explain to the group that they are going to write the text for a cartoon about the superhero Mole Man. This time, his arch-enemy, the Big Slug, is spoiling the South Pole.
- *Look at the first picture. What is the Big Slug eating? (pizza) Have you ever seen pizza being cooked in a pizza oven? A pizza oven gets very hot. The Big Slug has made the world's biggest pizza oven right under the South Pole and it is making the snow melt.*

- *Turn to a partner and think of the challenge facing Mole Man. You will be writing a picture caption in the present tense. Start your sentence: 'The snow at the South Pole is melting because ...'.*
- Share the children's ideas.

Demonstration Writing   4 minutes
- *I am going to write:* **The snow at the South Pole is melting because the Big Slug has made the world's biggest pizza oven under it.** *As I write the word 'snow', I want you to practise it in the Have a go box.*
- *Which word shows that an explanation is following? ('because') Can you remember a way to help you spell the word 'because'?*
- *Why have I used an apostrophe in 'world's'? On this occasion the apostrophe does not indicate a missing letter, but instead shows that the pizza is the biggest in the world.*
- *Look at the word 'biggest' and write it in the Have a go box.*
- Read the sentence together.

> Remind children of the mnemonic for 'because': Big Elephants Can Always Understand Small Elephants.

Independent Writing   3 minutes
- Allow the children 20 seconds to study your sentence then wipe your board clean, leaving the words 'South Pole' and 'oven' for them to copy.
- Ask the children to turn to a partner and repeat what they are going to write.
- Tell them to cover their practised words and then to write the sentence.
- Check the children's work.

Talk for Writing   2 minutes
- *Who do we think is going to save the South Pole? This sounds like just the job for Mole Man!*
- *Turn to a partner and think of a sentence starting: 'This is a job for ...'.*
- Share the children's ideas.

Demonstration Writing   2 minutes
- *I am going to write:* **This is a job for Mole Man!** *As I write the word 'This', I want you to write it with a capital letter in the Have a go box.*
- *Have I used the present tense? (yes) Which word tells you this? ('is')*
- *Why have I used an exclamation mark? (To show the reader that Mole Man is special.)*
- Read the sentence together.

Independent Writing   2 minutes
- Allow the children 10 seconds to study the sentence, then wipe your board clean.
- Ask the children to turn to a partner and repeat what they are going to write.
- Tell them to cover their practised words and then to write the sentence.
- Check the children's work.

Rounding Off   2 minutes
- What evil thing has the Big Slug done? (built a pizza oven under the South Pole)
- Ask the children if it matters if the snow at the South Pole melts. Who will suffer? (penguins, polar bears and other animals that live at the South Pole)

Review   3 minutes
- Write the adjective 'big' on the board. Ask the children what happens to the word 'big' when we add 'er' or 'est' (we double the 'g'). Help the children to think of a sentence using all three words: 'big', 'bigger', 'biggest'. (For example 'This house is big, but a mansion is bigger, and a palace is the biggest place to live.)
- Tell the children to work with a partner and to practise rereading their writing in the voice of a superhero comic narrator.
- How well do the children think they did? Ask them to colour in one of the thumbs.
- Share the joke!

15.1

UNIT 15

SAVE THE POLE! *SESSION 2*

Outcome:
- A superhero comic

Writing targets:
- Target words: 'oven', 'hole', 'freezes'
- Revision word: 'faster'
- Sentences: one complex sentence, one compound sentence, one expression

You will need:
- Writing Logs page 10
- Whiteboards and pens
- Card for covering spellings

> The word 'oven' is irregular in that the letter 'o' makes the 'uh' sound.

Warm Up

Spelling: 'oven' *2 minutes*
- Explain that 'oven' is an irregular word so they will learn to spell it using letter names.
- Demonstrate how to spell the word 'oven', saying the letter names as you write.
- Wipe your board clean and ask the children to trace the word with their finger on their whiteboard, saying the letter names as they do so. Then ask them to write 'oven' on their whiteboards.
- Tell the children to wipe their boards clean, then write the word three times in the Spelling box.

Phonics: 'hole' *2 minutes*
- Robot-speak the word 'h/oh/l' then ask the children to blend the phonemes to make the word.
- Listen as they robot-speak and then blend the whole word.
- As they robot-speak 'hole' again, write the letters on the board. Ask the children to identify which letters are making the long vowel 'oh' sound. Tell the children to link the 'o' and 'e'.
- Wipe your board clean and ask the children to write the word on their boards.
- Tell the children to wipe their boards clean and write 'hole' three times in the Phonics box.

> Ensure that children realise that the letter 's' is making a 'z' sound.

Phonics: 'freezes' *2 minutes*
- Robot-speak the word 'f/r/ee/z/e/s' then ask the children to blend the phonemes to make the word.
- Listen as they robot-speak and then blend the whole word.
- As they robot-speak 'freezes' again, write the letters on the board.
- Wipe your board clean, then ask the children to write the word on their whiteboards and add phoneme buttons.
- Tell the children to wipe their boards clean and to write 'freezes' three times in the Phonics box.

Guiding the Writing

Talk for Writing *3 minutes*
- Ask the children to recall what evil thing the Big Slug has done this time. (He's made a pizza oven under the South Pole.)
- *What are Mole Man's superpowers?* (He can smell trouble; he can dig faster than the speed of light.) Turn to a partner and think of a sentence in the present tense to describe what Mole Man does to stop the Big Slug. Start your sentence: 'Faster than the speed of light, Mole Man digs ...'.
- Share the children's ideas.

78

Demonstration Writing   3 minutes
- *I am going to write:* **Faster than the speed of light, Mole Man digs down to the pizza oven.** *As I write the word 'speed', I want you to practise it in the Have a go box.*
- *I have put a comma after 'light' because I need to separate that opening phrase from the main part of the sentence which says what Mole Man did.*
- *As I write the sentence, I want you to write 'faster' in your Have a go box.*
- *Read the sentence together.*

> point out that 'faster' is just 'fast' with 'er'.

Independent Writing   3 minutes
- Allow the children 20 seconds to study your sentence then wipe your board clean.
- Ask the children to turn to a partner and repeat the sentence.
- Tell them to cover their practised words and then write the sentence.
- Check the children's work.

Talk for Writing   2 minutes
- *Look at the pictures. Now we are going to write how Mole Man gets the penguins at the South Pole to help him. What are the penguins doing?* (blowing icy breath down the hole that Mole Man has dug) *What has happened to the pizza oven and the Big Slug?* (They are frozen!)
- *Turn to a partner and think of a sentence that starts: 'He gets the penguins to …'.*
- Share the children's ideas.

Demonstration Writing   4 minutes
- *I am going to write:* **He gets the penguins to blow down the hole and the pizza oven freezes!** *As I write the word 'blow', I want you to write it in the Have a go box.*
- *Have I used the present tense?* (yes) *How can you tell?* (from the words: 'gets', 'freezes')
- *What punctuation have I put at the end of the sentence?* (an exclamation mark) *Why?* (because it shows the reader that Mole Man is doing something amazing)
- *Read the sentence together.*
- *To round off the comic I am going to write on a new line:* **Job done, Mole Man!**
- *Read the sentences together.*

> Point out that you have added a comma after 'Job done' to indicate a short pause.

Independent Writing   3 minutes
- Allow the children 20 seconds to study the sentences, then wipe your board clean, leaving the word 'penguins' for them to copy.
- Ask the children to turn to a partner and repeat what they are going to write.
- Tell them to cover their practised words and then to write the sentences.
- Check the children's work.

Rounding Off   3 minutes
- *How did Mole Man use his superpowers to stop the Big Slug?* (He dug the hole down to the pizza oven very, very fast.)
- Remind the children that Mole Man can dig 'faster than the speed of light'. *Why is this a good way to describe a superpower?* (It is extreme and beyond anything a normal person can do.)
- Ask the children what they like best about superhero stories (the amazing things they can do; the enemies being crazy and often silly; the fact that it is good versus evil).

Review   3 minutes
- Ask the children to find all of the present tense verbs in the sentences ('digs', 'gets', 'blow', 'freezes') *Why is the present tense good to use in a cartoon?* (It makes it sound as though the action is happening there and then.)
- Ask the children why we did not repeat the words 'Mole Man' at the start of the second sentence. (The pronoun 'He' refers back to Mole Man, who was mentioned in the first sentence.)
- How well do the children think they did? Ask them to colour in one of the thumbs.
- Share the joke!

> Go to the orange box on page 21 in the Writing Log for an unaided writing activity.
> See page 142 of this Teaching Guide for guidance notes.

15.2

UNIT 16

RACE TO THE POLE: SESSION 1

Outcome:
- A diary entry

Writing targets:
- Target words: 'sledges', 'ourselves', 'believe'
- Sentences: two simple sentences, one compound sentence

You will need:
- Writing Logs page 11
- Whiteboards and pens
- Card for covering spellings

Warm Up

Spelling: 'sledges' — 2 minutes
- Explain that 'sledges' is an irregular word so they will learn to spell it using letter names.
- Demonstrate how to spell the word 'sledges', saying the letter names as you write.
- Wipe your board clean and ask the children to trace the word with their finger on their whiteboard, saying the letter names as they do so. Then ask them to write 'sledges' on their whiteboards.
- Tell the children to wipe their boards clean, then write the word three times in the Spelling box.

Spelling: 'ourselves' — 2 minutes
- Ask the children what word they can hear at the start of 'ourselves'. Remind them they have practised 'our' in a previous session.
- Explain that 'ourselves' is an irregular word so they will learn to spell it using letter names.
- Demonstrate how to spell 'ourselves', saying the letter names as you write.
- Wipe your board clean and ask the children to trace the word with their finger on their whiteboard, saying the letter names as they do so. Then ask them to write 'ourselves' on their whiteboards.
- Tell the children to wipe their boards clean, then write the word three times in the Spelling box.

Spelling: 'believe' — 2 minutes
- Explain that 'believe' is an irregular word so they will learn to spell it using letter names.
- Demonstrate how to spell the word 'believe', saying the letter names as you write.
- Wipe your board clean and ask the children to trace the word with their finger on their whiteboard, saying the letter names as they do so. Then ask them to write 'believe' on their whiteboards.
- Tell the children to wipe their boards clean, then write the word three times in the Spelling box.

Guiding the Writing

Talk for Writing — 4 minutes
- Explain to the children that in 1912 the explorer Captain Scott and his team tried to be the first to reach the South Pole. At the same time, a team from Norway led by a man called Amundsen was also trying to get to the South Pole.
- Tell them that they are going to write a diary entry by one of Captain Scott's team for day 40 of their journey across the Antarctic to the South Pole.

- *The weather was terrible and soon all of Scott's horses and dogs had died. Look at the photograph. What did the men do after the dogs died? (They pulled the sledges themselves.)*
- *You are going to write about the day the dogs died. The freezing winds and deep snow were too much for the dogs. Turn to a partner and think of two sentences. Start your first sentence with: 'The freezing winds have been …' and your second sentence with: 'One by one they …'.*
- *Share the children's ideas.*

Demonstration Writing   4 minutes
- *I am going to write:* **The freezing winds have been too much for the dogs.** *As I write my sentence I want you to study the word 'freezing'. Say the letter names to yourself and then write the word in the Have a go box.*
- *Now I am going to write:* **One by one they have died.** *As I write that sentence I want you to write 'died' in the Have a go box.*
- *Read the sentences together.*

> Point out that they have practised 'freezes' before. The word 'freezing' just has 'ing' instead of 'es' at the end.

Independent Writing   3 minutes
- Allow the children 20 seconds to study your sentences, then wipe your board clean.
- Ask the children to turn to a partner and repeat what they are going to write.
- Tell them to cover their practised words and then to write the sentences in the diary.
- Check the children's work.

Talk for Writing   3 minutes
- *Now we are going to explain that Scott's team had to drag the sledges themselves. This meant that they were slower, but Scott believed they could still be first.*
- *Turn to a partner and think of a sentence. Start your sentence: 'Now we must drag …' and then continue it with: 'but we still believe …'.*
- *Share the children's ideas.*

Demonstration Writing   3 minutes
- *I am going to write:* **Now we must drag the sledges ourselves but we still believe we can be first.** *As I write my sentence, I want you to write 'first' in the Have a go box.*
- *Instead of writing two short sentences I have joined the second part of my sentence with the word 'but'.*
- *Read the sentence together.*

Independent Writing   3 minutes
- Allow the children 20 seconds to study your sentence, then wipe your board clean.
- Ask the children to turn to a partner and repeat what they are going to write.
- Tell them to cover their practised words and then to write the sentence in the diary.
- Check the children's work.

Rounding Off   2 minutes
- Ask the children what went wrong for Captain Scott (bad weather; their horses and dogs died; the men had to pull the sledges).
- Do they think he and his team were brave or foolish to continue to try to get to the South Pole? Why?

Review   2 minutes
- Ask the children how they might remember the correct way to spell 'believe'. (They could use the mnemonic: 'You should never believe a lie.') Challenge them to write it on their whiteboards.
- Which sentence do they think is the most powerful in the diary entry?
- How well do the children think they did? Ask them to colour in one of the thumbs.
- Share the joke!

16.1

UNIT 16

RACE TO THE POLE: *SESSION 2*

Outcome:
- A diary entry

Writing targets:
- Target words: 'nothing', 'hope'
- Revision word: 'our'
- Sentences: three simple sentences, one complex sentence

You will need:
- Writing Logs page 11
- Whiteboards and pens
- Card for covering spellings

Explain that it is easier to spell 'nothing' if they split the word into the two shorter words 'no' and 'thing'.

Warm Up
Spelling: 'nothing' — 2 minutes
- Explain that 'nothing' is an irregular word so they will learn to spell it using letter names.
- Demonstrate how to spell the word 'nothing', saying the letter names as you write.
- Wipe your board clean and ask the children to trace the word with their finger on their whiteboard, saying the letter names as they do so. Then ask them to write 'nothing' on their whiteboards.
- Tell the children to wipe their boards clean, then write the word three times in the Spelling box.

Phonics: 'hope' — 2 minutes
- Robot-speak the word 'h/oh/p' then ask the children to blend the phonemes to make the word.
- Listen as they robot-speak and then blend the whole word.
- As they robot-speak 'hope' again, write the letters on the board. Ask the children to identify which letters are making the long vowel 'oh' sound. Tell the children to link the 'o' and 'e'.
- Wipe your board clean, then ask the children to write the word on their whiteboards.
- Tell the children to wipe their boards clean and to write 'hope' three times in the Phonics box.

Revision: 'our' — 2 minutes
- Remind the children that they practised the word 'our' when they learned to write 'ourselves' in an earlier session.
- Write the word on your board, saying the letter names as you write. Point at each letter and ask the children to say the letter names as you do so.
- Tell the children to study the word for five seconds, then wipe your board clean and ask them to write 'our' in the Have a go box.

Guiding the Writing
Talk for Writing — 4 minutes
- Explain to the children that they are going to write a diary entry by a member of Captain Scott's team for day 79 of their expedition.
- *When Scott and his team got to the Pole they saw a flag flying. They realised that they had been beaten by Amundsen. With heavy hearts they turned around and started to make their way back. All their hard work had been for nothing.*
- Turn to a partner and think of two sentences. Start the first sentence: 'All our hard work …' and the second sentence: 'We were not …'.
- Share the children's ideas.

Demonstration Writing — 3 minutes
- *I am going to write:* **All our hard work was for nothing.** *As I write 'work', I want you to tell me how to spell it.*
- *Now I am going to write:* **We were not the first.** *As I write that sentence I want you to write 'were' in the Have a go box.*
- Read the sentences together.

Independent Writing — 2 minutes
- Allow the children 20 seconds to study the sentences, then wipe your board clean.
- Ask the children to turn to a partner and repeat what they are going to write.
- Tell them to cover their practised words and then to write the sentences.
- Check the children's work.

Talk for Writing — 3 minutes
- *Now we are going to say how the writer felt. Do you think he was happy to be going back or sad that they had lost the race?*
- *Turn to a partner and think of two sentences. Your first sentence should start with: 'It is very sad …'. Our second sentence will show that he was worried that they might never get back, and start with: 'I hope …'.*
- Share the children's ideas.

Demonstration Writing — 3 minutes
- *I am going to write:* **It is very sad to go back knowing that we have lost.**
- *Look at the word 'knowing' and say the letter names to yourself, then write the word in the Have a go box.*
- *Finally, I am going to write:* **I hope we make it.**
- Read the sentences together.

> Remind the children that they have practised 'know' previously. The word 'knowing' is just the same with 'ing' on the end.

Independent Writing — 3 minutes
- Allow the children 20 seconds to study your sentence, then wipe your board clean.
- Ask the children to turn to a partner and repeat what they are going to write.
- Tell them to cover their practised words and then to write the sentence in the diary.
- Check the children's work.

Rounding Off — 3 minutes
- Tell the children that the weather got worse and worse and the food began to run out. The men got weaker and weaker. Only 18 kilometres from their base, they pitched their tent for the last time and all of them died. Now there is a memorial stone in Antarctica to the brave men who lost their lives.
- Ask the children to read the dairy entries with expression to show how the writer's feelings changed between the first entry and the second entry.

Review — 3 minutes
- Ask the children which sentence shows the reader the most about how the writer was feeling. ('All our hard work was for nothing.')
- Ask them to write the word 'hope' on their whiteboards. Then show the group how to write 'hopeless' by adding 'less'. Next, challenge them to try writing 'care' and then 'careless'.
- How well do the children think they did? Ask them to colour in one of the thumbs.
- Share the joke!

16.2

UNIT 17

UNSOLVED MYSTERY: *SESSION 1*

Outcome:
- An article for a magazine about unsolved mysteries

Writing targets:
- Target words: 'started', 'smoke', 'scared'
- Sentences: one complex sentence, one simple sentence, one compound sentence

You will need:
- Writing Logs page 13
- Whiteboards and pens
- Card for covering spellings

Warm Up

Phonics: 'started' — 2 minutes
- Robot-speak the word 's/t/ar/t/e/d' then ask the children to blend the phonemes to make the word.
- Listen as they robot-speak and then blend the whole word.
- As they robot-speak 'started' again, write the letters on the board.
- Wipe your board clean, then ask the children to write the word on their whiteboards and add phoneme buttons.
- Tell the children to wipe their boards clean and to write 'started' three times in the Phonics box.

Phonics: 'smoke' — 2 minutes
- Robot-speak the word 's/m/oh/k' then ask the children to blend the phonemes to make the word.
- Listen as they robot-speak and then blend the whole word.
- As they robot-speak 'smoke' again, write the letters on the board. Ask the children to identify which letters are making the long vowel 'oh' sound. Tell the children to link the 'o' and 'e'.
- Wipe your board clean, then ask the children to write the word on their whiteboards.
- Tell the children to wipe their boards clean and to write 'smoke' three times in the Phonics box.

Spelling: 'scared' — 2 minutes
- Explain that 'scared' is an irregular word so they will learn to spell it using letter names.
- Demonstrate how to spell the word 'scared', saying the letter names as you write.
- Wipe your board clean and ask the children to trace the word with their finger on their whiteboard, saying the letter names as they do so. Then ask them to write 'scared' on their whiteboards.
- Tell the children to wipe their boards clean, then write the word three times in the Spelling box.

If children are familiar with the letters 'ar' making the 'air' sound, and 'ed' making the 'd' sound, then this word could be taught using phonics.

Guiding the Writing

Talk for Writing — 4 minutes
- Explain that they are going to write an article for a magazine about unsolved mysteries. An unsolved mystery is a mystery that no-one can explain.
- *We are going to write from the point of view of a girl who was in school when a fire broke out. The smoke was so thick that she couldn't see the way out. What might the unsolved mystery be? (How did she get out?)*

- *Turn to a partner and think of how the girl will describe what it was like when she couldn't find her way out of the burning building. Remember, the smoke was so thick that she couldn't see. Start your sentence: 'When the fire started there was so much …'.*
- Share the children's ideas.

Demonstration Writing　　　　　　　　　　　　　　3 minutes
- *I am going to write:* **When the fire started there was so much smoke, I couldn't see.** *As I write the word 'fire', I want you to practise it in the Have a go box.*
- *Why have I put an apostrophe in 'couldn't'? (To show a letter is missing.)*
- *I have used a comma after 'smoke' to give the reader a little pause between the two parts of the sentence.*
- Read the sentence together.

> Remind the children of the mnemonic 'O U Lucky Duck' to help them with the 'ould' pattern in 'couldn't'.

Independent Writing　　　　　　　　　　　　　　　3 minutes
- Allow the children 10 seconds to study your sentence, then wipe your board clean.
- Ask the children to turn to a partner and repeat what they are going to write.
- Tell them to cover their practised words and then to write the sentence.
- Check the children's work.

Talk for Writing　　　　　　　　　　　　　　　　　3 minutes
- *Now we are going to write two more sentences that will build up the tension of how the girl felt when she was trapped in the building. Look at the second picture. She couldn't find a way out and was very scared. What might she be scared of? (dying in the fire)*
- *Turn to a partner and think of a sentence starting: 'I couldn't find …'. Then think of another sentence starting: 'I was very …' and then continuing: 'and I thought I …'.*
- Share the children's ideas.

Demonstration Writing　　　　　　　　　　　　　　3 minutes
- *I am going to write:* **I couldn't find a way out.** *Look at the word 'find'. What sound is the letter 'i' making? (the long vowel sound 'igh') Practise writing 'find' in the Have a go box.*
- *Next I am going to write:* **I was very scared and I thought I was going to die.** *As I write the word 'thought' I want you to write it in the Have a go box.*
- Read the sentences together.

Independent Writing　　　　　　　　　　　　　　　3 minutes
- Allow the children 20 seconds to study the sentences then wipe your board clean.
- Ask the children to turn to a partner and repeat what they are going to write.
- Tell them to cover their practised words and then to write the sentences.
- Check the children's work.

Rounding Off　　　　　　　　　　　　　　　　　　3 minutes
- How can we tell that the girl was panicking from what she has said? (She says she thought she was going to die.)
- What would be the scariest part of being trapped in a building full of smoke? (not being able to see the way out; not being able to breathe; the heat)
- How do we know the girl did not die in the fire? (She survived to tell her story.)

Review　　　　　　　　　　　　　　　　　　　　　2 minutes
- Which word links the two parts of the third sentence? ('and')
- Write the word 'couldn't' on the board. Ask the children to explain how they will remember to spell it correctly ('O U Lucky Duck'). Wipe your board clean, then challenge the children to write 'couldn't' and 'shouldn't' on the board.
- How well do the children think they did? Ask them to colour in one of the thumbs.
- Share the joke!

17.1

UNIT 17

UNSOLVED MYSTERY: *SESSION 2*

Outcome:
- An article for a magazine about unsolved mysteries

Writing targets:
- Target words: 'suddenly', 'appeared', 'thank'
- Sentences: three compound sentences

You will need:
- Writing Logs page 14
- Whiteboards and pens
- Card for covering spellings

Warm Up

Phonics: 'suddenly' — 2 minutes
- Robot-speak the word 's/u/dd/e/n/l/y' then ask the children to blend the phonemes to make the word.
- Listen as they robot-speak and then blend the whole word.
- As they robot-speak 'suddenly' again, write the letters on the board.
- Wipe your board clean, then ask the children to write the word on their whiteboards and add phoneme buttons.
- Tell the children to wipe their boards clean and to write 'suddenly' three times in the Phonics box.

Ensure that children realise the 'ee' sound at the end of the word is made with the letter 'y'.

Spelling: 'appeared' — 2 minutes
- Explain that 'appeared' is an irregular word so they will learn to spell it using letter names.
- Demonstrate how to spell the word 'appeared', saying the letter names as you write.
- Wipe your board clean and ask the children to trace the word with their finger on their whiteboard saying the letter names as they do so. Then ask them to write 'appeared' on their whiteboards.
- Tell the children to wipe their boards clean, then write the word three times in the Spelling box.

If children are familiar with 'ed' making the 'd' sound, then this word could be taught using phonics.

Phonics: 'thank' — 2 minutes
- Robot-speak the word 'th/a/n/k' then ask the children to blend the phonemes to make the word.
- Listen as they robot-speak and then blend the whole word.
- As they robot-speak 'thank' again, write the letters on the board.
- Wipe your board clean, then ask the children to write the word on their whiteboards and add phoneme buttons.
- Tell the children to wipe their boards clean and to write 'thank' three times in the Phonics box.

Ensure that children know that the letters 'th' represent one phoneme.

Guiding the Writing

Talk for Writing — 4 minutes
- Ask the children to reread the dramatic account of the girl who was trapped in the fire. Remind them that they are writing about an unsolved mystery.
- *Look at the picture. How did the girl get out of the building? The girl says that a boy appeared and led her out, but when she turned to thank him he had vanished! Had he ever been there?*
- *Turn to a partner and think of what the girl will say as she describes how she got out of the burning building. Start your first sentence: 'Suddenly a boy appeared and ...' and your second sentence: 'I turned to thank ...'.*
- Share the children's ideas.

Demonstration Writing — 4 minutes
- *For the first sentence I am going to write:* **Suddenly a boy appeared and led me out.** *As I write the word 'boy', I want you to practise it in the Have a go box.*
- *For the second sentence I will write:* **I turned to thank him but he had vanished!** *As I write the word 'vanished', I want you to practise it in the Have a go box.*
- *Why have I put an exclamation mark after 'vanished'? (To make the reader aware of how surprising it was that the boy was there one minute and gone the next.)*
- Read the sentences together.

Independent Writing — 3 minutes
- Allow the children 20 seconds to study your sentences, then wipe your board clean.
- Ask the children to turn to a partner and repeat what they are going to write.
- Tell them to cover their practised words and then to write the sentences.
- Check the children's work.

> Remind the children that they should write 'Suddenly' with a capital letter because it is at the start of a sentence.

Talk for Writing — 3 minutes
- *In our final sentence the girl is going to explain how some people do not believe that there was a boy at all. They think that she managed to find her own way out. What do you think? Do you think there was really a mysterious boy who saved her life?*
- *Turn to a partner and think of a sentence starting: 'People say that …' and then continuing: 'but I know …'.*
- Share the children's ideas.

Demonstration Writing — 3 minutes
- *I am going to write:* **People say that there was no boy, but I know he saved my life.** *As I write the word 'saved', I want you to write it in the Have a go box.*
- *I will put a comma after the word 'boy' to make the sentence easier for the reader to follow.*
- Read the sentence together.

> Point out that they have learned 'save' in a previous session. The word 'saved' just has a 'd' on the end.

Independent Writing — 2 minutes
- Allow the children 10 seconds to study the sentence, then wipe your board clean.
- Ask the children to turn to a partner and repeat what they are going to write.
- Tell them to cover their practised words and then to write the sentence.
- Check the children's work.

Rounding Off — 3 minutes
- Ask the children what effect starting the first sentence with 'Suddenly' has. (It sounds dramatic and mysterious; it makes the reader wonder where the boy appeared from so quickly.)
- What effect does the word 'vanished' have? (It makes it sound like the boy's disappearance was magical.)
- Who could the boy have been? (a ghost who had died in the school a long time ago; someone with superhuman powers)

Review — 2 minutes
- Which word links the two parts of the third sentence? ('but') Why is it important? (because it shows the contrast between what some people think and what the girl believes)
- Ask the children for a good strategy for remembering how to spell 'people' (mispronounce it as 'pe-ople'; learn it as the letter names: 'p/e/o/p/l/e').
- How well do the children think they did? Ask them to colour in one of the thumbs.
- Share the joke!

17.2

UNIT 18

THE LOCH NESS MONSTER: *SESSION 1*

Outcome:
- Email correspondence

Writing targets:
- Target words: 'guess', 'monster'
- Sentences: one expression, one compound sentence using 'when', two simple sentences

You will need:
- Writing Logs page 15
- Whiteboards and pens
- Card for covering spellings

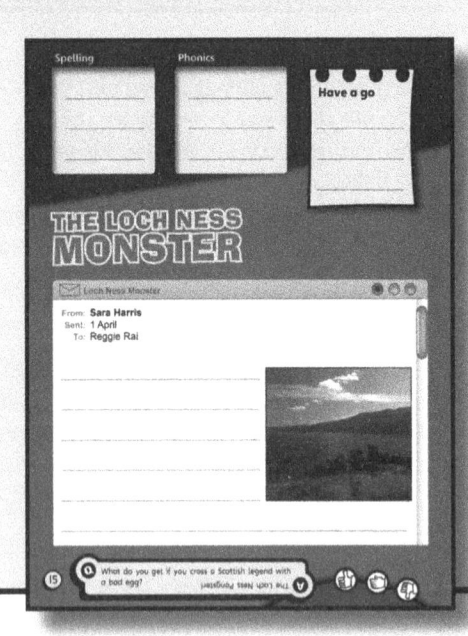

If the children are familiar with the letters 'gu' making the 'g' sound, then this word could be taught using phonics.

Warm Up

Spelling: 'guess' — 2 minutes
- Explain that 'guess' is an irregular word so they will learn to spell it using letter names.
- Demonstrate how to spell the word 'guess', saying the letter names as you write. Point out that the 'u' is not sounded when the word is spoken.
- Wipe your board clean and ask the children to trace the word with their finger on their whiteboard, saying the letter names as they do so. Then ask them to write 'guess' on their whiteboards.
- Tell the children to wipe their boards clean, then write the word three times in the Spelling box.

Phonics: 'monster' — 2 minutes
- Robot-speak the word 'm/o/n/s/t/er' then ask the children to blend the phonemes to make the word.
- Listen as they robot-speak and then blend the whole word.
- As they robot-speak 'monster' again, write the letters on the board.
- Wipe your board clean, then ask the children to write the word on their whiteboards and add phoneme buttons.
- Tell the children to wipe their boards clean and to write 'monster' three times in the Phonics box.

Guiding the Writing

Talk for Writing — 3 minutes
- Explain to the children that they are going to write an email from one friend to another, telling them that they were by Loch Ness when a monster came up out of the water.
- *What do you know about the Loch Ness monster? The loch is very deep and some people think that a monster of some kind could live undiscovered in its waters.*
- *Your email will be chatty and start with: 'Guess what?'. Turn to a partner and think of the next sentence. It should start with: 'We were by Loch Ness when ...'.*
- Share the children's ideas.

Demonstration Writing   4 minutes
- *I am going to write:* **Guess what?** *I'll put that on a line by itself to draw more attention to the question.*
- *Then I am going to write:* **We were by Loch Ness when a huge monster came up out of the water.** *As I write my sentence, I want you to write the words 'came' and 'water' in the Have a go box.*
- Read the sentences together.

Independent Writing   3 minutes
- Allow the children 20 seconds to study your sentences, then wipe your board clean, leaving 'Loch Ness' for them to copy.
- Ask the children to turn to a partner and repeat what they are going to write.
- Tell them to cover their practised words and then to write the sentences.
- Check the children's work.

> Remind the children to put the first sentence on a line by itself.

Talk for Writing   4 minutes
- *Now we are going to explain how you felt and what you did. Would you believe your eyes? Would you try to get a photo or a video of it?*
- *Turn to a partner and think of two sentences. Your first sentence will be about how you felt when you thought you'd seen a monster, and start with: 'I couldn't ...'. Your second sentence will say what you did next and start with: 'I grabbed my ...'.*
- Share the children's ideas.

Demonstration Writing   3 minutes
- *I am going to write:* **I couldn't believe it!** *What have I put at the end of my sentence? Why do you think I have put an exclamation mark? (To emphasise how amazing this was.)*
- *Then I am going to write what I did:* **I grabbed my camera.** *As I write my sentence, I want you to try to write 'grabbed' in the Have a go box.*
- Read the sentences together.

> Tell the children to make sure that they put two 'b's in 'grabbed'.

Independent Writing   3 minutes
- Allow the children 20 seconds to study your sentences, then wipe your board clean, leaving the word 'camera' for them to copy.
- Ask the children to turn to a partner and repeat what they are going to write.
- Tell them to cover their practised words and then to write the sentences.
- After they've written the sentences, ask them to sign their name.
- Check the children's work.

Rounding Off   3 minutes
- Ask the children if they would believe a friend who said they had seen the Loch Ness monster.
- What evidence would they want before they could be sure it was true?
- Have they ever had anything very surprising happen to them that not everyone believed?

Review   3 minutes
- Ask the children how they would start an email to their friend. Would they start a letter to the headteacher in the same way? How would it be different?
- Write 'couldn't', 'wouldn't' and 'shouldn't' on your whiteboards. Remind the group that the 'n't' stands for the word 'not', but that when we talk or write to a friend we often write as if we are speaking. Challenge the children to pick one of these words and write it as one word, then as two words.
- How well do the children think they did? Ask them to colour in one of the thumbs.
- Share the joke!

18.1

UNIT 18

THE LOCH NESS MONSTER: *SESSION 2*

Outcome:
- Email correspondence

Writing targets:
- Target words: 'wait', 'photo', 'date'
- Sentences: one compound sentence, three simple sentences

You will need:
- Writing Logs page 16
- Whiteboards and pens
- Card for covering spellings

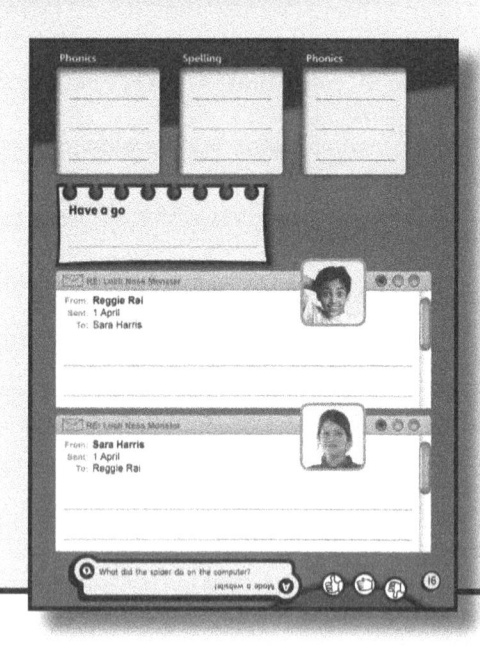

Warm Up

Phonics: 'wait' — 2 minutes
- Robot-speak the word 'w/ay/t' then ask the children to blend the phonemes to make the word.
- Listen as they robot-speak and then blend the whole word.
- As they robot-speak 'wait' again, write the letters on the board.
- Wipe your board clean, then ask the children to write the word on their whiteboards and add phoneme buttons (w/ai/t).
- Tell the children to wipe their boards clean and write 'wait' three times in the Phonics box.

> Ensure that children understand that the letters 'ai' represent one phoneme making the long vowel 'ay' sound.

Spelling: 'photo' — 2 minutes
- Explain that 'photo' is an irregular word so they will learn it using letter names.
- Demonstrate how to spell the word 'photo', saying the letter names as you write.
- Wipe your board clean and ask the children to trace the word with their finger on their whiteboard, saying the letter names as they do so. Then ask them to write 'photo' on their whiteboards.
- Tell the children to wipe their boards clean, then write the word three times in the Spelling box.

> The word 'photo' is irregular because the 'f' sound is made with a 'ph' and the two 'o's both make the long vowel sound 'oh'.

Phonics: 'date' — 2 minutes
- Robot-speak the word 'd/ay/t' then ask the children to blend the phonemes to make the word.
- Listen as they robot-speak and then blend the whole word.
- As they robot-speak 'date' again, write the letters on the board. Ask the children to identify which letters are making the long vowel 'ay' sound. Tell the children to link the 'a' and 'e'.
- Wipe your board clean, then ask the children to write the word on their whiteboards.
- Tell the children to wipe their boards clean and to write 'date' three times in the Phonics box.

Guiding the Writing

Talk for Writing — 3 minutes
- Explain to the children that they are going to write some more emails that were sent between these two friends about seeing the Loch Ness monster. First they are going to imagine they are the friend who received the email from last time.
- *Would you have been very excited to read that your friend actually saw a monster? Would you want to see the photo? If they have got a real photo of the monster, it would be worth lots of money, so they could sell it.*

90

- *Turn to a partner and think of two sentences. The first sentence should start: 'Can't wait ...'. The second sentence should tell them what to do and start with: 'You could sell ...'. Try to use some of the words you've just practised in your sentences.*
- Share the children's ideas.

Demonstration Writing   3 minutes
- *I am going to write:* **Can't wait to see the photo! You could sell it and make a million.** *I have put an exclamation mark after 'photo' to show how excited the friend is.*
- *As I write my sentences, I want you to practise the words 'Can't' (with a capital letter) and 'sell' in the Have a go box.*
- Read the sentences together.

> Ensure that children know where to put the apostrophe in 'Can't'.

Independent Writing   3 minutes
- Allow the children 20 seconds to study your sentences, then wipe your board clean.
- Ask the children to turn to a partner and repeat what they are going to write.
- Tell them to cover their practised words and then write the sentences in the first email.
- Check the children's work.

Talk for Writing   3 minutes
- *Now we are going to send a reply from the friend who saw the monster. Look back at the email you wrote last time. Do you notice anything interesting about when it was sent? The first email was sent on April 1st. What is that day famous for? (It is a day when people try to trick their friends into believing something that is not true.) We need to tell our friend he has had an April fool's joke played on him!*
- *Turn to a partner and think of a sentence starting: 'Check out ...'. Then think of a final sentence starting 'I can't believe you ....'*
- Share the children's ideas.

Demonstration Writing   3 minutes
- *I am going to write:* **Check out the date!** *Look carefully at the word 'Check'. How many phonemes are there? (three – 'ch/e/ck') I will put an exclamation mark at the end of the sentence to emphasise how silly it was that the friend fell for it.*
- *I am going to finish by writing:* **I can't believe you fell for it!** *As I write that sentence I want you to write 'believe' in the Have a go box.*
- Read the sentences together.

> Remind the children that they have learned 'believe' in a previous session. Ask them if they can remember the mnemonic 'never bel<u>ie</u>ve a lie'.

Independent Writing   3 minutes
- Allow the children 20 seconds to study the sentences, then wipe your board clean.
- Ask the children to turn to a partner and repeat what they are going to write.
- Tell them to cover their practised words and then to write the sentences in the second email.
- Check the children's work.

Rounding Off   3 minutes
- Ask the children if they have ever been fooled on April Fool's Day. What happened?
- Do they think this trick about the Loch Ness monster was a good April fool trick?
- Can they think of a good April fool trick to play on a friend or a teacher next April 1st?

Review   3 minutes
- Discuss different ways of writing the date with the group. What ways are there? (using only numbers; writing the month out in words) Can they write their date of birth in two different ways on their whiteboards?
- In what two different ways is the long 'ay' sound written in the words 'wait' and 'date'? ('ai', with the 'a' and the 'e')
- How well do the children think they did? Ask them to colour in one of the thumbs.
- Share the joke!

18.2

UNIT 19

A REAL ALIEN? *SESSION 1*

Outcome:
- A report

Writing targets:
- Target words: 'lied', 'about', 'alien'
- Sentences: one complex sentence, one simple sentence

You will need:
- Writing Logs page 17
- Whiteboards and pens
- Card for covering spellings

Warm Up

Phonics: 'lied'   2 minutes
- Robot-speak the word 'l/igh/d' then ask the children to blend the phonemes to make the word.
- Listen as they robot-speak and then blend the whole word.
- As they robot-speak 'lied', write the letters on the board.
- Wipe your board clean, then ask the children to write the word on their whiteboards and add phoneme buttons (l/ie/d).
- Tell the children to wipe their boards clean and to write 'lied' three times in the Phonics box.

> Ensure that children understand that the letters 'ie' represent one phoneme.

Phonics: 'about'   2 minutes
- Robot-speak the word 'a/b/ow/t' then ask the children to blend the phonemes to make the word.
- Listen as they robot-speak and then blend the whole word.
- As they robot-speak 'about' again, write the letters on the board.
- Wipe your board clean, then ask the children to write the word on their whiteboards and add phoneme buttons (a/b/ou/t).
- Tell the children to wipe their boards clean and to write 'about' three times in the Phonics box.

> Ensure that children understand that the 'ow' sound is represented by the letters 'ou'.

Spelling: 'alien'   2 minutes
- Explain that 'alien' is an irregular word so they will learn to spell it using letter names.
- Demonstrate how to spell the word 'alien', saying the letter names as you write.
- Wipe your board clean and ask the children to trace the word with their finger on their whiteboard, saying the letter names as they do so. Then ask them to write 'alien' on their whiteboards.
- Tell the children to wipe their boards clean, then write the word three times in the Spelling box.

Guiding the Writing

Talk for Writing   4 minutes
- Look at the pictures. Explain that Kate and Harry like to investigate mysteries. They have interviewed Josh who claims that he saw a UFO in the sky and took a photo to prove it. Ask the children what a UFO is (an Unidentified Flying Object – a mysterious craft in the sky).
- *Kate has managed to prove that Josh faked the photo with a toy spaceship and some clever camera work, but no-one can work out how an alien got in the photo! Josh has owned up to trying to trick everyone, but says he too has no idea how the alien got there.*

- *We are going to write Harry's report on the mystery. Harry is convinced that Josh doesn't know how the alien got in the photo, so this is what he will say in his report. Turn to a partner and think of Harry's first sentence, starting: 'I know Josh lied about ...' and then continuing: 'but I believe him when he says ...'.*
- Share the children's ideas.

Demonstration Writing   4 minutes
- *I am going to write:* **I know Josh lied about seeing a UFO, but I believe him when he says he didn't put the alien in the photo.** *As I write the words 'know' and 'didn't', I want you to practise them in the Have a go box.*
- *I am going to add a comma after 'UFO' to break up the long sentence and to make it easier to read.*
- Read the sentence together.

Independent Writing   3 minutes
- Allow the children 20 seconds to study your sentence, then wipe your board clean.
- Ask the children to turn to a partner and repeat what they are going to write.
- Tell them to cover their practised words and then to write the sentence. Remind them about the three capital letters for UFO.
- Check the children's work.

> Check that children remember the 'k' at the beginning of the word 'know'.

Talk for Writing   3 minutes
- *Now we are going to write one rounding-off sentence where Harry will state what he believes about the alien in the photo.*
- *Turn to a partner and think of a sentence starting: 'I think it was ...'.*
- Share the children's ideas.

Demonstration Writing   2 minutes
- *I am going to write:* **I think it was a real alien.** *As I write the word, 'real' I want you to practise it in the Have a go box.*
- Read the sentence together.

Independent Writing   2 minutes
- Allow the children 10 seconds to study the sentence, then wipe your board clean.
- Ask the children to turn to a partner and repeat what they are going to write.
- Tell them to cover their practised words and then to write the sentence.
- Check the children's work.

Rounding Off   3 minutes
- Why does Harry think Josh is telling the truth? (It would be very difficult to get a tiny alien in the model.)
- Ask the group if they believe Josh when he says he didn't put the alien in the fake photo.
- Why might the alien have come to Earth? (To learn about how we live; to plan an attack.)

Review   3 minutes
- Which word links the two parts of the first sentence ('but'). Why is it important? (because it shows the contrast between what some people think and what Harry believes)
- Write the word 'lied' on your board. Write the letters: 'tr', 'cr', 'fr'. Challenge the children to write three rhyming words on their whiteboards with those letters.
- How well do the children think they did? Ask them to colour in one of the thumbs.
- Share the joke!

19.1

UNIT 19

A REAL ALIEN? *SESSION 2*

Outcome:
- A report

Writing targets:
- Target words: 'only', 'sure', 'clever'
- Revision words: 'photo', 'everyone'
- Sentences: two compound sentences

You will need:
- Writing Logs page 18
- Whiteboards and pens
- Card for covering spellings

Warm Up

Spelling: 'only' — *2 minutes*
- Explain that 'only' is an irregular word so they will learn to spell it using letter names.
- Demonstrate how to spell the word 'only', saying the letter names as you write.
- Wipe your board clean and ask the children to trace the word with their finger on their whiteboard, saying the letter names as they do so. Then ask them to write 'only' on their whiteboards.
- Tell the children to wipe their boards clean, then write the word three times in the Spelling box.

Spelling: 'sure' — *2 minutes*
- Explain that 'sure' is an irregular word so they will learn to spell it using letter names.
- Demonstrate how to spell the word 'sure', saying the letter names as you write.
- Wipe your board clean and ask the children to trace the word with their finger on their whiteboard, saying the letter names as they do so. Then ask them to write 'sure' on their whiteboards.
- Tell the children to wipe their boards clean, then write the word three times in the Spelling box.

> The word 'sure' is irregular as the 'sh' sound at the beginning of the word is made with the letter 's'.

Phonics: 'clever' — *2 minutes*
- Robot-speak the word 'c/l/e/v/er' then ask the children to blend the phonemes to make the word.
- Listen as they robot-speak and then blend the whole word.
- As they robot-speak 'clever', write the letters on the board.
- Wipe your board clean, then ask the children to write the word on their whiteboards and add phoneme buttons.
- Tell the children to wipe their boards clean and then to write 'clever' three times in the Phonics box.

> Ensure that children understand that the letters 'er' represent one phoneme.

Guiding the Writing

Talk for Writing — *3 minutes*
- Remind the children that last time they wrote Harry's report in which he said that he thought Josh was telling the truth about the alien in the flying saucer. Now they are going to write Kate's report. She thinks the opposite of Harry so what will she think about Josh's story? (that he made it up, just like he faked the picture of the UFO)
- *Turn to a partner and think about what Kate will write in her report. Start your first sentence: 'Josh not only lied about ...' and then continue it with: 'but he lied about ...'.*
- Share the children's ideas.

Demonstration Writing   3 minutes
- *I am going to write:* **Josh not only lied about seeing a UFO but he lied about the alien too.** *As I write the word 'seeing', I want you to practise it in the Have a go box.*
- Point out that 'UFO' is written in capital letters because it is a shortened version of a phrase. Ask the children if they can remember what these letters stand for ('Unidentified Flying Object').
- Read the sentence together.

Independent Writing   3 minutes
- Allow the children 20 seconds to study your sentence. Ask them to repeat the three letters in 'UFO', then wipe your board clean.
- Ask the children to turn to a partner and repeat what they are going to write.
- Tell them to cover their practised words and then to write the sentence.
- Check the children's work.

Talk for Writing   3 minutes
- *Now we are going to write one final sentence which will state what Kate believes about the alien in the photo.*
- *Look at the photo. Kate thinks that Josh is trying to trick everyone with a toy alien and a clever photo. Turn to a partner and think of a sentence starting: 'I am sure the alien was ...' and continuing: 'and he took ...'.*
- Share the children's ideas.

Demonstration Writing   3 minutes
- *I am going to write:* **I am sure the alien was a toy and he took a clever photo to trick everyone.** *What sound can you hear at the beginning of 'photo'? ('f') What letters represent that sound? ('ph') As I write the word 'photo', I want you to write it in the Have a go box.*
- Ask the children which two words make up 'everyone' ('every' + 'one'). Tell them to say the letter names as you point at each letter. Tell them to close their eyes and repeat the letter names, and then to write the word in their Have a go box.
- Read the sentence together.

Independent Writing   3 minutes
- Allow the children 20 seconds to study the sentence, then wipe your board clean.
- Ask the children to turn to a partner and repeat what they are going to write.
- Tell them to cover their practised words and then to write the sentence.
- Check the children's work.

Rounding Off   3 minutes
- Why might Josh have taken a clever photo to make it look like an alien in a UFO? (he wanted to trick people; he wanted to be famous)
- Which words suggest that Kate knows she is right? ('I am sure')
- Who do you think is right – Kate or Harry? Why?

Review   3 minutes
- Which word at the end of the first sentence means 'as well'? ('too')
- Write the word 'every' on the board. Then write the words: 'thing', 'one', 'where'. Tell the children to study the words, then wipe your board clean and challenge them to write the three compound words.
- How well do the children think they did? Ask them to colour in one of the thumbs.
- Share the joke!

19.2

UNIT 20
UFOs

Outcome:
- A questionnaire

Writing targets:
- Target words: 'disappeared', 'before', 'contact'
- Sentences: one compound sentence, two questions

You will need:
- Writing Logs page 19
- Whiteboards and pens
- Card for covering spellings

Warm Up

Spelling: 'disappeared' — 3 minutes
- Write the word 'appear' on your board and explain that it is an irregular word so they will learn it using letter names.
- Demonstrate how to spell the word 'appear', saying the letter names as you write.
- Remind the children that they learned the word 'appear' in an earlier session.
- Explain that they are now going to write 'disappeared'. What letters do they think make the prefix 'dis'? Tell them to add 'dis' to the beginning of 'appear' on the whiteboards and then to add 'ed' to the end of the word. Say the word together.
- Tell the children to wipe their boards clean, then write 'disappeared' three times in the Spelling box.

> Ensure that children understand that the prefix 'dis' changes the meaning of the word.

Spelling: 'before' — 2 minutes
- Explain that 'before' is an irregular word so they will learn to spell it using letter names.
- Demonstrate how to spell the word 'before', saying the letter names as you write.
- Wipe your board clean and ask the children to trace the word with their finger on their whiteboard, saying the letter names as they do so. Then ask them to write 'before' on their whiteboard.
- Tell the children to wipe their boards clean, then write the word three times in the Spelling box.

Phonics: 'contact' — 2 minutes
- Robot-speak the word 'c/o/n/t/a/c/t' then ask the children to blend the phonemes to make the word.
- Listen as they robot-speak and then blend the whole word.
- As they robot-speak 'contact', write the letters on the board.
- Wipe your board clean, then ask the children to write the word on their whiteboards and add phoneme buttons.
- Tell the children to wipe their boards clean and to write 'contact' three times in the Phonics box.

Guiding the Writing

Talk for Writing — 3 minutes
- Look together at the pictures. Ask the children whether they know the expression 'flying saucer'. Why do they think people call some UFOs 'flying saucers'?
- *You are going to write a questionnaire to find out if people think UFOs are really visitors from space. Some people say they have seen a UFO, but that it disappeared before they could take the photo.*

96

- *Turn to a partner and think of a sentence starting: 'Some people say ...' and then continuing: 'but it disappeared ...'. Try to use some of the words you've just practised in your sentence.*
- Share the children's ideas.

Demonstration Writing   3 minutes
- *I am going to write:* **Some people say they have seen a UFO but it disappeared before they could take a photo.**
- *As I write my sentence, I want you to write the words 'people' and 'take' in the Have a go box.*
- Read the sentence together.

> Remind children that they have met the words 'people' and 'take' in previous sessions.

Independent Writing   3 minutes
- Allow the children 20 seconds to study your sentence, then wipe your board clean.
- Ask the children to turn to a partner and repeat what they are going to write.
- Tell them to cover their practised words and then to write the sentence.
- Check the children's work.

Talk for Writing   3 minutes
- *Now we need to ask two questions to find out if people believe there are such things as UFOs. Some people believe that aliens are trying to make contact with us. Do you think this is possible?*
- *Turn to a partner and think of two questions. The first question is going to ask the reader whether they think that there are other beings in outer space trying to contact us. Start your first question: 'Do you believe aliens ...'. The second question is going to ask whether the reader thinks UFOs exist. Start this question: 'Are there ...'.*
- Share the children's ideas.

Demonstration Writing   3 minutes
- *I am going to write:* **Do you believe aliens are trying to contact us?** *As I write that sentence, I want you to practise 'trying' in the Have a go box.*
- *Finally I will finish the survey by asking a very direct question:* **Are there UFOs?**
- Read the questions together.

> Point out that you have not put an apostrophe before the 's' because we are just adding an 's' to a noun to make it plural.

Independent Writing   2 minutes
- Allow the children 20 seconds to study your sentences then wipe your board.
- Ask the children to turn to a partner and repeat what they are going to write.
- Tell them to cover their practised words and then to write the questions, being careful not to write on the short lines.
- Check the children's work.

Rounding Off   3 minutes
- Tell the children to think about how they might answer the two questions and then to write either 'Yes' or 'No' against them on the short lines. Then add up the answers to find out the result of the questionnaire.
- Ask the children if they have ever seen a film or a programme about UFOs.
- Ask them what they would do if they thought they saw a UFO.

Review   3 minutes
- Ask the children what the verb 'appear' means (something has come into sight). What happens to the meaning if the prefix 'dis' is added? (It means the opposite; it vanishes.) Challenge them to write the following: 'appear'/'disappear'; 'like'/'dislike'; 'agree'/'disagree'.
- Write the following words on your whiteboard and ask the children what you need to do to make them plural: 'moon', 'saucer', 'alien', 'photo', 'UFO' (add an 's' to all of them).
- How well do the children think they did? Ask them to colour in one of the thumbs.
- Share the joke!

20.1

UNIT 20

WRITE IT! *ASSESSMENT*

Outcome:
- Assessment of skills covered in Book 8

Writing assessments:
- Spelling: independent spelling of 32 key words
- Writing: accurately writing four sentences

You will need:
- Writing Logs page 20
- Whiteboards and pens

Writing Task

Assessment 1 — 7 minutes
- *Look at the first picture. Do you remember the two children who found the man filling bottles from a hosepipe? They asked him to stop but he was very angry.*
- *Tell the children that they are going to write the sentence: When the two children saw what he was doing they told him to stop.*
- *How many words are there in the sentence? (14) What will you remember about starting a sentence and finishing it? What strategies can you use to help you with the spelling of the words? Say the sentence to yourself and then spell each word carefully. Also think about forming each letter accurately as you write it.*
- *Warn the children that you will only say the sentences once.*
- Dictate the sentence: **When the two children saw what he was doing, they told him to stop.**

Revision: 'scared' — 2 minutes
- *In a minute you are going to spell the word 'scared'. How are you going to remember how to spell that word? Have a go at writing the word on your whiteboard.*

Assessment 2 — 7 minutes
- *Look at the second picture. Remember writing a story about Emily who said she had been rescued from a fire by a strange boy.*
- *Tell the children that they are going to write the sentence: I was very scared and I thought I was going to die.*
- *How many words are there in that sentence? (12) What will you remember about starting a sentence and finishing it? What strategies can you use to help you with the spelling of the words? Say the sentence to yourself and then spell each word carefully. Also think about forming each letter accurately as you write it.*
- *Warn the children you will only say the sentence once.*
- Dictate the sentence: **I was very scared and I thought I was going to die.**

Check Points

As the children write, observe:
- letter formation
- spelling strategies
- strategies to recall the sentence (rereading what they have written so far, saying the sentence to themselves).

After the children have written the sentence, ask them to check it and to decide if they have:
- remembered to write every word
- spelt each word correctly.

- Encourage the children to picture the word 'scared'.

As the children write, observe:
- letter formation
- spelling strategies
- strategies to recall the sentence (rereading what they have written so far, saying the sentence to themselves).

After the children have written the sentence, ask them to check it and to decide if they have:
- remembered to write every word
- spelt each word correctly.

Revision: 'million' *2 minutes*
- In a minute you are going to spell the word 'million'. How are you going to remember how to spell that word? How many 'l's are there in the word? Have a go at writing the word on your whiteboard.

Assessment 3 *7 minutes*
- Look at the third picture Do you remember writing an email to a friend saying you had seen a monster? Your friend thought you could sell the photo and make loads of money.
- Tell the children they are going to write the sentences: Can't wait to see the photo. You could sell it and make a million.
- How many words are there in the first sentence? (six) How many words are there in the second sentence? (eight) What will you remember about starting sentences? What punctuation will you put at the end of the sentences? (An exclamation mark and a full stop.) What strategies can you use to help you with the spelling of the words? Say the sentences to yourself and then spell each word carefully. Also think about forming each letter accurately as you write it.
- Warn the children that you will only say the sentences once.
- Dictate the sentences: **Can't wait to see the photo! You could sell it and make a million.**

- Encourage the children to picture the word 'million'.

As the children write, observe:
- letter formation
- spelling strategies
- strategies to recall the sentence (rereading what they have written so far, saying the sentence to themselves).

After the children have written the sentences, ask them to check them and to decide if they have:
- remembered to write every word
- spelt each word correctly.

Review *5 minutes*
- Encourage children to reread their writing. Are there any words that they think they might have got wrong? Tell them to put a little line under any letters they think might be wrong.
- Ask the children to look back through their book. Which writing activity did they like best? Which is their best writing?
- What have they learned? Encourage them to talk about: capital letters, full stops, exclamation marks, spelling strategies, captions, labels, first-person writing.
- Share the joke!

Go to the orange box on page 22 in the Writing Log for an unaided writing activity.
See page 144 of this Teaching Guide for guidance notes.

20.2

UNIT 21

MERLIN MYSTERY: *SESSION 1*

Outcome:
- Two dramatic paragraphs

Writing targets:
- Target words: 'voice', 'whispered', 'trainer'
- Revision words: 'someone', 'who's'
- Sentences: one short sentence, two sentences with phrases, one sentence of dialogue

You will need:
- Writing Logs page 1
- Whiteboards and pens
- Card for covering spellings

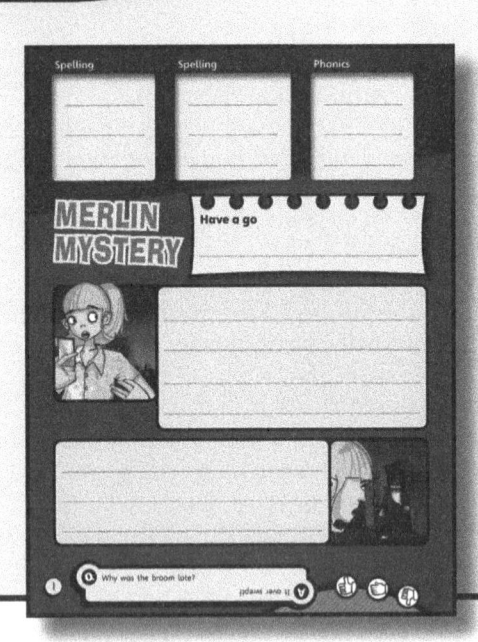

Warm Up

Spelling: 'voice' *2 minutes*
- Explain that 'voice' is an irregular word so they will learn to spell it using letter names.
- Demonstrate how to spell the word 'voice', saying the letter names as you write.
- Wipe your board clean and ask the children to trace the word with their finger on their whiteboard, saying the letter names as they do so. Then ask them to write 'voice' on their whiteboards.
- Tell the children to wipe their boards clean, then write the word three times in the Spelling box.

> Point out to the children that the word 'ice' can be found in 'voice'.

Spelling: 'whispered' *2 minutes*
- Explain that 'whispered' is an irregular word so they will learn to spell it using letter names.
- Demonstrate how to spell the word 'whispered', saying the letter names as you write.
- Wipe your board clean and ask the children to trace the word with their finger on their whiteboard, saying the letter names as they do so. Then ask them to write 'whispered' on their whiteboards.
- Tell the children to wipe their boards clean, then write the word three times in the Spelling box.

> Ensure that the children realise that 'whispered' is 'whisper' + 'ed'.

Phonics: 'trainer' *2 minutes*
- Robot-speak the word 't/r/ay/n/er' then ask the children to blend the phonemes to make the word.
- Listen as they robot-speak and then blend the whole word.
- As they robot-speak 'trainer' again, write the letters on the board.
- Wipe your board clean, then ask the children to write the word on their whiteboards and add phoneme buttons (t/r/ai/n/er).
- Tell the children to wipe their boards clean and to write 'whispered' three times in the Phonics box.

> Ensure that children understand that the 'ay' sound is being made by the letters 'ai'.

Guiding the Writing

Talk for Writing *4 minutes*
- Explain to the group that they are going to write a dramatic paragraph in the middle of a mystery story. There is a legend that, at the time of an eclipse, the magician Merlin's face appears on one of the stones of Stonehenge, and Carla and Rob have gone to find out if it is true. An eclipse is when the moon goes in front of the sun and blocks out its light. Explain that Carla and Rob are brother and sister and that they love playing tricks on each other. Why might that be important in the plot? (One of them might pretend to be Merlin.)

100

- *I want to grab the reader's attention from the start so the first sentence will be: '"Carla," a voice whispered.' By saying 'a voice', I am not giving away who is speaking. Then Carla will spin round to see who it is.*
- *Turn to a partner and think of a three-word sentence starting: 'Carla spun …' and a second sentence starting: 'In the dim light she could see …'.*
- Share the children's ideas.

Demonstration Writing 4 minutes
- *First I am going to write:* **"Carla," a voice whispered.**
- *Then I will write:* **Carla spun round.** *The word 'spun' suggests how spooked she is by the whispering voice. As I write 'round', practise it in the Have a go box.*
- *Next I am going to write:* **In the dim light, she could see someone in a long robe.** *As I write 'someone', I want you to write it in the Have a go box. Next, look at the word 'robe'. Which two letters make the long vowel 'oh' sound? ('o', 'e')*

> Point out that the speech marks around the word 'Carla' show that it is spoken.

> Point out that 'someone' is made up of 'some' and 'one'.

Independent Writing 3 minutes
- Allow the children 30 seconds to study your sentences, then wipe your board clean.
- Ask the children to turn to a partner and repeat what they are going to write.
- Tell them to cover their practised words and then write the three sentences.
- Check the children's work.

> Check that children put speech marks around the word 'Carla'.

Talk for Writing 3 minutes
- *Now we are going to write what Carla says when she sees the mystery figure in the dim light. What might she ask? ('Who's that?') What speech verb could we use instead of 'said'? ('asked', 'called')*
- *Look at the second picture. Can you see anything strange about Merlin? (He's wearing trainers.) Who do you think is pretending to be Merlin? (Rob)*
- *In the last sentence, we want the reader to be able to work out who is wearing the robe, but without actually telling them. Turn to a partner and think of a sentence starting: 'Then she saw …'.*
- Share the children's ideas.

Demonstration Writing 3 minutes
- *First I am going to write:* **"Who's that?" she called.** *Which two words are in 'Who's'? ('Who', 'is') The apostrophe shows that the letter 'i' is missing.*
- *Next I am going to write:* **Then she saw a trainer under the robe.** *As I write the word 'under' I want you to practise it in the Have a go box.*
- Read the sentences together.

> Check that children understand that the question mark goes before the closing speech marks.

Independent Writing 3 minutes
- Allow the children 20 seconds to study your sentences then wipe your board clean.
- Ask the children to turn to a partner and repeat what they are going to write.
- Tell them to cover their practised words and then to write the sentences.
- Check the children's work.

Rounding Off 2 minutes
- Ask the children why they didn't let the reader know straight away that the person in the robe was Rob (to make it more mysterious). How did they hide his identity? (by saying 'a voice' and 'someone')
- How did Carla realise that the figure could not be Merlin? (an ancient magician would not be wearing trainers)

Review 2 minutes
- Write the word 'train' on your board. Tell children to work with a partner and to write as many words as they can that have 'train' as the root. ('trains', 'trained', 'training').
- Ask the children which speech verbs they used ('whispered', 'called'). Why are they more effective than 'said'? ('whispered' makes it more scary; 'called' suggests that Carla was nervous.)
- How well do the children think they did? Ask them to colour in one of the thumbs.
- Share the joke!

21.1

UNIT 21

MERLIN MYSTERY: *SESSION 2*

Outcome:
- Two dramatic paragraphs

Writing targets:
- Target words: 'front', 'darker', 'stones'
- Revision word: 'getting'
- Sentences: two simple sentences, a compound sentence, a question

You will need:
- Writing Logs page 2
- Whiteboards and pens
- Card for covering spellings

The word 'front' is treated as irregular because the letter 'o' is unusually making the 'u' sound.

Point out that the letters 'er' at the end of the word make the sound 'uh'. This is called the unstressed vowel.

Warm Up

Spelling: 'front' — 2 minutes
- Explain that 'front' is an irregular word so they will learn to spell it using letter names.
- Demonstrate how to spell the word 'front', saying the letter names as you write.
- Wipe your board clean and ask the children to trace the word with their finger on their whiteboard, saying the letter names as they do so. Then ask them to write 'front' on their whiteboards.
- Tell the children to wipe their boards clean, then write the word three times in the Spelling box.

Phonics: 'darker' — 2 minutes
- Robot-speak the word 'd/ar/k/uh' then ask the children to blend the phonemes to make the word.
- Listen as they robot-speak and then blend the whole word.
- As they robot-speak 'darker' again, write the letters on the board.
- Wipe your board clean, then ask the children to write the word on their whiteboards and add phoneme buttons (d/ar/k/er).
- Tell the children to wipe their boards clean and to write 'darker' three times in the Phonics box.

Phonics: 'stones' — 2 minutes
- Robot-speak the word 's/t/oh/n/s' then ask the children to blend the phonemes to make the word.
- Listen as they robot-speak and then blend the whole word.
- As they robot-speak 'stones' again, write the letters on the board. Ask the children to identify which letters are making the long vowel 'oh' sound. Tell the children to link the 'o' and 'e'.
- Wipe your board clean, then ask the children to write the word on their whiteboards.
- Tell the children to wipe their boards clean and to write 'stones' three times in the Phonics box.

Guiding the Writing

Talk for Writing — 4 minutes
- Ask the children where the action of the story is taking place (Stonehenge). What is an eclipse? (when the moon goes in front of the sun and blocks out its light) What did the legend say happened at the time of an eclipse? (the face of Merlin appears on one of the stones) What trick did Rob play on Carla? (pretended to be Merlin) Why was the light dim? (because the eclipse had started)

- *Look at the second picture. Rob has gone over to Carla after playing his trick on her. What is he pointing at? (a mysterious face on one of the stones) This time Rob thinks that Carla has somehow managed to play a trick on him, but Carla doesn't know anything about it.*
- *First we will make the atmosphere scarier by describing how it's getting darker. We will do this in two short sentences. Turn to a partner and think of one sentence starting: 'The moon went ...' and a second sentence starting: 'It was getting ...'.*
- *Share the children's ideas.*

Demonstration Writing   3 minutes
- *I am going to write:* **The moon went in front of the sun.** *As I write 'moon', I want you to write it in the Have a go box.*
- *For the next sentence I am going to write:* **It was getting darker and darker.** *As I write the word 'getting', I want you to tell me how to spell it and then write it in the Have a go box.*
- *Read the sentences together.*

> Point out the two 't's in 'getting'.

Independent Writing   2 minutes
- Allow the children 20 seconds to study the sentences, then wipe your board clean.
- Ask the children to turn to a partner and repeat what they are going to write.
- Tell them to cover their practised words and then write the sentences.
- Check the children's work.

Talk for Writing   3 minutes
- *In mystery stories, a good way to draw the reader into the action is to ask them a question. Whose face does the author want us to think it is? (Merlin's) So in the second question we could ask that directly.*
- *Turn to a partner and think of a question starting: 'Was it a trick of the light or ...'. Then think of a direct second question starting with: 'Could it ...'.*
- *Share the children's ideas.*

Demonstration Writing   3 minutes
- *First I am going to write:* **Was it a trick of the light or was that a face on one of the stones?** *As I write 'light', I want you to practise it in the Have a go box. Why have I put a question mark after 'stones'? (It is a question.)*
- *Next I am going to write:* **Could it be Merlin?**
- *Read the sentences together.*

Independent Writing   3 minutes
- Allow the children 20 seconds to study the sentences, then wipe your board clean.
- Ask the children to turn to a partner and repeat what they are going to write.
- Tell them to cover their practised words and then to write the two sentences.
- Check the children's work.

Rounding Off   3 minutes
- Ask the children if they can tell you some of the writing 'tricks' they used to make the reader more interested. (They built up the suspense by describing it getting darker and darker; they drew the reader in by asking a question.)
- What do the children think caused the face to appear on the stone? Was there a face at all or were Carla and Rob just imagining it?
- Ask the children what we call a block of writing, not just single sentences (a paragraph).

Review   3 minutes
- Write the word 'darker' on the board and underline 'er'. Then write: 'cold', 'fast', 'new'. Challenge the children to write the adjectives with 'er' on the end.
- Tell the children to work with a partner and to take it in turns to read both paragraphs. Can they make it sound really scary?
- How well do the children think they did? Ask them to colour in one of the thumbs.
- Share the joke!

21.2

UNIT 22

STONEHENGE: *SESSION 1*

Outcome:
- An explanation

Writing targets:
- Target words: 'built', 'machines', 'roads'
- Sentences: two simple sentences, one complex sentence

You will need:
- Writing Logs page 3
- Whiteboards and pens
- Card for covering spellings

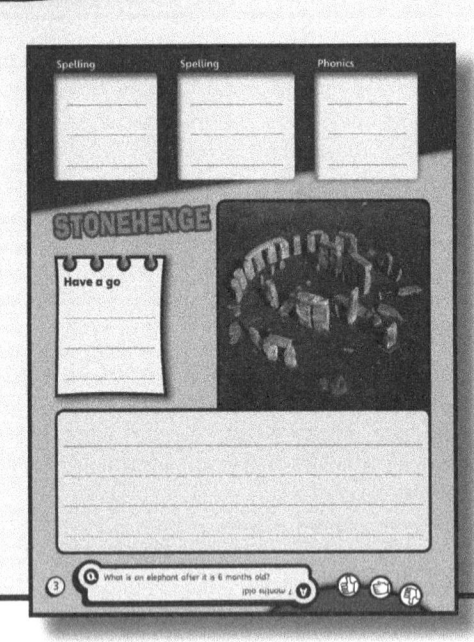

Warm Up

Spelling: 'built' *2 minutes*
- Explain that 'built' is an irregular word so they will learn to spell it using letter names.
- Demonstrate how to spell the word 'built', saying the letter names as you write.
- Wipe your board clean and ask the children to trace the word with their finger on their whiteboard, saying the letter names as they do so. Then ask them to write 'built' on their whiteboards.
- Tell the children to wipe their boards clean, then write the word three times in the Spelling box.

Spelling: 'machines' *2 minutes*
- Explain that 'machines' is an irregular word so they will learn to spell it using letter names.
- Demonstrate how to spell the word 'machines', saying the letter names as you write.
- Wipe your board clean and ask the children to trace the word with their finger on their whiteboard, saying the letter names as they do so. Then ask them to write 'machines' on their whiteboards.
- Tell the children to wipe their boards clean, then write the word three times in the Spelling box.

> The word 'machines' is irregular because the letters 'ch' makes a 'sh' sound and the letter 'i' makes an 'ee' sound.

Phonics: 'roads' *2 minutes*
- Robot-speak the word 'r/oh/d/s' then ask the children to blend the phonemes to make the word.
- Listen as they robot-speak and then blend the whole word.
- As they robot-speak 'roads' again, write the letters on the board.
- Wipe your board clean and ask the children to write the word on their whiteboards and add phoneme buttons (r/oa/d/s).
- Tell the children to wipe their boards clean and to write 'roads' in the Phonics box three times.

> Ensure that children understand that the letters 'oa' represent the long vowel 'oh' sound.

Guiding the Writing

Talk for Writing *4 minutes*
- Look together at the photo of Stonehenge. Ask the children if any of them have visited it.
- *Archaeologists believe that Stonehenge was built over 5000 years ago and was probably for a religious purpose – but no-one really knows. Stonehenge was made from 82 huge stones, some weighing more than five large elephants!*

104

- *We are going to write an explanation about how archaeologists think Stonehenge was built. First we need to tell the reader that Stonehenge is a ring of stones that was built 5000 years ago. Turn to a partner and think of a sentence starting: 'Stonehenge is ...'. Start your second sentence, which you will start: 'It was built ...'.*
- Share the children's ideas. If they haven't already, encourage them to include an adjective to improve their first sentence (for example 'huge').

Demonstration Writing   3 minutes
- *I am going to write:* **Stonehenge is a ring of huge stones.** *As I write this sentence, I want you to write the word 'huge' in the Have a go box.*
- *Then I am going to write:* **It was built 5000 years ago.** *As I write that sentence I want you to write 'ago' in the Have a go box.*
- Read the sentences together.

> Point out to the children that if the number is more than ten it is often written in figures rather than in letters.

Independent Writing   3 minutes
- Allow the children 20 seconds to study your sentences, then wipe your board clean, leaving 'Stonehenge' for them to copy.
- Ask the children to turn to a partner and repeat what they are going to write.
- Tell them to cover their practised words and then write the sentences.
- Check the children's work.

Talk for Writing   3 minutes
- *Now we need to ask a question which we will answer next time. Remember, we want to explain how archaeologists thought Stonehenge was built.*
- *It is amazing that people managed to move the stones to Stonehenge when there were no roads or machines to help them.*
- *Turn to a partner and think of a question. Start your question: 'How did people ...'.*
- Share the children's ideas.

Demonstration Writing   3 minutes
- *I am going to write:* **How did people, so long ago, move such big stones when they had no machines or roads?** *As I write the sentence I want you to write 'people' in the Have a go box.*
- *I have put commas around 'so long ago' because I want the reader to pause at the commas to separate this piece of information from the rest of the question.*
- Read the sentence together.

Independent Writing   3 minutes
- Allow the children 20 seconds to study your question, then wipe your board clean.
- Ask the children to turn to a partner and repeat what they are going to write.
- Tell them to cover their practised words and then to write the question.
- Check the children's work.

> Remind the children to put commas round the phrase 'so long ago'.

Rounding Off   3 minutes
- Ask the children if they can think of how the people might have moved the stones.
- *Why do you think the people wanted to use such huge stones? (They were building something very important; they wanted people to see it from far away.)*
- *What other ancient buildings were built so that people would see them from far away? (castles, churches)*

Review   2 minutes
- Ask the children what the following words have in common: 'road', 'roast', 'coat', 'coast'. (The long vowel 'oh' sound is made with the letters 'oa'.) Ask them to write 'road' and 'roast' on their whiteboards.
- Why do writers sometimes start an explanation with a question? (because they are going to explain the answer)
- How well do the children think they did? Ask them to colour in one of the thumbs.
- Share the joke!

22.1

UNIT 22

STONEHENGE: *SESSION 2*

Outcome:
- An explanation

Writing targets:
- Target words: 'hundreds', 'dragged', 'rollers'
- Sentences: two complex sentences, one simple sentence

You will need:
- Writing Logs page 4
- Whiteboards and pens
- Card for covering spellings

Warm Up

Phonics: 'hundreds' — 2 minutes
- Robot-speak the word 'h/u/n/d/r/e/d/s' then ask the children to blend the phonemes to make the word.
- Listen as they robot-speak and then blend the whole word.
- As they robot-speak 'hundreds' again, write the letters on the board.
- Wipe your board clean, then ask the children to write the word on their whiteboards and add phoneme buttons.
- Tell the children to wipe their boards clean and to write 'hundreds' three times in the Phonics box.

Phonics: 'dragged' — 2 minutes
- Robot-speak the word 'd/r/a/gg/d' then ask the children to blend the phonemes to make the word.
- Listen as they robot-speak and then blend the whole word.
- As they robot-speak 'dragged' again, write the letters on the board.
- Wipe your board clean, then ask the children to write the word on their whiteboards and add phoneme buttons ('d/r/a/gg/ed').
- Tell the children to wipe their boards clean and to write dragged three times in the Phonics box.

> Point out that 'dragged' has two 'g's and that the final 'd' sound is made with the letters 'ed'.

Spelling: 'rollers' — 2 minutes
- Explain that 'rollers' is an irregular word so they will learn to spell it using letter names.
- Demonstrate how to spell the word 'rollers', saying the letter names as you write.
- Wipe your board clean and ask the children to trace the word with their finger on their whiteboard, saying the letter names as they do so. Then ask them to write 'rollers' on their whiteboards.
- Tell the children to wipe their boards clean, then write the word three times in the Spelling box.

Guiding the Writing

Talk for Writing — 4 minutes
- Remind the children that they are writing an explanation about how archaeologists think Stonehenge was built. Ask them to reread their writing from the previous session.
- Tell the children that they are now going to answer the question they wrote last time and explain how the stones were moved.

- *Look at the picture. What are the men doing? (pulling a huge stone) Archaeologists think that about 500 men would have been needed to drag the stones over the ground. They think that the stones were moved by putting rollers made from tree trunks under the stones.*
- *Turn to a partner and think of a long sentence that explains how the stones were moved. Start your sentence: 'Hundreds of men dragged ...' and continue it with 'by putting ...'.*
- *Share the children's ideas.*

Demonstration Writing   3 minutes
- *I am going to write:* **Hundreds of men dragged the huge stones by putting rollers under the stones.** *As I write this sentence, I want you to write the word 'putting' in the Have a go box.*
- *Read the sentence together.*

> Remind the children about doubling the 't' in 'putting'.

Independent Writing   2 minutes
- *Allow the children 20 seconds to study the sentence, then wipe your board clean.*
- *Ask the children to turn to a partner and repeat what they are going to write.*
- *Tell them to cover their practised words and then write the sentence.*
- *Check the children's work.*

Talk for Writing   4 minutes
- *Look at the picture. It shows the men using long ropes to pull the stones over the rollers. Do you think this was easy?*
- *In an explanation we need to tell the readers things in a logical order. We have already explained how they put huge rollers under the stones. Now we need to explain how this helped the men move them.*
- *Turn to a partner and think of two sentences. The first sentence needs to explain how they used long ropes to move the stones over the rollers. In the final sentence we will tell the reader that this was very hard work. Start your first sentence: 'Then they used ...' and the final sentence: 'It was very ...'.*
- *Share the children's ideas.*

Demonstration Writing   3 minutes
- *I am going to write:* **They used long ropes to pull the stones over the rollers.** *As I write, I want you to practise 'used' and 'over' in the Have a go box.*
- *I will finish my explanation by saying:* **It was very hard work.**
- *Read the sentences together.*

Independent Writing   2 minutes
- *Allow the children 20 seconds to study the sentences, then wipe your board clean.*
- *Ask the children to turn to a partner and repeat what they are going to write.*
- *Tell them to cover their practised words and then to write both sentences.*
- *Check the children's work.*

Rounding Off   3 minutes
- *Tell the children to work with a partner and ask one to explain what Stonehenge is and the other to explain how the stones reached Stonehenge.*
- *If they could ask the people that built Stonehenge anything, what would they ask?*

Review   3 minutes
- *Talk about the features of an explanation: starting with a question; giving reasons in the answer; explaining things in a logical order. How well do they think they have explained how Stonehenge was built.*
- *How well do the children think they did? Ask them to colour in one of the thumbs.*
- *Share the joke!*

22.2

UNIT 23

DANGER AT SEA: *SESSION 1*

Outcome:
- A plan of a dramatic plot

Writing targets:
- Target words: 'crashes', 'knocked', 'filling'
- Sentences: two compound sentences and two simple sentences

You will need:
- Writing Logs page 5
- Whiteboards and pens
- Card for covering spellings

Warm Up

Phonics: 'crashes' *2 minutes*
- Robot-speak the word 'c/r/a/sh/e/s' then ask the children to blend the phonemes to make the word.
- Listen as they robot-speak and then blend the whole word.
- As they robot-speak 'crashes' again, write the letters on the board.
- Wipe your board clean then ask the children to write the word on their whiteboards and add phoneme buttons.
- Tell the children to wipe their boards clean and to write 'crashes' three times in the Phonics box.

Phonics: 'knocked' *2 minutes*
- Robot-speak the word 'kn/o/ck/t' then ask the children to blend the phonemes to make the word.
- Listen as they robot-speak and then blend the whole word.
- As they robot-speak 'knocked' again, write the letters on the board.
- Wipe your board clean then ask the children to write the word on their whiteboards and add phoneme buttons (kn/o/ck/ed).
- Tell the children to wipe their boards clean and write 'knocked' three times in the Phonics box.

> Ensure that children understand that the 't' sound at the end of 'knocked' is represented by the letters 'ed'.

Phonics: 'filling' *2 minutes*
- Robot-speak the word 'f/i/ll/i/ng' then ask the children to blend the phonemes to make the word.
- Listen as they robot-speak and then blend the whole word.
- As they robot-speak 'filling' again, write the letters on the board.
- Wipe your board clean, then ask the children to write the word on their whiteboards and add phoneme buttons.
- Tell the children to wipe their boards clean and to write 'filling' three times in the Phonics box.

> Ensure that children put one phoneme button for 'll' and one for 'ng'.

Guiding the Writing

Talk for Writing *3 minutes*
- Explain to the children that they will be writing a plan outlining how, at first, things go wrong for the characters, Karl and Adam.
- *Karl and Adam are on board Karl's uncle's boat when a storm blows up. Another boat crashes into them and makes a hole in their boat.*
- *So let's recap on the problems so far: there is a storm, then a boat crashes into them, making a hole in their boat.*

108

- *We will write the problems in the order that they occur, and in the present tense. Turn to a partner and think of the first problem starting: 'A storm …'. Then think of the second problem starting: 'A boat crashes …'.*
- Share the children's ideas.

Demonstration Writing *3 minutes*
- *First I am going to write:* **A storm blows up.**
- *Then I am going to write:* **A boat crashes into them and makes a hole in their boat.** *As I write the word 'hole', I want you to practise it in the Have a go box.*
- Read the sentences together, then ask one child to underline the verbs.

> Remind the children that story plans use the present tense, i.e. 'blows', 'crashes', 'makes'.

Independent Writing *3 minutes*
- Allow the children 20 seconds to study the first two problems, then wipe your board clean.
- Ask the children to turn to a partner and repeat what they are going to write.
- Tell them to cover their practised words and then write the problems next to the first picture.
- Check the children's work.

Talk for Writing *4 minutes*
- *Look at the second picture. Karl is knocked out when the crash happens and now he is lying in the hold and the boat is filling with water. What can Adam do to help Karl? (try to lift him out of the hold)*
- *Now I need to write the next problems. What happens to Karl when the other boat crashes into them? (He is knocked out.) What is happening to their boat? (It is filling with water.) This is building up the tension in the narrative.*
- *Turn to a partner and think of a sentence starting: 'Karl is knocked out …'. Then start the next sentence with: 'Adam can't lift …'.*
- Share the children's ideas.

Demonstration Writing *3 minutes*
- *I am going to write:* **Karl is knocked out and the boat is filling with water.** *As I write 'boat' and 'water', I want you to practise them in the Have a go box.*
- *Next I am going to write:* **Adam can't lift Karl up the steps.**
- Read the problems together.

> Break the characters' names into phonemes to help the children spell them: 'K/ar/l', 'A/d/a/m'.

Independent Writing *3 minutes*
- Allow the children 20 seconds to study your writing, then wipe your board clean.
- Ask the children to turn to a partner and repeat what they are going to write.
- Tell them to cover their practised words and then to write the problems next to the last two pictures.
- Check the children's work.

> Check that children have put the apostrophe in 'can't' in the correct place.

Rounding Off *2 minutes*
- Explain that you have not used any adjectives in the story map. Can the children think why not? (They will be added when the story is written in full. A story map just outlines the action.)
- Why is it important to let the reader know that Adam can't lift Karl up the steps? (It makes the story more dramatic if the reader feels that a problem in the story can't be solved.)

Review *3 minutes*
- Write the word 'fill' on your board. Tell children to write as many words as they can that have 'fill' as the root ('fills', 'filled', 'filling').
- What's different about writing part of a story and writing a plan or story map? (A story map just lists the events in time sequence. It does not describe the characters' feelings or say what they said.)
- How well do the children think they did? Ask them to colour in one of the thumbs.
- Share the joke!

23.1

DANGER AT SEA: *SESSION 2*

Outcome:
- A plan of a dramatic plot

Writing targets:
- Target words: 'won't', 'last', 'manages'
- Sentences: four simple sentences, one with a phrase of time, one compound sentence

You will need:
- Writing Logs page 6
- Whiteboards and pens
- Card for covering spellings

Warm Up

Spelling: 'won't' — 2 minutes
- Explain that 'won't' is an irregular word so they will learn to spell it using letter names.
- Demonstrate how to spell the word 'won't', saying the letter names as you write. Explain that it is short for 'will not' and draw attention to the apostrophe between the 'n' and the 't'.
- Wipe your board clean and ask the children to trace the word with their finger on their whiteboard, saying the letter names as they do so. Then ask them to write 'won't' on their whiteboards.
- Tell the children to wipe their boards clean, then write the word three times in the Spelling box.

Phonics: 'last' — 2 minutes
- Robot-speak the word 'l/a/s/t' then ask the children to blend the phonemes to make the word.
- Listen as they robot-speak and then blend the whole word.
- As they robot-speak 'last' again, write the letters on the board.
- Wipe your board clean, then ask the children to write the word on their whiteboards and add phoneme buttons.
- Tell the children to wipe their boards clean and to write 'last' three times in the Phonics box.

> In regions where the 'a' is pronounced 'ar', you may prefer to teach 'last' using letter names.

Spelling: 'manages' — 2 minutes
- Explain that 'manages' is an irregular word so they will learn to spell it using letter names.
- Demonstrate how to spell the word 'manages', saying the letter names as you write.
- Wipe your board clean and ask the children to trace the word with their finger on their whiteboard, saying the letter names as they do so. Then ask them to write 'manages' on their whiteboards.
- Tell the children to wipe their boards clean, then write the word three times in the Spelling box.

Guiding the Writing

Talk for Writing — 3 minutes
- Ask the children why a plan is helpful when writing a story. (It helps the writer remember the events in sequence; it ensures that the story has plenty of action because you list problems for the characters to overcome.)
- Ask the children to recap on the problems facing Karl and Adam so far.

- *Look at the pictures. Adam is trying to drag Karl up the steps. The water is getting deeper. What will happen if Adam can't pull Karl out on to the deck? (Karl will drown.) In a story we need to make the reader care about what happens to the characters, so we will make Karl sound brave. He will tell Adam to leave him in the hold, and save himself.*
- *Turn to a partner and think of two more events for the plot. Start the first sentence: 'Karl tells Adam to ...' and continue with: 'but ...'. Start a second sentence: 'He tries to drag Karl ...'.*
- Share the children's ideas.

Demonstration Writing   3 minutes
- *I am going to write:* **Karl tells Adam to leave him, but Adam won't give up on Karl.** *As I write 'leave', I want you to write it in the Have a go box.*
- *Next I am going to write:* **He tries to drag Karl up the steps.** *Look at the verb 'tries'. Which tense is it in? (present tense) Remember that the present tense is used in story plans.*

> Point out that there is a comma after 'him' to break up the sentence into manageable chunks for the reader.

Independent Writing   3 minutes
- Allow the children 20 seconds to study your writing, then wipe your board clean.
- Ask the children to turn to a partner and repeat what they are going to write.
- Tell them to cover their practised words and then write the sentences.
- Check the children's work.

Talk for Writing   3 minutes
- *Now I am going to remind the reader that the water is getting deeper. That will build up the tension in the story. Turn to a partner and think of the next challenge. Start the entry: 'The water is ...'.*
- *Finally we need to reach a solution. What would be a happy ending? (Adam manages to pull Karl up on the deck. Start the final entry on the plan: 'At last Adam manages ...'.*
- Share the children's ideas.

Demonstration Writing   3 minutes
- *I am going to write:* **The water is getting deeper.** *As I write 'deeper', I want you to practise it in the Have a go box.*
- *Next I am going to write:* **At last Adam manages to pull Karl on to the deck.**
- Read the final problem and the happy ending together.

Independent Writing   3 minutes
- Allow the children 20 seconds to study your writing, then wipe your board clean.
- Ask the children to turn to a partner and repeat what they are going to write.
- Tell them to cover their practised words and then write the entries.
- Check the children's work.

Rounding Off   3 minutes
- Ask the children what phrase they used to indicate to the reader that it was the final part of the story map ('At last').
- How did they keep the tension going in the story? (by reminding the reader that the water is getting deeper)
- Who do they think is the hero of the story? Karl or Adam? Why?

Review   3 minutes
- Tell the children to draw a graph to show how the dramatic tension of the story builds up across their plan. They should start at a low level when the storm blows up, then track how each event makes the story more and more tense. Which is the most dramatic moment? Where will they place the ending on the graph? Do they think the graph line is going back towards the lower level?
- How well do the children think they did? Ask them to colour in one of the thumbs.
- Share the joke!

23.2

UNIT 24

FIRE! *SESSION 1*

Outcome:
- A bulleted list of instructions

Writing targets:
- Target words: 'door', 'open', 'crawl'
- Sentences: a heading, four instructions

You will need:
- Writing Logs page 7
- Whiteboards and pens
- Card for covering spellings

Warm Up

Phonics: 'door' — 2 minutes
- Robot-speak the word 'd/oor' then ask the children to blend the phonemes to make the word.
- Listen as they robot-speak and then blend the whole word.
- As they robot-speak 'door' again, write the letters on the board.
- Wipe your board clean, then ask the children to write the word on their whiteboards and add phoneme buttons.
- Tell the children to wipe their boards clean and to write 'door' three times in the Phonics box.

Point out that the letters 'oor' make one phoneme.

Phonics: 'open' — 2 minutes
- Robot-speak the word 'oh/p/e/n' then ask the children to blend the phonemes to make the word.
- Listen as they robot-speak and then blend the whole word.
- As they robot-speak 'open' again, write the letters on the board.
- Wipe your board clean, then ask the children to write the word on their whiteboards and add phoneme buttons (o/p/e/n).
- Tell the children to wipe their boards clean and to write 'open' three times in the Phonics box.

Phonics: 'crawl' — 2 minutes
- Robot-speak the word 'c/r/aw/l' then ask the children to blend the phonemes to make the word.
- Listen as they robot-speak and then blend the whole word.
- As they robot-speak 'crawl' again, write the letters on the board.
- Wipe your board clean, then ask the children to write the word on their whiteboards and add phoneme buttons.
- Tell the children to wipe their boards clean and to write 'crawl' three times in the Phonics box.

Point out that the letters 'aw' make one phoneme.

Guiding the Writing

Talk for Writing — 5 minutes
- Tell the children that they are going to write the instructions for what to do in a fire. Have they heard or seen the fire instructions in school?
- Look at the heading: 'What to do in a fire'. Why do you think it is important to make the heading stand out? (To draw attention, to show it is important, to inform the reader.)
- If you saw a fire, what would you do first? If you can you should phone 999.
- Then you need to see how close the fire is to you. You should touch the door handle: if it is cold you can open the door.

112

- *Turn to a partner and think of two instructions. Start your first instruction: 'If you can …'. Start your second instruction: 'If the door handle …'.*
- Share the children's ideas.

Demonstration Writing   3 minutes
- *As we are writing these in a list, I am going to put a number before each instruction. The list will show the order in which people should do things.*
- *First I will write:* **1. If you can, call 999.**
- *Then I will write:* **2. If the door handle is cold, open the door.** *I have put a comma after 'cold' so the reader pauses and then is given the instruction.*
- Read the sentences together.

Independent Writing   3 minutes
- Allow the children 20 seconds to study your sentences, then wipe your board clean, leaving the word 'handle' for them to copy.
- Ask the children to turn to a partner and repeat what they are going to write.
- Tell them to cover their practised words and then to write the two instructions.
- Check the children's work.

> Remind the children that we are numbering each instruction in the list.

Talk for Writing   3 minutes
- *We must finish by telling people what to do after they have opened the door. If there is smoke but no flames, they should get down and crawl out of the building because it is easier to breathe down on the floor. It's very important that they do not go back into the building to look for anything.*
- *Turn to a partner and think of two sentences. Start the first sentence: 'If you see smoke …' and the second sentence: 'Don't go …'.*
- Share the children's ideas.

Demonstration Writing   3 minutes
- *I am going to write* **3. If you see smoke, get down and crawl out.** *As I write the sentence, I want you to write 'down' in the Have a go box.*
- *Then I will write:* **4. Don't go back in.** *As I write this sentence, I want you to write 'Don't', with a capital 'D', in the Have a go box.*
- Read the sentences together.

Independent Writing   3 minutes
- Allow the children 20 seconds to study the sentences, then wipe your board clean.
- Ask the children to turn to a partner and repeat what they are going to write.
- Tell them to cover their practised words, then to write two further instructions.
- Check the children's work.

Rounding Off   2 minutes
- Tell the children to read the instructions. Are the instructions clear?
- Ask them to think of some quiz questions to challenge each other with, for example 'What is the first instruction?', 'Why should you touch the door handle?'.

Review   2 minutes
- Remind the children that they wrote 'door' and 'crawl' at the start of the session. Ask them what sound these two words have in common ('or'). What different letters made the sound 'or'? ('oor', 'aw')
- Why did they number the instructions? (To show the order of importance.)
- How well do the children think they did? Ask them to colour in one of the thumbs.
- Share the joke!

24.1

UNIT 24

FIRE! SESSION 2

Outcome:
- A bulleted list of instructions

Writing targets:
- Target words: 'window', 'handle', 'clothes'
- Sentences: four instructions

You will need:
- Writing Logs page 8
- Whiteboards and pens
- Card for covering spellings

Point out the word 'hand' in 'handle' and tell the children to remember to add the suffix 'le'.

Warm Up

Phonics: 'window' *2 minutes*
- Robot-speak the word 'w/i/n/d/oh' then ask the children to blend the phonemes to make the word.
- Listen as they robot-speak and then blend the whole word.
- As they robot-speak 'window' again, write the letters on the board.
- Wipe your board clean, then ask the children to write the word on their whiteboards and add phoneme buttons (w/i/n/d/ow).
- Tell the children to wipe their boards clean and to write 'window' three times in the Phonics box.

Spelling: 'handle' *2 minutes*
- Explain that 'handle' is an irregular word so they will learn to spell it using letter names.
- Demonstrate how to spell the word 'handle', saying the letter names as you write.
- Wipe your board clean and ask the children to trace the word with their finger on their whiteboard, saying the letter names as they do so. Then ask them to write 'handle' on their whiteboards.
- Tell the children to wipe their boards clean, then write the word three times in the Spelling box.

Phonics: 'clothes' *2 minutes*
- Robot-speak the word 'c/l/oh/th/s' then ask the children to blend the phonemes to make the word.
- Listen as they robot-speak and then blend the whole word.
- As they robot-speak 'clothes' again, write the letters on the board. Ask the children to identify which letters are making the long vowel 'oh' sound. Tell the children to link the 'o' and 'e'.
- Wipe your board clean and ask the children to write the word on their whiteboards.
- Tell the children to wipe their boards clean and to write 'clothes' three times in the Phonics box.

Guiding the Writing

Talk for Writing *3 minutes*
- Tell the children that they we are going to complete their instructions for what to do in a fire. Reread the instructions that they wrote in the previous session.
- *Now we need to say what to do if the door handle is hot. Why shouldn't you open the door if the handle is hot? It would mean that the fire was just outside the door, so it would be dangerous to open it.*
- *In order to stop any smoke coming into the room, they should use their clothes to block up the gap under the door.*

114

- *Turn to a partner and think of two instructions. The first one should start: 'If the door handle is ...'. The second instruction should start: 'Use your clothes ...'.*
- Share the children's ideas.

Demonstration Writing 4 minutes
- *I am going to write:* **5. If the door handle is hot, don't open the door.** *I have put a comma after 'hot' because I want the reader to pause and then to emphasise the word 'don't'.*
- *Then I am going to write:* **6. Use your clothes to block any gaps under the door.** *As I write that sentence, I want you to write 'block' in the Have a go box.*
- Read the instructions together.

Independent Writing 3 minutes
- Allow the children 20 seconds to study your writing, then wipe your board clean.
- Ask the children to turn to a partner and repeat what they are going to write.
- Tell them to cover their practised words and then write the two instructions.
- Check the children's work.

> Remind the children to put a comma in the correct place in the first sentence.

Talk for Writing 3 minutes
- *It is important that people know which room you are in so they can help you. You should go to a window and shout for help. You could hang a sheet out of the window so they can see where you are.*
- *Turn to a partner and think of two more instructions. Start your first instruction: 'Go to a ...' and the next instruction: 'Hang a ...'.*
- Share the children's ideas.

Demonstration Writing 3 minutes
- *I am going to write:* **7. Go to a window and shout for help.**
- *For the last instruction I will write:* **8. Hang a sheet from the window.** *As I write my sentence, I want you to write 'hang' and 'sheet' in the Have a go box.*
- Read the sentences together.

> Point out the phonemes in 'hang' (h/a/ng) and 'sheet' (sh/ee/t).

Independent Writing 3 minutes
- Allow the children 20 seconds to study the writing, then wipe your board clean.
- Ask the children to turn to a partner and repeat what they are going to write.
- Tell them to cover their practised words and then to write the instructions.
- Check the children's work.

Rounding Off 3 minutes
- Ask the children to close their books and then to take it in turns to tell you what to do in a fire. Remind them that they should try to tell you in the correct order.
- Ask the children why we put numbers next to each instruction rather than just using bullet points. (To show the correct order; to help people remember that there are six steps.)

Review 2 minutes
- What features of instructions have they used in this session and the previous one? (a heading; a numbered list; short sentences)
- Why was there a comma in the instructions 1, 2, 3 and 5? (To make the reader pause; to emphasise the importance of the next word.)
- How well do the children think they did? Ask them to colour in one of the thumbs.
- Share the joke!

24.2

UNIT 25

ROBBERS! *SESSION 1*

Outcome:
- Writing dialogue to move action forward

Writing targets:
- Target words: 'later', 'evening', 'I'll'
- Sentences: one compound sentence, four simple sentences in direct speech

You will need:
- Writing Logs page 9
- Whiteboards and pens
- Card for covering spellings

Warm Up
Spelling: 'later' *2 minutes*
- Explain that 'later' is an irregular word so they will learn to spell it using letter names.
- Demonstrate how to spell the word 'later', saying the letter names as you write.
- Wipe your board clean and ask the children to trace the word with their finger on their whiteboard, saying the letter names as they do so. Then ask them to write 'later' on their whiteboards.
- Tell the children to wipe their boards clean, then write the word three times in the Spelling box.

Spelling: 'evening' *2 minutes*
- Explain that 'evening' is an irregular word so they will learn to spell it using letter names.
- Demonstrate how to spell the word 'evening', saying the letter names as you write.
- Wipe your board clean and ask the children to trace the word with their finger on their whiteboard, saying the letter names as they do so. Then ask them to write 'evening' on their whiteboards.
- Tell the children to wipe their boards clean, then write the word three times in the Spelling box.

Spelling: 'I'll' *2 minutes*
- Explain that 'I'll' is a short way to write the words: 'I will'. The letters 'w' and 'i' are omitted and we use an apostrophe to show this.
- Demonstrate how to spell the word 'I'll', saying the letter names as you write.
- Wipe your board clean and ask the children to trace the word with their finger on their whiteboard, saying the letter names as they do so. Then ask them to write 'I'll' on their whiteboards.
- Tell the children to wipe their boards clean, then write the word three times in the Spelling box.

> As you demonstrate how to spell the word, say: 'I apostrophe double l'.

Guiding the Writing
Talk for Writing *4 minutes*
- Explain to the children that they will be creating some dialogue and using it to move the action forward in a story. Karl and Adam have gone out and while the house is empty, two thieves break in to steal cash, the TV and the DVD player.
- *Look at the picture. It shows one of the thieves, Liz, slowly opening the window and climbing into Adam's house. What time of day is it?* (the evening) *How do you think she might open the window?* (quietly, slowly) *Why?* (because they wouldn't want to be heard)
- *At first we won't say who Liz is to make it sound more mysterious. We will just describe her as 'a girl'.*

- *First we need to write a sentence that sets the scene. Turn to a partner and think of a sentence starting: 'Later that evening, the window slowly opened and …'.*
- Share the children's ideas.

Demonstration Writing 2 minutes
- *I am going to write:* **Later that evening, the window slowly opened and a girl climbed in.** *As I write 'slowly', I want you to write it in the Have a go box.*
- *I have put a comma after 'evening' to tell the reader to take a short pause after reading 'Later that evening'.*
- Read the sentence together.

> Remind the children that the word 'slowly' is just 'slow' with 'ly' at the end.

Independent Writing 2 minutes
- Allow the children 10 seconds to study the sentence, then wipe your board clean.
- Ask the children to turn to a partner and repeat what they are going to write.
- Tell them to cover their practised words and then to write the sentence.
- Check the children's work.

Talk for Writing 3 minutes
- *Now I need to write the dialogue between the thieves – Rick and Liz. What will they want to know as soon as they get into the house? (that no-one is there) Liz climbs in first so she will speak to Rick to tell him that it's OK. What did we say they intended to steal? (cash, the TV and the DVD player) Liz is going to look for cash while Rick handles the TV and DVD player.*
- *Turn to a partner and think of what Liz will say first, starting: '"It's OK, Rick," said Liz …'. Then think of Rick's reply, starting: '"I'll grab the …"'.*
- Share the children's ideas.

Demonstration Writing 5 minutes
- *I am going to write:* **"It's OK, Rick," said Liz.** *Which words does Liz actually say? ('It's OK, Rick') So those are the words I will put inside the speech marks. I have put a comma before 'Rick' to indicate a short pause and another just before the closing speech marks because the sentence continues with 'said Liz'.*
- *Then I am going to write what Liz goes on to say:* **"No-one is here. I'll look for cash."** *Liz says all those words so the speech marks need to go around them.*
- *Finally, I am going to write Rick's reply:* **"I'll grab the TV and the DVD player," said Rick.** *As I write 'grab', I want you to write it in the Have a go box.*
- Read the dialogue together.

> Point out to the children that the full stop at the end of the sentence goes inside the speech marks.

Independent Writing 3 minutes
- Allow the children 30 seconds to study your writing, then wipe your board clean.
- Ask the children to turn to a partner and repeat what they are going to write.
- Tell them to cover their practised words and then to write the dialogue.
- Check the children's work.

Rounding Off 2 minutes
- Ask the children why 'grab' is a good word for Rick to use. (It suggests he's in a hurry because he does not want to be caught.)
- Why do the short sentences suit the action? (It makes it sound as though they are speaking quickly because they want to grab the stuff and get away.)

Review 3 minutes
- *Which word describes how the window was opened? ('slowly') What kind of word is it? (an adverb – it tells us more about how the window was opened)*
- Tell the children to work with a partner and to read just the dialogue. Can they make it sound nervous and edgy?
- How well do the children think they did? Ask them to colour in one of the thumbs.
- Share the joke!

25.1

UNIT 25

ROBBERS! SESSION 2

Outcome:
- Writing dialogue to move action forward

Writing targets:
- Target words: 'heard', 'noise', 'phone'
- Revision word: 'through'
- Sentences: one complex sentence, one simple sentence, four sentences of direct speech

You will need:
- Writing Logs page 9
- Whiteboards and pens
- Card for covering spellings

Warm Up

Spelling: 'heard' — 2 minutes
- Explain that 'heard' is an irregular word so they will learn to spell it using letter names.
- Demonstrate how to spell the word 'heard', saying the letter names as you write.
- Wipe your board clean and ask the children to trace the word with their finger on their whiteboard, saying the letter names as they do so. Then ask them to write 'heard' on their whiteboards.
- Tell the children to wipe their boards clean, then write the word three times in the Spelling box.

Point out the word 'hear' in 'heard'.

Spelling: 'noise' — 2 minutes
- Explain that 'noise' is a tricky word so they will learn to spell it using letter names.
- Demonstrate how to spell the word 'noise' saying the letter names as you write.
- Wipe your board clean and ask the children to trace the word with their finger on their whiteboard, saying the letter names as they do so. Then ask them to write 'noise' on their whiteboards.
- Tell the children to wipe their boards clean, then write the word three times in the Spelling box.

If children are familiar with the letters 'oi' making the 'oy' sound and the letters 'se' making the 's' sound, this word could be taught using phonics.

Phonics: 'phone' — 2 minutes
- Robot-speak the word 'ph/oh/n' then ask the children to blend the phonemes to make the word.
- Listen as they robot-speak and then blend the whole word.
- As they robot-speak 'phone' again, write the letters on the board. Ask the children to identify which letters are making the long vowel 'oh' sound. Tell the children to link the 'o' and 'e'.
- Wipe your board clean and ask the children to write the word on their whiteboards.
- Tell the children to wipe their boards clean and to write 'phone' three times in the Phonics box.

Ensure that children realise that the 'f' sound at the beginning of 'phone' is made with the letters 'ph'.

Guiding the Writing

Talk for Writing — 3 minutes
- Remind the children that they are writing some dialogue to move the action forward in a story.
- Karl and Adam have come back. They hear a noise so Karl thinks that his mum must be in. What phrase could we use to make Karl and Adam's return more dramatic? ('Just then') So the first sentence will be: 'Just then, Karl and Adam came back.'
- Turn to a partner and think of the next sentence using the words 'heard' and 'noise' which you have just practised. It will be: 'They heard a noise.'

118

- *Then we need Karl to speak. He is looking through the window and he thinks the noise is his Mum. Remember, Karl is speaking so we will write 'said Karl'. Turn to a partner and think of a sentence starting: '"Mum must be back," said Karl as he …'.*
- Share the children's ideas.

Demonstration Writing 4 minutes
- *I am going to write:* **Just then, Karl and Adam came back. They heard a noise.**
- *Then I am going to write:* **"Mum must be back," said Karl as he looked through the window.** *As you write the word 'through' say the letter names and ask the children to repeat them. Ask them to write it in the Have a go box.*
- Wipe out the speech marks and invite a child to add them back in. Point out the comma before the closing speech marks.

> Point out that none of this is direct speech, so we don't need speech marks.

Independent Writing 3 minutes
- Allow the children 20 seconds to study the sentences, then wipe your board clean.
- Ask the children to turn to a partner and repeat what they are going to write.
- Tell them to cover their practised words and then write the sentences.
- Check the children's work.

Talk for Writing 3 minutes
- *Look at the picture. Karl has seen the robbers stealing his stuff and is calling the police while Adam watches them.*
- *I want to write what Karl and Adam said to each other when Karl first saw the robbers. To keep the action well-paced, I am going to have Karl asking to use Adam's phone to call the police. I don't need to tell the reader exactly what he saw because the reader knows what is going on from what we wrote in the last session.*
- *Turn to a partner and think of what Karl will say, starting: 'Quick, give me …'.*
- *Adam hasn't seen the robbers through the window yet and isn't sure what is going on, so he will say: 'What's up?' What one word could Karl use to describe Liz and Rick? ('robbers')*
- Share the children's ideas.

Demonstration Writing 3 minutes
- *I am going to write:* **"Quick, give me your phone," he said.**
- *Next I am going to write Adam's reply:* **"What's up?" asked Adam.** *As I write 'asked', I want you to write it in the Have a go box.*
- *Finally I am going to write:* **"Robbers!" whispered Karl.** *I've used the word 'whispered' because Karl does not want Liz and Rick to hear him.*
- Read the dialogue together.

> Talk about the speech punctuation. Remind the children that it goes around the actual words spoken.

Independent Writing 3 minutes
- Allow the children 20 seconds to study your writing, then wipe your board clean.
- Ask the children to turn to a partner and repeat what they are going to write.
- Tell them to cover their practised words and then to write the dialogue.
- Check the children's work.

Rounding Off 2 minutes
- What does the reader know at the start that Karl and Adam do not know? (that the noise is not Karl's mum but the robbers, Rick and Liz) Why is it a good idea for an author to use this technique? (It makes it more dramatic.)
- Ask the group what they think will happen to Rick and Liz. (The police will come, Rick and Liz will be charged with theft.)

> Go to the orange box on page 21 in the Writing Log for an unaided writing activity.
> See page 145 of this Teaching Guide for guidance notes.

Review 3 minutes
- Which three speech verbs are used in the dialogue? ('said', 'asked', 'whispered') Why is it a good idea to have a variety of speech verbs? (To tell the reader how the words are spoken.)
- Tell the children to work with a partner and to read just the dialogue of the dramatic paragraphs right from the beginning. Then swap roles.
- How well do the children think they did? Ask them to colour in one of the thumbs.
- Share the joke!

25.2

UNIT 26

MAN'S BEST FRIEND: *SESSION 1*

Outcome:
- A personal account

Writing targets:
- Target words: 'blind', 'guide', 'safe'
- Sentences: one simple sentence, one compound sentence, two complex sentences.

You will need:
- Writing Logs page 11
- Whiteboards and pens
- Card for covering spellings

If the children understand that the letter 'i' represents the long vowel sound 'igh', then this word could be taught using phonics.

Warm Up
Spelling: 'blind' — 2 minutes
- Explain that 'blind' is an irregular word so they will learn to spell it using letter names.
- Demonstrate how to spell the word 'blind', saying the letter names as you write.
- Wipe your board clean and ask the children to trace the word with their finger on their whiteboard, saying the letter names as they do so. Then ask them to write 'blind' on their whiteboards.
- Tell the children to wipe their boards clean, then write the word three times in the Spelling box.

Spelling: 'guide' — 2 minutes
- Explain that 'guide' is an irregular word so they will learn to spell it using letter names.
- Demonstrate how to spell the word 'guide', saying the letter names as you write.
- Wipe your board clean and ask the children to trace the word with their finger on their whiteboard, saying the letter names as they do so. Then ask them to write 'guide' on their whiteboards.
- Tell the children to wipe their boards clean, then write the word three times in the Spelling box.

Phonics: 'safe' — 2 minutes
- Robot-speak the word 's/ay/f' then ask the children to blend the phonemes to make the word.
- Listen as they robot-speak and then blend the whole word.
- As they robot-speak 'safe' again, write the letters on the board. Ask the children to identify which letters are making the long vowel 'ay' sound. Tell the children to link the 'a' and 'e'.
- Wipe your board clean and ask the children to write the word on their whiteboards.
- Tell the children to wipe their boards clean and to write 'safe' three times in the Phonics box.

Guiding the Writing
Talk for Writing — 3 minutes
- We are going to write a personal account about a man called Omar Rivera, who is blind, and his guide dog, Salty. How do guide dogs help blind people? (They help them to get around.)
- In a personal account we have to imagine that we are Omar and we are telling the story of what happened to him.
- The Twin Towers in New York were hit by planes in 2001. Look at the photo. Omar was working in the Twin Towers when they were hit by planes.

120

- *Turn to a partner and think of two sentences. Start the first sentence: 'My name is Omar and …' and the next sentence: 'My guide dog, Salty …'.*
- Share the children's ideas.

Demonstration Writing 3 minutes
- *I am going to write:* **My name is Omar and I'm blind.** *As I write this sentence, I want you to write the word 'I'm' in the Have a go box.*
- *Then I am going to write:* **My guide dog, Salty, helps me.** *I have put commas around 'Salty' to tell the reader to pause and to show that this is extra information. I could have left his name out and the sentence would still make sense.*
- Read the sentences together.

Independent Writing 2 minutes
- Allow the children 20 seconds to study your sentences, then wipe your board clean, leaving the names 'Omar' and 'Salty' for them to copy.
- Ask the children to turn to a partner and repeat what they are going to write.
- Tell them to cover their practised words and then write both sentences.
- Check the children's work.

> Remind the children to put commas before and after the name 'Salty'.

Talk for Writing 4 minutes
- *Now we need to tell the listeners what happened to Omar. On 11th September 2001, Omar was in the Twin Towers when the planes hit. Ever since that day people have referred to it as '9.11'. In America they put the number of the month before the day. '9.11' means 11th September.*
- *Omar thought he would not be able to find his way out, but he wanted to save Salty so he told Salty to get out.*
- *Turn to a partner and think of two more sentences. Start your first sentence: 'I was in the …' and continue it with: 'when …'. Start the next sentence: 'I wanted to save …' and continue it with: 'so …'.*
- Share the children's ideas.

Demonstration Writing 4 minutes
- *I am going to write:* **I was in the Twin Towers when the planes hit.** *As I write my sentence, I want you to write 'planes' in the Have a go box.*
- *For the next sentence I am going to write:* **I wanted to save Salty, so I told him to get out.** *Study the word 'wanted' and say the letter names. Then write it in the Have a go box.*
- Read the sentences together.

Independent Writing 3 minutes
- Allow the children 20 seconds to study your sentences, then wipe your board clean, leaving the word 'Salty' for them to copy.
- Ask the children to turn to a partner and repeat what they are going to write.
- Tell them to cover their practised words and then to write the sentences.
- Check the children's work.

> Remind the children to put capital letters for 'Twin Towers' as that was the name of the towers.

Rounding Off 2 minutes
- Ask the children to read the account so far with intonation and expression.
- Do they think Omar was brave to send Salty away? Would they have tried to save their dog?

Review 3 minutes
- Ask the children why we have used the words 'My' and 'I' (because we are writing as if we were Omar).
- Ask the children why we put commas round the word 'Salty' in the second sentence. (because it makes the reader pause; because it separated out the extra information)
- How well do the children think they did? Ask them to colour in one of the thumbs.
- Share the joke!

26.1

UNIT 26

MAN'S BEST FRIEND: *SESSION 2*

Outcome:
- A personal account

Writing targets:
- Target words: 'stuck', 'floor', 'hours'
- Sentences: one complex sentence, two compound sentences, one simple sentence

You will need:
- Writing Logs page 12
- Whiteboards and pens
- Card for covering spellings

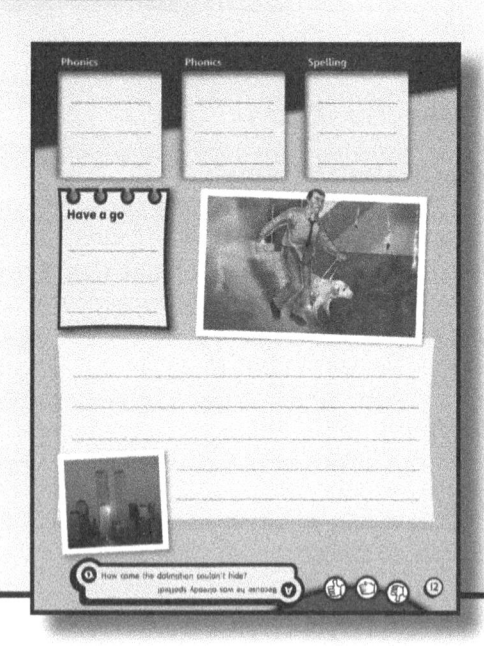

Warm Up

Phonics: 'stuck'   2 minutes
- Robot-speak the word 's/t/u/ck' then ask the children to blend the phonemes to make the word.
- Listen as they robot-speak and then blend the whole word.
- As they robot-speak 'stuck' again, write the letters on the board.
- Wipe your board clean, then ask the children to write the word on their whiteboards and add phoneme buttons.
- Tell the children to wipe their boards clean and to write 'stuck' three times in the Phonics box.

Phonics: 'floor'   2 minutes
- Robot-speak the word 'f/l/oor' then ask the children to blend the phonemes to make the word.
- Listen as they robot-speak and then blend the whole word.
- As they robot-speak 'floor' again, write the letters on the board.
- Wipe your board clean, then ask the children to write the word on their whiteboards and add phoneme buttons.
- Tell the children to wipe their boards clean and to write 'floor' three times in the Phonics box.

> Ensure that children understand that the letters 'oor' represent the 'or' sound.

Spelling: 'hours'   2 minutes
- Explain that 'hours' is an irregular word so they will learn to spell it using letter names.
- Demonstrate how to spell the word 'hours', saying the letter names as you write.
- Wipe your board clean and ask the children to trace the word with their finger on their whiteboard, saying the letter names as they do so. Then ask them to write 'hours' on their whiteboards.
- Tell the children to wipe their boards clean, then write the word three times in the Spelling box

> Point out that the smaller word 'our' is in the word 'hours'. Remind the children that they have learned 'our' previously.

Guiding the Writing

Talk for Writing   3 minutes
- *We are going to continue Omar's personal account of what happened, and as we are writing as if we are Omar we will continue to use 'I' and 'we'.*
- *When the planes hit the Twin Towers the rooms were filled with smoke and fire so Omar could not find his way out. He was stuck on the 71st floor. How many floors are there in this school? Imagine how high 71 floors must have been. Suddenly Omar felt something by his leg. What do you think it was? Salty had come back for him!*

- *Turn to a partner and think of a sentence starting: 'I was stuck on the …'. Remember to continue to speak as if you were Omar and tell the listeners your account. Start the second sentence: 'Then I felt …'. When you come to write about Salty try to think of a word to describe him and put that in your sentence.*
- Share the children's ideas.

Demonstration Writing   5 minutes
- *I am going to write:* **I was stuck on the 71st floor in the fire and smoke.** *As I write this sentence, I want you to write the word 'smoke' in the Have a go box. Look again at '71st'. The 'st' is short for 'first'.*
- *Then I am going to write:* **Then I felt something by my leg – brave Salty had come back!** *I have put a dash in that sentence to make the reader really pause before the exciting news, and I have used 'brave' to describe Salty. I have finished my sentence with an exclamation mark because it was so amazing that Salty came back and found his master.*
- Read the sentences together.

> Remind the children that they have learned the words 'fire' and 'smoke' in an earlier session.

Independent Writing   4 minutes
- Allow the children 20 seconds to study your sentences, then wipe your board clean, leaving the name 'Salty' for them to copy.
- Ask the children to turn to a partner and repeat what they are going to write.
- Tell them to cover their practised words and then write the sentences.
- Check the children's work.

Talk for Writing   2 minutes
- *Now we need to say how Omar got out. What do you think Salty did? He led Omar down the steps. It took them 1½ hours to get down, but they reached the bottom just before the two towers collapsed.*
- *Turn to a partner and think of two more sentences. Start your first sentence: 'He led me …'. The next sentence should start with: 'It took …' and continue with: 'but …'.*
- Share the children's ideas.

Demonstration Writing   3 minutes
- *I am going to write:* **He led me down.**
- *For the last sentence I am going to write:* **It took 1½ hours but we got down just in time.** *Look carefully at how we write 1½ and then write it in the Have a go box. Then practise 'time' in the Have a go box.*
- Read the sentences together.

> Explain to the children that we often write a length of time in numbers rather than letters.

Independent Writing   3 minutes
- Allow the children 20 seconds to study your sentences, then wipe your board clean.
- Ask the children to turn to a partner and repeat what they are going to write.
- Tell them to cover their practised words and then to write the sentences.
- Check the children's work.

Rounding Off   2 minutes
- Ask the children to find a partner and to read the whole account with intonation and expression.
- Ask the children if they think that telling this story as if they were Omar makes it more interesting and personal. Point out they could have written: 'A blind man, called Omar, was in the twin Towers …'. Which version do they think is better?

Review   2 minutes
- Challenge the children to write '71st floor' and '1½ hours' on their whiteboards.
- What makes this writing a personal account? (It is someone's story told from their own point of view; it tells the events as that person experienced them.)
- How well do the children think they did? Ask them to colour in one of the thumbs.
- Share the joke!

26.2

UNIT 27

THE CLEAN TEAM: *SESSION 1*

Outcome:
- Dialogue in a reality TV show

Writing targets:
- Target words: 'those', 'maggots', 'disgusting'
- Revision word: 'crawling'
- Sentences: seven simple sentences, a one-word sentence

You will need:
- Writing Logs page 13
- Whiteboards and pens
- Card for covering spellings

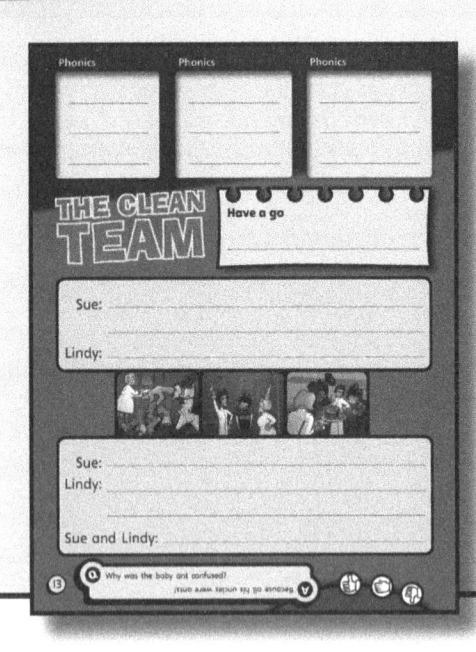

Warm Up

Phonics: 'those' — 2 minutes
- Robot-speak the word 'th/oh/s' then ask the children to blend the phonemes to make the word.
- Listen as they robot-speak and then blend the whole word.
- As they robot-speak 'those' again, write the letters on the board. Ask the children to identify which letters are making the long vowel 'oh' sound. Tell the children to link the 'o' and 'e'.
- Wipe your board clean, then ask the children to write the word on their whiteboards.
- Tell the children to wipe their boards clean and to write 'those' three times in the Phonics box.

Phonics: 'maggots' — 2 minutes
- Robot-speak the word 'm/a/gg/o/t/s' then ask the children to blend the phonemes to make the word.
- Listen as they robot-speak and then blend the whole word.
- As they robot-speak 'maggots' again, write the letters on the board.
- Wipe your board clean, then ask the children to write the word on their whiteboards and add phoneme buttons.
- Tell the children to wipe their boards clean and to write 'maggots' three times in the Phonics box.

> Ensure that children realise that the 'g' sound is made with the double 'g'.

Phonics: 'disgusting' — 2 minutes
- Robot-speak the word 'd/i/s/g/u/s/t/i/ng' then ask the children to blend the phonemes to make the word.
- Listen as they robot-speak and then blend the whole word.
- As they robot-speak 'disgusting' again, write the letters on the board.
- Wipe your board clean, then ask the children to write the word on their whiteboards and add phoneme buttons.
- Tell the children to wipe their boards clean and to write 'disgusting' three times in the Phonics box.

> Ensure that children realise that the letters 'ng' represent one sound.

Guiding the Writing

Talk for Writing — 3 minutes
- Tell the children that they are going to write a dialogue. Lindy and Sue are presenters on a reality TV show, inspecting how clean people's houses are. They have come to Josh's room.
- *In the first picture Lindy and Sue have found a smelly football sock. First of all Sue will say that the room stinks because Josh never opens his window. Turn to a partner and think of what she will say, starting with: 'What a stink! I bet you ...'. Then think of what Lindy will say when she finds the sock.*
- Share the children's ideas.

Demonstration Writing 3 minutes
- *I am going to write:* **What a stink! I bet you never open your window**. *As I write 'stink', I want you to sound out the phonemes ('s/t/i/n/k') and write the word in the Have a go box. I have put an exclamation mark after stink because that will show how the words should be spoken.*
- *Next I am going to write what Lindy says:* **Yuk! A smelly football sock!**
- Read the sentences together.

> Point out that the exclamation mark after 'Yuk' tells the reader how Lindy says the word.

Independent Writing 2 minutes
- Allow the children 20 seconds to study the sentences, then wipe your board clean.
- Ask the children to turn to a partner and repeat what they are going to write.
- Tell them to cover their practised words and then write the first sentence next to 'Sue' and the second sentence next to 'Lindy'.
- Check the children's work.

Talk for Writing 3 minutes
- *Look at the second picture. Now Sue and Lindy have noticed the dead flies and the rotten food that Josh has left lying around in his room. Flies have laid their eggs on the food and the eggs have hatched into crawling maggots, so Sue will say: 'Look at all those dead flies!'*
- *Turn to a partner and think of a sentence that Lindy will say, starting: 'This food is …'. Then think of another sentence starting: 'There are maggots …'.*
- *Finally, Lindy and Sue are going to speak together and sum up what they think about Josh's room. Think of a sentence that uses a word from the start of the session and starts: 'Your room is …'.*
- Share the children's ideas.

Demonstration Writing 4 minutes
- *For Sue's words, I am going to write:* **Look at all those dead flies!** *As I write 'dead', I want you to practise it in the Have a go box.*
- *Next I am going to write Lindy's words:* **This food is rotten. There are maggots crawling all over it.** *As I write 'rotten', I want you to sound out the phonemes ('r/o/tt/e/n') and write it in the Have a go box.*
- *Look again at the word 'crawling'. Ask a child to add phoneme buttons to the word. Which letters are making the 'or' sound? ('aw')*
- *Finally I will write:* **Your room is disgusting!**
- Read the sentences together.

Independent Writing 4 minutes
- Allow the children 20 seconds to study your writing, then wipe your board clean.
- Ask the children to turn to a partner and repeat what they are going to write.
- Tell them to cover their practised words and then to write the sentences.
- Check the children's work.

> Ensure that the children write the sentences next to the correct names.

Rounding Off 2 minutes
- Ask the children why we used so many exclamation marks in the script (to show the reader how to read the play; to show how disgusted Sue and Lindy are at the state of Josh's room).
- Ask the children if they keep their rooms tidy. Have they ever left food in their room that has gone off? What did their parents say?

Review 3 minutes
- Ask the children why we have not used speech marks (in a script of dialogue we just write the spoken words next to the name of the character).
- Tell the children to work with a partner and to read one of the parts each. Then swap roles. Can they make it sound dramatic?
- How well do the children think they did? Ask them to colour in one of the thumbs.
- Share the joke!

27.1

UNIT 27

THE CLEAN TEAM: *SESSION 2*

Outcome:
- Dialogue in a reality TV show

Writing targets:
- Target words: 'untidy', 'clean', 'room'
- Sentences: three simple sentences, a one-word sentence, one compound sentence.

You will need:
- Writing Logs page 14
- Whiteboards and pens
- Card for covering spellings

Warm Up

Spelling: 'untidy' — 2 minutes
- Explain that 'untidy' is an irregular word so they will learn to spell it using letter names.
- Demonstrate how to spell the word 'untidy', saying the letter names as you write.
- Wipe your board clean and ask the children to trace the word with their finger on their whiteboard, saying the letter names as they do so. Then ask them to write 'untidy' on their whiteboards.
- Tell the children to wipe their boards clean, then write the word three times in the Spelling box.

> Check that children understand that the 'ee' sound at the end of 'untidy' is made with the letter 'y'.

Phonics: 'clean' — 2 minutes
- Robot-speak the word 'c/l/ee/n' then ask the children to blend the phonemes to make the word.
- Listen as they robot-speak and then blend the whole word.
- As they robot-speak 'clean' again, write the letters on the board.
- Wipe your board clean, then ask the children to write the word on their whiteboards and add phoneme buttons (c/l/ea/n).
- Tell the children to wipe their boards clean and to write 'clean' three times in the Phonics box.

> Ensure that children understand that the 'ee' sound is made with the letters 'ea'.

Phonics: 'room' — 2 minutes
- Robot-speak the word 'r/oo/m' then ask the children to blend the phonemes to make the word.
- Listen as they robot-speak and then blend the whole word.
- As they robot-speak 'room' again, write the letters on the board.
- Wipe your board clean, then ask the children to write the word on their whiteboards and add phoneme buttons.
- Tell the children to wipe their boards clean and to write 'room' three times in the Phonics box.

> In some accents the 'oo' in 'room' is sounded as in the word 'book'. If children do this, then this word could be taught using letter names.

Guiding the Writing

Talk for Writing — 4 minutes
- Ask the children what Lindy and Sue found in Josh's room (a smelly football sock, dead flies, rotten food with maggots).
- *Josh tries to explain about the state of his room. He admits that it's untidy but he doesn't think it is disgusting. Of course, Lindy and Sue say that they think rotten food, dead flies and maggots are disgusting.*
- *First think of what Josh will say, starting: 'I know my room is untidy but …'. Then write Sue's reply, starting: 'Rotten food …'.*
- Share the children's ideas.

Demonstration Writing — *4 minutes*
- *For Josh I am going to write:* **I know my room is untidy but I don't think it's disgusting.** *As I write 'it's' I want you to write it in the Have a go box. In this sentence we are using it to mean 'it is' so you must put an apostrophe between the 't' and 's'.*
- *Next I will write Sue's reply:* **Rotten food, dead flies and maggots are disgusting.**
- Read the sentences together.

Independent Writing — *3 minutes*
- Allow the children 20 seconds to study the sentences, then wipe your board clean.
- Ask the children to turn to a partner and repeat what they are going to write.
- Tell them to cover their practised words and then write Josh's dialogue next to 'Josh' and Sue's dialogue next to 'Sue'.
- Check the children's work.

> Check that children put the apostrophe in the right place in 'it's'.

Talk for Writing — *3 minutes*
- *Now Josh is going to respond. Look at the picture. Do you think he feels bad about the disgusting state of his room? Do you think he likes having maggots in his room? What will he promise to do?* (clean up his room)
- *Josh will respond with three sentences. The first sentence will just be: 'OK.' Turn to a partner and think of the next two sentences. Start the first sentence: 'I'll …', including the word 'clean'. Start the final sentence: 'I don't want …', including the word 'maggots'.*
- Share the children's ideas.

Demonstration Writing — *2 minutes*
- *For Josh's words I am going to write:* **OK. I'll clean up my room. I don't want maggots in my bed!** *As I write 'don't', I want you to practise it in the Have a go box.*
- Read the sentences together.

> Ensure that children put the apostrophe in 'don't' in the right place.

Independent Writing — *3 minutes*
- Allow the children 10 seconds to study the sentences, then wipe your board clean.
- Ask the children to turn to a partner and repeat what they are going to write.
- Tell them to cover their practised words and then to write Josh's dialogue.
- Check the children's work.

Rounding Off — *2 minutes*
- What persuades Josh to clean up his room? (The thought of maggots in his bed!)
- Ask the children how they would feel if the Clean Team inspected their bedroom. Do they think that the Clean Team would find anything that they'd say was disgusting?

Review — *3 minutes*
- Which sentence is just one word in length? ('OK.') Why is this word good to use in a TV reality show dialogue? (It makes it sound like real people talking because it's informal.)
- Tell the children to work with in threes and to reread the complete dialogue, each taking on a character's role. Then ask them to swap roles. Make sure they use expression.
- How well do the children think they did? Ask them to colour in one of the thumbs.
- Share the joke!

27.2

UNIT 28

SNEEZES SPREAD DISEASES! *SESSION 1*

Outcome:
- A leaflet to persuade people not to spread diseases

Writing targets:
- Target words: 'matter', 'cover', 'sneeze'
- Sentences: two complex sentences, two simple sentences

You will need:
- Writing Logs page 15
- Whiteboards and pens
- Card for covering spellings

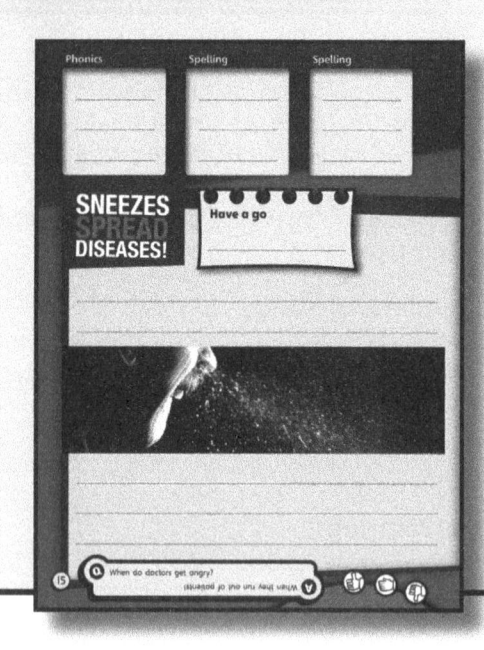

Warm Up
Phonics: 'matter' *2 minutes*
- Robot-speak the word 'm/a/tt/er' then ask the children to blend the phonemes to make the word.
- Listen as they robot-speak and then blend the whole word.
- As they robot-speak 'matter' again, write the letters on the board.
- Wipe your board clean, then ask the children to write the word on their whiteboards and add phoneme buttons.
- Tell the children to wipe their boards clean and to write 'matter' three times in the Phonics box.

> Point out that there are two 't's in 'matter' in order to keep the 'a' sound short.

Spelling: 'cover' *2 minutes*
- Explain that 'cover' is an irregular word so they will learn to spell it using letter names.
- Demonstrate how to spell the word 'cover', saying the letter names as you write.
- Wipe your board clean and ask the children to trace the word with their finger on their whiteboard, saying the letter names as they do so. Then ask them to write 'cover' on their whiteboards.
- Tell the children to wipe their boards clean, then write the word three times in the Spelling box.

Spelling: 'sneeze' *2 minutes*
- Explain that 'sneeze' is an irregular word so they will learn to spell it using letter names.
- Demonstrate how to spell the word 'sneeze', saying the letter names as you write.
- Wipe your board clean and ask the children to trace the word with their finger on their whiteboard, saying the letter names as they do so. Then ask them to write 'sneeze' on their whiteboards three times.
- Tell the children to wipe their boards clean, then write the word three times in the Spelling box.

> 'Sneeze' is treated as irregular because it has 'ee' in the middle and also an 'e' at the end.

Guiding the Writing
Talk for Writing *3 minutes*
- Tell the children that they are going to write a leaflet to persuade people to cover their nose when they sneeze. A persuasive leaflet tries to change people's behaviour. First we need to tell the reader what happens when a person sneezes and point out how it could spread germs.
- *Look at the photo of the man sneezing. Do you think this photo will help people to understand how important it is to cover their nose when they sneeze?*
- *It is a good idea to start a persuasive text by asking the reader a question.*

128

- *Turn to a partner and think of a question starting: 'Does it matter if …'. Then write your answer starting: 'Yes …'.*
- Share the children's ideas.

Demonstration Writing   3 minutes
- *I am going to write:* **Does it matter if you don't cover your nose when you sneeze?** *As I write, I want you to write 'nose' in the Have a go box.*
- *I am going to answer the question with:* **Yes it does!** *Why have I put an exclamation mark at the end of this sentence? (To emphasise the answer.) I am going to write this on a new line so that the answer stands out from the question.*
- Read the sentences together.

Independent Writing   3 minutes
- Allow the children 20 seconds to study your sentences, then wipe your board clean.
- Ask the children to turn to a partner and repeat what they are going to write.
- Tell them to cover their practised words and then write the question and answer.
- Check the children's work.

> Remind the children to put the answer to their question on a new line.

Talk for Writing   3 minutes
- *Now we need to tell the reader what happens when they sneeze. Did you know that millions of germs are sent out of your nose at 60 miles an hour? These germs could give your cold to other people.*
- *Turn to a partner and think of a sentence that tells the reader what happens. Start your sentence: 'When you sneeze you send …'. Then think of another sentence starting: 'These germs can make …'.*
- Share the children's ideas.

Demonstration Writing   4 minutes
- *I am going to write:* **When you sneeze you send out millions of germs at more than 60 miles an hour.** *As I write that sentence, I want you to write 'millions' in the Have a go box.*
- *Next I will write:* **These germs can make someone ill.**
- Read the sentences together.

> Remind the children that it is usual to write numbers over ten as figures.

Independent Writing   3 minutes
- Allow the children 30 seconds to study your sentences, then wipe your board clean leaving the word 'germs' for them to copy.
- Ask the children to turn to a partner and repeat what they are going to write.
- Tell them to cover their practised words and then to write both sentences.
- Check the children's work.

Rounding Off   3 minutes
- Ask the children whether they have ever had a bad cold. Did any of their family or friends catch a cold from them?
- Ask the children whether they have ever tried to persuade people to do something they did not want to do. How did they try to persuade them?

Review   2 minutes
- Ask the children why it is good to start a piece of persuasive writing with a question (it makes people think about what they are reading).
- Why did they put the answer 'Yes it does' on a new line? (To make it stand out; to draw attention to it.)
- How well do the children think they did? Ask them to colour in one of the thumbs.
- Share the joke!

28.1

UNIT 28

SNEEZES SPREAD DISEASES! *SESSION 2*

Outcome:
- A leaflet to persuade people not to spread diseases

Writing targets:
- Target words: 'breathe', 'spread', 'yourself'
- Sentences: one compound sentence, one complex sentence, one simple sentence

You will need:
- Writing Logs page 16
- Whiteboards and pens
- Card for covering spellings

Warm Up

Spelling: 'breathe' *2 minutes*
- Explain that 'breathe' is an irregular word so they will learn to spell it using letter names.
- Demonstrate how to spell the word 'breathe', saying the letter names as you write.
- Wipe your board clean and ask the children to trace the word with their finger on their whiteboard, saying the letter names as they do so. Then ask them to write 'breathe' on their whiteboards.
- Tell the children to wipe their boards clean, then write the word three times in the Spelling box.

Spelling: 'spread' *2 minutes*
- Explain that 'spread' is an irregular word so they will learn to spell it using letter names.
- Demonstrate how to spell the word 'spread', saying the letter names as you write.
- Wipe your board clean and ask the children to trace the word with their finger on their whiteboard, saying the letter names as they do so. Then ask them to write 'spread' on their whiteboards.
- Tell the children to wipe their boards clean, then write the word three times in the Spelling box.

> If children are familiar with the letters 'ea' representing the short vowel 'e' sound, this word could be taught using phonics.

Spelling: 'yourself' *2 minutes*
- Ask the children which two words they can hear in the word 'yourself'.
- Explain that 'yourself' is an irregular word so they will learn to spell it using letter names.
- Demonstrate how to spell 'yourself', saying the letter names as you write.
- Wipe your board clean and ask the children to trace the word with their finger on their whiteboard, saying the letter names as they do so. Then ask them to write 'yourself' on their whiteboards.
- Tell the children to wipe their boards clean, then write the word three times in the Spelling box.

> Remind the children to think of the two words as they write as this helps to break up the spelling and makes it easier to spell.

Guiding the Writing

Talk for Writing *3 minutes*
- Remind the children that they are going to finish the persuasive leaflet that they started last time.
- *Now we need to really persuade the reader to be careful not to pass their germs on to anyone else when they have a cold. If other people breathe in your germs, they could catch your cold.*
- *Turn to a partner and think of a sentence starting: 'People can breathe …'.*
- Share the children's ideas.

Demonstration Writing   3 minutes
- *I am going to write:* **People can breathe in your germs and catch your cold.** *As I write this sentence, I want you to write the word 'people' in the Have a go box.*
- Read the sentence together.

> Remind the children that they may find it easier to remember how to spell 'people' by mispronouncing it as 'pe-ople'.

Independent Writing   2 minutes
- Allow the children 10 seconds to study your sentence, then wipe your board clean, leaving the word 'germs' for them to copy.
- Ask the children to turn to a partner and repeat what they are going to write.
- Tell them to cover their practised words and then write the sentence.
- Check the children's work.

Talk for Writing   3 minutes
- If there are germs on your hands and someone touches something you have touched, they could get your cold.
- Turn to a partner and think of a sentence starting: 'If there are germs on your hands and then …'.
- To finish our leaflet, we need to write a slogan that summarises what we want people to do and is easy for them to remember. Turn to a partner and think of a slogan starting: 'Keep your germs …'.
- Share the children's ideas.

Demonstration Writing   4 minutes
- *I am going to write:* **If there are germs on your hands and then you touch something, this can also spread your cold.** *To help you to remember that sentence think of the three parts; first explain where the germs are, then say what you might do and finally how this spreads the cold.*
- *As I write that sentence I want you to write 'touch' in the Have a go box.*
- *I will finish by writing a short sentence that people will remember:* **Keep your germs to yourself!** *We will write our slogan on a new line to make it stand out.*
- Read the sentences together.

> Point out the exclamation mark at the end of the sentence.

Independent Writing   4 minutes
- Allow the children 30 seconds to study your sentences, then wipe your board clean, leaving the word 'germs' for them to copy.
- Ask the children to turn to a partner and repeat the first sentence.
- Tell them to cover their practised words and then to write that sentence. When they have finished, ask them to say the slogan and then write it on a new line.
- Check the children's work.

Rounding Off   2 minutes
- Ask the children if they think people will try to remember to cover their noses when they have read this leaflet.
- Ask the children what else they might say to persuade people to cover their noses when they sneeze (that they would not like someone sneezing near them).

Review   3 minutes
- Challenge the children to tell you the features of a persuasive piece of writing (often starting with a question; telling the reader facts; making the reader sympathise with your point of view; ending with a summary statement).
- Write the word 'spread' on your whiteboard, then write: 'head', 'bread', 'instead'. Ask the children what these words have in common ('ead'). Why is this unusual? (because the letters 'ea' are making the short vowel sound 'e')
- How well do the children think they did? Ask them to colour in one of the thumbs.
- Share the joke!

28.2

UNIT 29

HAVE YOU GOT TALENT? *SESSION 1*

Outcome:
- The climax of a story

Writing targets:
- Target words: 'judges', 'groaned'
- Revision word: 'across'
- Sentences: two simple sentences, two compound sentences

You will need:
- Writing Logs page 17
- Whiteboards and pens
- Card for covering spellings

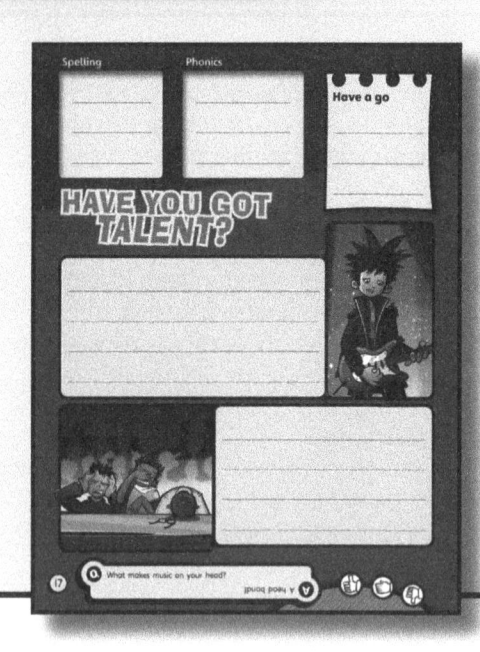

Warm Up
Spelling: 'judges' — 2 minutes

If children are familiar with the letters 'dg' representing the 'j' sound, this word could be taught using phonics.

- Explain that 'judges' is an irregular word so they will learn to spell it using letter names.
- Demonstrate how to spell the word 'judges', saying the letter names as you write.
- Wipe your board clean and ask the children to trace the word with their finger on their whiteboard, saying the letter names as they do so. Then ask them to write 'judges' on their whiteboards.
- Tell the children to wipe their boards clean, then write the word three times in the Spelling box.

Phonics: 'groaned' — 2 minutes

Point out that the 'oh' sound is made with the letters 'oa' and that the 'd' sound at the end of 'groaned' is made with the letters 'ed'.

- Robot-speak the word 'g/r/oh/n/d' then ask the children to blend the phonemes to make the word.
- Listen as they robot-speak and then blend the whole word.
- As they robot-speak 'groaned' again, write the letters on the board.
- Wipe your board clean, then ask the children to write the word on their boards and add phoneme buttons (g/r/oa/n/ed).
- Tell the children to wipe their boards clean and to write 'groaned' three times in the Phonics box.

Revision: 'across' — 2 minutes
- Remind the children that they practised 'across' in an earlier session. Write the word 'cross' on the board and ask the children what you need to add to make the word 'across' ('a').
- Ask one child to add phoneme buttons to the word ('a/c/r/o/ss'). Wipe your board clean and challenge the children to spell 'across' in the Have a go box.

Guiding the Writing
Talk for Writing — 3 minutes
- Ask the children whether they have ever watched a talent show on TV. What did they like about it? Tell the children that they are going to write the climax of a story in which a boy called Josh is on a reality TV talent show.
- *Look at the first picture. What do you think Josh is hoping? (that he will make it in the pop world) Who are you trying to impress on a talent show? (the judges)*
- *In the first sentence, we need to set the scene for the reader explaining why Josh has gone on the talent show. In the second sentence, we need to get across that feeling of anxiety – has he played well enough to impress the judges?*
- *Turn to a partner and think of a sentence starting: 'Josh really wanted ...' and another sentence starting: 'He thought he played well but ...'.*
- Share the children's ideas.

Demonstration Writing — 4 minutes

- *I am going to write:* **Josh really wanted to make it in the pop world.** *As I write 'wanted' I want you to practise it in the Have a go box.*
- *For the second sentence I will write:* **He thought he played well, but what would the judges think?** *I have added a comma after 'well' to emphasise the contrast between what Josh thought and what the judges might think. What punctuation finishes that sentence? Why? (a question mark, because it's a question) By asking the reader a question we are drawing them in to the decision making.*
- *Why did I start the second sentence with 'He'? (We do not need to repeat 'Josh' because it is obvious to the reader that 'He' will refer to Josh.)*

> Point out that the word 'really' is just 'real' with 'ly' at the end.

Independent Writing — 4 minutes

- *Allow the children 20 seconds to study the sentences, then wipe your board clean.*
- *Ask the children to turn to a partner and repeat what they are going to write.*
- *Tell them to cover their practised words and then write the sentences next to the first picture.*
- *Check the children's work.*

Talk for Writing — 3 minutes

- *We need to build the tension for the reader. We don't want to give away the ending too quickly, so we are going to describe how Josh tries to guess what the judges thought of his playing.*
- *Look at the second picture. Do you think the judges were impressed by Josh's playing? What has one judge done? (put his head in his hands) Which verb did you practise at the start of the session? ('groaned') What does that tell you about the judge's opinion?*
- *Turn to a partner and think of one sentence starting: 'He looked across ...' and then another sentence starting: 'One judge groaned and ...'.*
- *Share the children's ideas.*

Demonstration Writing — 3 minutes

- *I am going to write:* **He looked across at them. One judge groaned and put his head in his hands.**
- *As I write 'head', I want you to practise it in the Have a go box.*
- *Read the sentences together.*

Independent Writing — 3 minutes

- *Allow the children 20 seconds to study your sentences, then wipe your board clean.*
- *Ask the children to turn to a partner and repeat what they are going to write.*
- *Tell them to cover their practised words and then to write the sentences next to the second picture.*
- *Check the children's work.*

Rounding Off — 2 minutes

- *Ask the children why it is a good idea to ask the reader a question. (It draws them in and makes them think of the answer before they have written it.)*
- *Ask the children if they would like to go on a TV talent show. What talent would they show?*

Review — 2 minutes

- *Look together at each pronoun and link them to the relevant nouns ('He', 'he', 'he' = Josh; 'them' = judges; 'his', 'his' = one of the judges).*
- *What evidence is there that the judges did not think much of Josh's performance? (One judge groaned and put his head in his hands.)*
- *How well do the children think they did? Ask them to colour in one of the thumbs.*
- *Share the joke!*

29.1

UNIT 29

HAVE YOU GOT TALENT? *SESSION 2*

Outcome:
- The climax of a story

Writing targets:
- Target words: 'shook', 'another'
- Revision word: 'last'
- Sentences: five simple sentences, four of them dialogue

You will need:
- Writing Logs page 18
- Whiteboards and pens
- Card for covering spellings

In some dialects the 'oo' sound in 'shook' is pronounced clearly, so you may prefer to teach it using phonics.

Warm Up

Spelling: 'shook' *2 minutes*
- Explain that 'shook' is an irregular word so they will learn to spell it using letter names.
- Demonstrate how to spell the word 'shook', saying the letter names as you write.
- Wipe your board clean and ask the children to trace the word with their finger on their whiteboard, saying the letter names as they do so. Then ask them to write 'shook' on their whiteboards.
- Tell the children to wipe their boards clean, then write the word three times in the Spelling box.

Spelling: 'another' *2 minutes*
- Explain that 'another' is a tricky word so they will learn to spell it using letter names.
- Demonstrate how to spell the word 'another', saying the letter names as you write.
- Wipe your board clean and ask the children to trace the word with their finger on their whiteboard saying the letter names as they do so. Then ask them to write 'another' on their whiteboards.
- Tell the children to wipe their boards clean, then write the word three times in the Spelling box.

In some dialects the 'a' sound in 'last' is a short vowel sound and so you may prefer to teach it using phonics.

Revision: 'last' *1 minute*
- Remind the children that they learned to spell 'last' in a previous session, Write it on the board. Say each letter name and, as you do so, ask the children to write 'last' on their whiteboards.
- Give the children three seconds to study the word and then wipe all the boards clean. Challenge them to write 'last' in the Have a go box.

Guiding the Writing

Talk for Writing *4 minutes*
- Remind the children that Josh is waiting for the verdict from the judges on a TV talent show.
- *What does Josh want to do? (He wants to make it as a pop star.) What was the clue last time that the judges didn't think much of his performance? (One groaned and put his head in his hands.)*
- *What question will Josh ask the judges? ('Will I make it as a pop star?') Which word from the start of this session might be a clue to the judges' answers? ('shook' – they shook their heads)*
- *Turn to a partner and think of the question Josh asks the judges. Then think of another sentence to show the judges' reaction, and include the word 'shook'.*
- Share the children's ideas.

Demonstration Writing   3 minutes
- *I am going to write:* **"Will I make it as a pop star?" asked Josh.** *As I write 'asked', I want you to practise it in the Have a go box. As I write the word 'star' I want you to sound out the phonemes: 's/t/ar'. Then write the word in your Have a go box.*
- *For the second sentence I will write:* **The judges shook their heads.**
- *Read the sentences together.*

> Ensure that children realise that the question mark goes before the closing speech marks.

Independent Writing   3 minutes
- Allow the children 20 seconds to study the sentences, then wipe your board clean.
- Ask the children to turn to a partner and repeat what they are going to write.
- Tell them to cover their practised words and then write the sentences.
- Check the children's work.

Talk for Writing   3 minutes
- *Now we need to write about the judges' verdicts. Each judge will speak and we will use a repetitive pattern to make it more amusing for the reader. What could be wrong with Josh's playing and singing? (It is out of tune and out of time.) What might the third, harsher judge say? ("Out of the show!")*
- *Tell each child to pretend to be one of the three judges and to deliver one of the verdicts starting: "Out of …".*
- Share the children's ideas.

Demonstration Writing   3 minutes
- *I am going to write:* **"Out of tune!" said one judge.** *As I write 'tune', I want you to practise it in the Have a go box.*
- *Next I will write:* **"Out of time!" said another.**
- *Finally I will write:* **"Out of the show!" said the last judge.**
- *Read the sentences together.*

Independent Writing   3 minutes
- Allow the children 20 seconds to study your sentences, then wipe your board clean.
- Ask the children to turn to a partner and repeat what they are going to write.
- Tell them to cover their practised words and then to write the sentences.
- Check the children's work.

Rounding Off   3 minutes
- Ask the children how they would feel if they heard those judges' comments about their performance in a talent show. What could Josh have done differently to get a better review from the judges? (practised more)
- Ask the children why it is a good idea to have the judges' responses very similar to each other. (It builds up the sense that Josh was no good; it makes it funnier for the reader, especially the final sentence.)

Review   3 minutes
- Ask the children how we built up to the final judgement given by the last judge (with the repetition of "Out of …").
- Which words go inside the speech marks? (the actual words spoken)
- How well do the children think they did? Ask them to colour in one of the thumbs.
- Share the joke!

29.2

UNIT 30
FOOTBALL FACTS

Outcome:
- A time line

Writing targets:
- Target words: 'agreed', 'rules', 'England'
- Sentences: three simple sentences, one compound sentence

You will need:
- Writing Logs page 19
- Whiteboards and pens
- Card for covering spellings

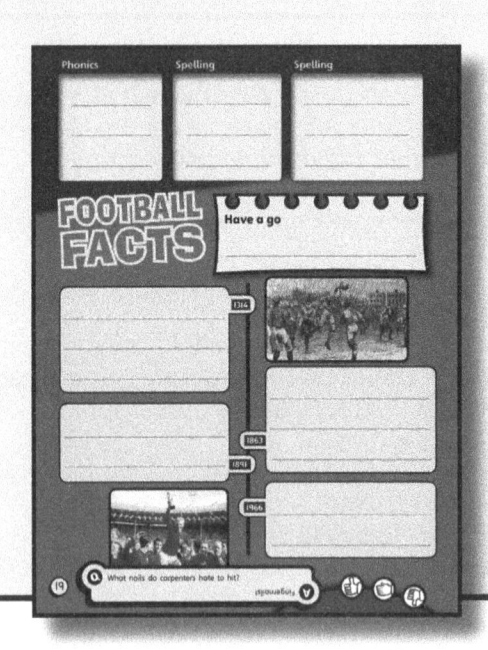

Warm Up

Phonics: 'agreed' — 2 minutes
- Robot-speak the word 'a/g/r/ee/d' then ask the children to blend the phonemes to make the word.
- Listen as they robot-speak and then blend the whole word.
- As they robot-speak 'agreed' again, write the letters on the board.
- Wipe your board clean, then ask the children to write the word on their whiteboards and add phoneme buttons.
- Tell the children to wipe their boards clean and to write 'agreed' three times in the Phonics box.

Spelling: 'rules' — 2 minutes
- Explain that 'rules' is an irregular word so they will learn to spell it using letter names.
- Demonstrate how to spell the word 'rules', saying the letter names as you write.
- Wipe your board clean and ask the children to trace the word with their finger on their whiteboard, saying the letter names as they do so. Then ask them to write 'rules' on their whiteboards.
- Tell the children to wipe their boards clean, then write the word three times in the Spelling box.

> If children are familiar with the letters 'u' and 'e' representing the 'oo' sound, then this word could be taught using phonics.

Spelling: 'England' — 2 minutes
- Explain that 'England' is an irregular word so they will learn to spell it using letter names.
- Demonstrate how to spell the word 'England', saying the letter names as you write.
- Wipe your board clean and ask the children to trace the word with their finger on their whiteboard, saying the letter names as they do so. Then ask them to write 'England' on their whiteboards.
- Tell the children to wipe their boards clean, then write the word three times in the Spelling box.

> Point out that 'England' is always written with a capital 'E' because it is the name of a country.

Guiding the Writing

Talk for Writing — 2 minutes
- Explain to the children that they are going make a time line to show a brief history of football. Look together at the line with the dates marked. Why do they think we call it a time line?
- *We will start by telling the reader about King Edward II, who in 1314, stopped people from playing football in London because he thought it was too noisy.*
- *Turn to a partner and think of a sentence starting: 'The king stopped ...'.*
- Share the children's ideas.

Demonstration Writing *2 minutes*
- *Beside the date 1314 I am going to write:* **The king stopped football games in London.** *As I write this sentence, I want you to write the word 'stopped'.*
- Read the sentence together.

> Remind the children that there are two 'p's in 'stopped'.

Independent Writing *2 minutes*
- Allow the children 10 seconds to study your sentence, then wipe your board clean.
- Ask the children to turn to a partner and repeat what they are going to write, leaving 'London' for them to copy.
- Tell them to cover their practised words and write the entry on the time line.
- Check the children's work.

> Make sure that the children write the sentence next to '1314' on the time line.

Talk for Writing *2 minutes*
- *Now we need to pick out some other important events. In 1863 the Football Association (F.A.) was set up and agreed the rules of football.*
- *Turn to a partner and think of a sentence starting: 'The F.A. was …' and continuing: 'and agreed …'.*
- Share the children's ideas.

Demonstration Writing *2 minutes*
- *I will write:* **The F.A. was set up and it agreed the rules of football.** *As I write the sentence, I want you to write 'football' in the Have a go box.*
- *I have just used the letters 'F.A.' as that stands for the Football Association.*
- Read the sentence together.

Independent Writing *2 minutes*
- Allow the children 20 seconds to study your sentence, then wipe your board clean.
- Ask the children to turn to a partner and repeat what they are going to write.
- Tell them to cover their practised words and to write the entry on the time line.
- Check the children's work.

> Remind the children to use capital letters for 'F.A.' and to put a full stop between each letter.

Talk for Writing *3 minutes*
- *Before 1891, football was played without nets. They just used posts.*
- *Turn to a partner and think of an entry for the date 1891, starting: 'The first time …'. For the last date, 1966, start your sentence: 'England …'.*
- *Can you guess what happened on the last date, 1966? It was when England won the World Cup. They beat Germany 4–2.*
- Share the children's ideas.

Demonstration Writing *3 minutes*
- *I am going to write:* **The first time a net was used.** *As I write that sentence, I want you to write 'used' in the Have a go box.*
- *Then for my last important fact I will write:* **England won the World Cup!**
- Read the sentences together.

> Point out that 'World' and 'Cup' have capital letters because it is the name of a tournament.

Independent Writing *2 minutes*
- Allow the children 20 seconds to study the sentences, then wipe your board clean.
- Ask the children to turn to a partner and repeat what they are going to write.
- Tell them to cover their practised words and to write the entries on the time line.
- Check the children's work.

Rounding Off *2 minutes*
- Ask the children why they think football is the most popular game in the UK.
- Which other sports would they like to find out about?

Review *2 minutes*
- What does a time line show? (important dates when things happened)
- Ask the children why we always write the names of countries with a capital letter. (because it is the name of a place) Why have we put capital letters for 'World Cup'? (because it is the name of the tournament)
- How well do the children think they did? Ask them to colour in one of the thumbs.
- Share the joke!

30.1

UNIT 30
WRITE IT! *ASSESSMENT*

Outcome:
- Assessment of skills covered in Writing Log 9

Writing targets:
- Independent spelling of 34 key words
- Accurate writing of three questions, including one in speech, and one simple sentence

You will need:
- Writing Logs page 20
- Whiteboards and pens

Writing Task

Assessment 1 — 7 minutes
- *Look at the first picture. Do you remember Carla and Rob, who were at Stonehenge when there was an eclipse? They were scared when they thought they saw a face on one of the stones.*
- Tell the children they are going to write: *'Was it a trick of the light or was that a face on one of the stones?'*
- *What kind of sentence is it? (a question) What strategies can you use to help you with the spelling of the words? (sounding out the phonemes; remembering what the word looks like and recalling the letter names) Say the sentences to yourself and then spell each word carefully. Also think about forming each letter accurately as you write it.*
- Warn the children that you will only say the sentence once and then dictate the sentence: **Was it a trick of the light or was that a face on one of the stones?**

Revision: 'sneeze' — 2 minutes
- *In a minute you are going to spell the word 'sneeze'. How are you going to remember how to spell that word? Think about how many 'e's there are in the middle of the word. Practise it now on your whiteboard.*

Assessment 2 — 7 minutes
- *Look at the third picture. Remember writing to persuade people to cover their noses when they sneeze? We asked a question for the reader to answer.*
- Tell the children they are going to write the question: *'Does it matter if you don't cover your nose when you sneeze?'*
- *How many words are in that sentence? (12) What kind of sentence is it? (a question) What strategies can you use to help you with the spelling of the words? (sounding out the phonemes; remembering what the word looks like and recalling the letter names) Say the sentence to yourself and then spell each word carefully. Also think about forming each letter accurately as you write it.*
- Warn the children that you will only say the sentence once and then dictate the sentence: **Does it matter if you don't cover your nose when you sneeze?**

Check Points

As the children write, observe:
- letter formation
- spelling strategies
- strategies to recall the sentence (rereading what they have written so far, saying the sentence to themselves).

After the children have written the sentence, ask them to check it and to decide whether they have:
- remembered to write every word
- spelt each word correctly.

- Encourage the children to picture the word 'sneeze'.

As the children write observe:
- letter formation
- spelling strategies
- strategies to recall the sentence (rereading what they have written so far, saying the sentence to themselves).

After the children have written the sentence, ask them to check it and to decide whether they have:
- remembered to write every word
- spelt each word correctly.

Revision: 'judges' — 2 minutes
- *In a minute you are going to spell the word 'judges'. How are you going to remember how to spell that word? Practise it now on your whiteboard.*

Assessment 3 — 7 minutes
- *Look at the second picture. Remember writing about Josh, who wanted to be a pop star but the judges of a talent show turned him down and said he was no good?*
- Tell the children that they are going to write: '"Will I make it as a pop star?" asked Josh. The judges shook their heads.'
- *What will you remember about starting a sentence and finishing it? (use a capital letter and full stop) Remember that Josh is speaking in the first sentence. What must you put around the words that Josh says? (speech marks) What strategies can you use to help you with the spelling of the words? (sounding out the phonemes; remembering what the word looks like; recalling the letter names) Say the sentences to yourself and then spell each word carefully. Also think about forming each letter accurately as you write it.*
- Warn the children that you will only say the sentences once but that you will write the word 'judges' on the board for them to copy. Dictate the sentences: **"Will I make it as a pop star?" asked Josh. The judges shook their heads.**

- Encourage the children to picture the word 'judges'.

As the children write, observe:
- letter formation
- spelling strategies
- strategies to recall the sentence (rereading what they have written so far, saying the sentence to themselves).

After the children have written the sentences, ask them to check them and to decide whether they have:
- remembered to write every word
- spelt each word correctly.

Review — 5 minutes
- Encourage children to reread their writing. Are there any words that they think they might have got wrong? Tell them to put a little line under any letters they think might be wrong.
- Ask the children to look back through their book. Which writing activity did they like best? Which is their best writing?
- What have they learned? Encourage them to talk about punctuation: capital letters, full stops, question marks and speech marks. Talk about different ways they have remembered how to spell words. Discuss the range of genre that they have written in: captions, labels, reports, instructions, plan, dialogue, personal account, leaflet, time line.
- How well do the children think they did? Ask them to colour in one of the thumbs.
- Share the joke!

Go to the orange box on page 22 in the Writing Log for an unaided writing activity.
See page 145 of this Teaching Guide for guidance notes.

30.2

Assessing writing

Rapid Writing and Assessment for Learning

Assessment for Learning (AfL) is a widely-used assessment practice. It is based on the idea that children will improve most if they understand the aim of their learning, where they are in relation to this aim and how they can achieve the aim. The main characteristics of AfL practices are:

- observing learning
- analysing and interpreting evidence of learning
- giving feedback to learners
- supporting learners in self-assessment.

Rapid Writing is perfectly aligned with the principles of AfL. During the structured 30-minute sessions the adult is able to:

- observe how the children in the group are tackling the word, sentence and text level tasks. In the Warm Up the adult will be able to assess phonic knowledge, letter name knowledge, spelling and handwriting.
- assess the memory of the sequence of words in a sentence, spelling and handwriting in the Independent Writing
- advise children on how to improve their writing. During Talk for Writing the adult can assess speaking and listening and the ability to organise words into sentences
- guide children to reflect upon their learning during the Rounding Off and Review parts of each session. This is concluded when the children select a thumb to colour to indicate how well they think they have completed the tasks.

In addition to the informal and on-going assessment opportunities in each *Rapid Writing* session, there are specific occasions for more formal assessments. These are:

1) Assessment of unaided writing (after five units and after ten units). Here children are given a visual prompt related to writing tasks they have practised earlier and are challenged to write appropriate sentences. The assessments will reveal progress in:

   – writing imaginatively
   – organising ideas into coherent sentences
   – spelling.

2) Assessment of dictated sentences (after ten units). Here children are challenged to spell and punctuate dictated sentences drawn from the previous units. The assessments will reveal progress in:

   – retaining a sequence of words to make a complete sentence
   – correctly spelling key vocabulary practised earlier
   – using punctuation accurately.

Assessing writing

Rapid Writing and Assessing Pupils' Progress

If you are using Assessing Pupils' Progress (APP) the assessment procedure published by the QCA and DCSF, you will be familiar with the eight Assessment Focuses (AFs) for writing:

AF1	Write imaginative, interesting and thoughtful texts
AF2	Produce texts that are appropriate to task, reader and purpose
AF3	Organise and present whole texts effectively, sequencing and structuring information, ideas and events
AF4	Construct paragraphs and use cohesion within and between paragraphs
AF5	Vary sentences for clarity, purpose and effect
AF6	Write with technical accuracy of syntax and punctuation in phrases, clauses and sentences
AF7	Select appropriate and effective vocabulary
AF8	Use correct spelling

APP recommends that assessment of writing should begin at sentence level (AF5 and AF6) before moving on to whole text structure and cohesion. This is the area of writing where *Rapid Writing* assessment can provide informative insight into children's growing control over the writing process.

Using *Rapid Writing* tasks to inform APP judgements

Rapid Writing targets all of the AFs. Rather than offering extended writing opportunities, the tasks in *Rapid Writing* provide children with practice in achieving cohesion within a paragraph. This means they are acquiring the skills that they will eventually need to be successful in longer writing tasks. They offer the chance to observe how well children are developing control over the organization of writing sentence by sentence. This mastery of sentence construction will give children the building blocks for the longer writing tasks they will undertake in whole class work.

Using the unaided writing tasks for assessment

When children have attempted the unaided writing tasks on pages 21 and 22 of the Writing Log (after five units and after ten units), it will be possible to assess their progress against some of the relevant National Curriculum Level Writing Assessment Guidelines. Read the criteria for the relevant level and determine if the child's writing is showing characteristics of those criteria. Start with AF5 (varied sentences) and AF6 (technical accuracy of syntax and punctuation), then assess against AF7 (appropriate vocabulary) and AF8 (correct spelling).

Although the children may only have written one or two sentences, it might be possible to assess whether these are imaginative and interesting (AF1) and appropriate to task, reader and purpose (AF2). The results will not be sufficient to determine an overall assessment; however it will be possible to highlight the criteria the child is showing some evidence of achieving.

Using the Write It! pages for assessment

When children have undertaken the Write It! assessed dictated sentences on page 20 of the Writing Log, it will be possible to assess their progress against AF6 and AF8. It will also be possible to make some judgements under the 'Handwriting and Presentation' criteria.

Assessing writing

Assessment of unaided writing

You can find the unaided writing tasks on pages 21 and 22 of each Writing Log, where they are included among a variety of word and pencil games that children will enjoy completing. This assessment could be undertaken in the group, provided that children are able to produce their own individual work rather than working with other children to create sentences.

What you need
- Writing Log Page 21 (Assessment after five units)
- Writing Log Page 22 (Assessment after ten units)
- Pen or pencil

What to do
Look together at the box with the orange outline on page 21 (or page 22) in the Writing Log. This shows some characters the children will have met in the preceding units. Talk to the children about the pictures and, in very general terms, discuss what they might write to accompany the pictures. Point out that they have limited writing space so they will need to construct sentences that suit the pictures but which will fit in the space provided.

Ask the children what writing skills they will need to take care with during the assessment. Talk about:

- handwriting
- spelling
- sentence construction
- sentence punctuation.

Ask the children what writing strategies they could use to help them. Talk about:

- segmenting words into phonemes before spelling them
- visualizing 'irregular' words before spelling them
- rehearsing the whole sentence before writing
- rereading the sentence to check they have written what they intended to write and have not left out any words
- checking they have used the correct punctuation.

Give the children approximately five minutes to complete the assessment. As they write, observe:

- letter formation
- spelling strategies
- whether they have rehearsed a sentence before writing it
- whether they reread what they have written to check it.

Using the *Rapid Writing* Pupil Software to assess unaided writing

The text-to-speech activities in the *Rapid Writing* Pupil Software will give further opportunity to assess children's unaided writing. In this feature, the child is provided with vocabulary prompts to create imaginative and interesting texts which the text-to-speech software will read back to them. The child's text is stored by the system so that you can review and assess their work once they have completed it.

Assessing writing

Example of unaided writing from Writing Log 7

Pupil Writing: "you have four leg's not two said Ziggy you are stupid."

Sentences are clear and suit purpose (AF5)
Alfie has given a clear answer to the prompt and used the picture to support his writing. He has captured the relationship between Ziggy and Pod with Ziggy being bossy and Pod getting things wrong.

Technical accuracy (AF6)
Alfie has used a capital letter for 'Ziggy' and he has finished his second sentence with a full stop but he has not demarcated the two sentences. He has partial understanding of the use of speech marks. He has not closed the speech marks after the first sentence or opened them for the second sentence. He has added an apostrophe in 'legs', suggesting confusion over the apostrophe to indicate possession.

Appropriate and effective vocabulary (AF7)
As Alfie is writing speech there is not much opportunity to reveal wider vocabulary choices, but the use of 'stupid' suggests linking word choices to character.

Spelling (AF8)
Alfie has spelt all high frequency words correctly (have, four, two, said, are).

Handwriting and presentation
Alfie has a neat print handwriting style with good orientation and mostly accurate line positioning. Occasionally there is confusion between upper and lower case ('y' in 'you' and 'L' in 'Legs'). He has not always finished letters accurately ('g' in 'legs').

Next steps

- Alfie needs to be encouraged to reread his writing to a partner to help him hear the sentence breaks.
- Encourage Alfie to read direct speech in his own writing to his partner and then to underline it. Then he should add in the speech marks.
- Alfie should be given the opportunity to practise the high frequency spelling words from List 6 (see page 149) using a joined handwriting style.
- In Shared Reading (and Guided Reading) draw attention to the fact that most nouns end in 's' to show a plural and that there is no need for an apostrophe.
- Continue teaching the spelling of high frequency words from List 7 (see page 149).
- Cross-reference this unaided writing with Alfie's performance on the mid unit dictated sentences and other written work.
- Provide Alfie with opportunities to use the *Rapid Writing* software, especially the tasks where he creates his own sentences.
- Alfie can now continue to work through Writing Log 7.

Assessing writing

Example of unaided writing from Writing Log 8

Pupil Writing:
- He can smell truble.
- He can dig a whole really fast.
- He save's the world.

Sentences are clear and suit purpose (AF5)
Lara was directed to use bullet points but she shows an understanding that bullet points are generally brief and focused. She has selected three relevant facts about Mole Man and written three characteristics which sum up his superhero status.

Technical accuracy (AF6)
Lara has accurately used capital letters and full stops for each bullet point. She is inclined to put an apostrophe before writing an 's' at the end of a word (save's). Although prompted to use bullet points, Lara shows an understanding of how sentences follow a bullet point, e.g. repeating the pronoun 'He'.

Appropriate vocabulary (AF7)
Lara has carefully selected words for the bullet points. She has used an adverb to qualify 'fast' and the expression 'saves the world' shows a good understanding of the superhero genre.

Spelling (AF8)
Lara correctly spells most words and has made a good phonic attempt at 'trouble'. The confusion with the homonym 'hole' (whole) suggests she is trying hard to do her best!

Handwriting and presentation
Lara's handwriting is in a neat joined style. The size is good, clear and readable. When she is concerned over spelling a word, the consistency of the slant is a little awry but otherwise the handwriting is swift and flowing.

Next steps

- Ask Lara to reflect on her writing to see if she can see the error with 'whole'. Set her a challenge of finding six words in her reading book which have homonyms (e.g. to, two; their, there; hear, here; some, sum).
- Ask Lara why she has put an apostrophe before the 's' in 'saves'. Talk about when we do need apostrophes. Remind her that most nouns end in 's' to show a plural and do not require an apostrophe.
- Cross-reference this unaided writing with Lara's performance on the mid unit dictated sentences and other written work.
- Provide Lara with opportunities to use the *Rapid Writing* software, especially the tasks where she creates her own sentences.
- Lara can now continue to work through Writing Log 8.

Assessing writing

Example of unaided writing from Writing Log 9

Pupil Writing: The Stones were rolled on tree trunks. They were pulled with AnimlX Animal ropes. The men had to be verey stong.

Sentences are clear and suit purpose (AF5)
Lauren's writing answers the question and she has adopted a formal style to suit a non-fiction report (generic pronouns: 'they'; passive tense: 'were pulled'; referring to 'the men' and not individuals).

Technical accuracy (AF6)
Lauren has written three short sentences and accurately demarcated them. She shows consistency of verb tense ('were rolled', 'were pulled'). The use of 'had to be' shows a good control of verb strings.

Spelling (AF8)
Lauren has spelt most high frequency words correctly (were, they, pulled, with). She self-corrects the word 'trunks' as she initially put a 'c' before the 'k'. She corrects the spelling of 'Animal' by rewriting the whole word. She has made an error in 'verey' but her handwriting suggests that she suspected it was incorrect. She has omitted the 'r' in 'strong'.

Handwriting and presentation
Lauren forms all letters correctly but there are some inconsistencies over upper and lower case. She has used a capital 'S' for stones and the lower case 'r' for 'rolled' is too big. She is able to confidently join most familiar words (were, men) but when she stops to think about a spelling, she writes the word in print (Animal). Some letters in the middle of words are a little squashed (the 'ed' in 'rolled'; the double 'l' in 'pulled').

Next steps

- In Shared and Guided reading, point out to Lauren examples of compound and complex sentences so that she becomes familiar with the variety of sentences types.
- Ask her to review her writing regarding use of inappropriate use of capital letters or over-large lower case letters.
- Foster Lauren's growing confidence to self-correct spelling errors and discourage her from thinking that crossing out is worse than making a mistake!
- Check Lauren can spell (and write in a joined hand) all the spelling high frequency words on List 8 (see page 149).
- Lauren could be encouraged to write slightly larger so that the patterning of each spelling is reinforced on rereading. This should be set as one of her Writing Targets.
- Cross-reference this unaided writing with Lauren's performance on the mid unit dictated sentences and other written work.
- Provide Lauren with opportunities to use the *Rapid Writing* software, especially the tasks where she creates her own sentences.
- Lauren can now continue to work through Writing Log 9.

Assessing writing

Correcting common errors

Handwriting

Unable to write letters of a regular size

Provide writing lines to indicate the height of ascenders, descenders and height of the body of the letters (see page 6 for examples of letter formation). Encourage the child to keep their letters within these lines.

Improving writing speed

If children are writing accurately but painfully slowly, challenge them to copy a sentence containing many high frequency words e.g. 'He saw a big dog in the park.' They should write it as carefully and neatly as they can. Then ask them to write the same line quickly and fluently without paying attention to neatness. Over time children will improve the overall speed of their writing.

Sentence demarcation and construction

Does not have a clear idea of what a sentence is

- Say a sentence starter and ask the child if it is a sentence e.g. 'When I got to …'. Ask the child to complete the sentence.
- Read half sentences from their reading book and ask them if this sounds like a whole sentence. Explain that half a sentence does not make sense and point out how the sentences in the book always make sense.
- Encourage children to plan sentences orally before they write them.

Cannot remember a rehearsed sentence at the point of writing

- Ask each child to repeat to their partner the sentence you want them to write.
- Then ask them to say the sentence in unison.
- If they forget the end of a sentence as they are writing, tell them to reread what they have written so far and to think about what would make sense to finish the sentence. You could repeat the whole sentence and they could work out which words they still need to write to complete the sentence.
- Say the sentence aloud from the beginning and support them if they still find it difficult to remember.

Does not start sentences with capital letters

- Point out capital letters at the start of sentences when reading.
- Teach the child the chant 'Every sentence starts with a capital letter'.
- Write a short sentence and omit the first letter of the first word e.g. '_hey went to the shop.' Challenge the children to work out what letter is missing and then to write it as a capital to start the sentence.

Does not end sentences with full stops

- Encourage the child to read with expression and point out the purpose of the full stop.
- Remind the child to put a full stop at the end of every sentence.

Is not sure when to use a question mark or an exclamation mark

- Children get a 'star' if they point out a question when reading. They only get the 'reward' if they read the whole question with intonation.
- When reading their own writing, encourage children to work with a partner and discuss if a sentence needs a question mark or exclamation mark.

Is not sure when to use speech marks

- Photocopy a page from a book that has plenty of dialogue. Give each child a copy. Read only the direct speech text to the group. They should underline the spoken words. Check children's work. Then go back and ask the children to circle all the pairs of speech marks. Tell the children to work with a partner and to take it in turns to read aloud only the underlined (spoken) text.

Assessing writing

- Write a simple sentence with speech on the board but omit the speech marks e.g. Can you help me? asked the man. Discuss with the children which are the actual words spoken. Invite a child to add the speech marks. Talk about placing the speech marks around the actual words spoken and after any end of sentence punctuation.

Phonics
Cannot segment CCVC (Consonant Consonant Vowel Consonant) or CVCC words

- Write a CCVC word (e.g. stop, help) and say the phonemes as you point to each one in turn. Ask the child to repeat the process. Indicate each separate phoneme with a dot (phoneme button) underneath.
- Say a CCVC word and then use 'robot speak' to separate the phonemes. Write the phonemes as you sound them. Add the phoneme buttons.
- Encourage the child to sound out the phonemes with you.
- Say a CCVC word and ask the child to segment it into its separate phonemes.

Cannot blend CCVC words

- With the children, devise easy mnemonics for each set of adjacent consonants e.g. 'cl' (clap your hands), 'bl' (blink your eyes), 'sn' (snip with your fingers as if making a cutting action).

Initial adjacent consonants:	Final adjacent consonants:
bl cl fl gl pl	ld nd lk nk sk lp mp
br cr dr fr gr pr tr	sp ct ft lt nt pt st
sc sk sl sm sn sp st sw	xt lf nch lth
tw qu	
scr spl spr squ shr str thr	

Spelling irregular sight words
Does not remember how to spell high frequency words

- Ensure that the child knows the letter names for all letters.
- Encourage the child to say the letter names as they write the word, using their 'writing finger' (that is, the forefinger of their writing hand) onto a tactile surface such as carpet or fine sandpaper.
- Encourage the child to visualise the word before asking them to write the word.
- Look for small words inside longer words, for example, 'hat' in 'what'.
- Some children find mnemonics a good way to remember how to spell tricky words. For example, remembering the 'ould' of 'could', 'would' and 'should' by saying: 'O U lucky duck'.
- Only select one or two words for child to learn.

Spelling strategies
Raps

- Teach words based on rap rhythms and using letter names. For example, teach 'because' as: 'b' 'e' / 'b' 'e' 'c' / 'b' 'e' 'c' 'a' 'u' 's' 'e' / This is how to learn 'because'. Or: Give me 'f'/ Give me 'r' / Give me 'fri' / Give me 'f' 'r' 'i' and 'e' 'n' 'd' / 'f' 'r' i' and 'e' 'n' 'd' / Put it together and what have we got: 'friend'!

Breaking words into syllables

- Help children to hear all the parts of multi-syllabic words by clapping (one clap for each syllable: 'yes/ter/day' (three claps).
- Get the children to tuck their elbows into the ribcage and then move their arms stiffly up and down (like a robot) to mark each syllable: 'some/thing' (two arm movements)
- Get the children to place their elbow on the table and form a fist with their hand. Put the fist under the chin. Model for them how to separate a word into its syllables e.g. 'sudd/en/ly'. As they say the syllables they will feel their chin pressing down on their fist.

Assessing writing

Progression in writing skills

Writing skill	Writing Log 7	Writing Log 8	Writing Log 9
Handwriting	handwriting is observed and monitored	handwriting is observed and monitored	handwriting is observed and monitored
Phonics	segmenting, blending and spelling CCVC and CVCC words; further practice with words with less usual Grapheme Phoneme Correspondence (GPC)	segmenting, blending and spelling CCVC and CVCC words; further practice with words with less GPC	segmenting, blending and spelling CCVC and CVCC words; further practice with words with less GPC
Spelling – high frequency words	memorizing and practising 20 high frequency words	memorizing and practising a further 20 high frequency words	memorizing and practising a further 20 high frequency words
Spelling – knowledge	recognizing compound words e.g. 'everyone'; adding 'ed' to words which double the consonant after a short vowel; using the apostrophe to show a letter is omitted e.g. 'doesn't'	recognizing compound words e.g. 'ourselves'; adding 'ed' to longer words e.g. 'appeared'; adding a prefix e.g. 'dis' to words ('disappeared')	adding 'ed' to longer words e.g. 'whispered' adding a prefix e.g. 'un' to words ('untidy'); using the apostrophe to show a letter is omitted e.g. 'I'll'
Sentence construction	writing simple and compound sentences after sentence starter prompt and oral rehearsal (Average sentence length = 12 words)	writing simple, compound and complex sentences after sentence starter prompt and oral rehearsal (Average sentence length = 13 words)	writing simple, compound and complex sentences after sentence starter prompt and oral rehearsal (Average sentence length = 15 words)
Punctuation	capital letters, full stops, question marks, dashes, exclamation marks, ellipses	capital letters, full stops, question marks, exclamation marks, speech marks, commas before closing speech marks, commas to mark clauses	capital letters, full stops, question marks, exclamation marks, speech marks, commas before closing speech marks, commas to mark clauses
Genre	report, captions, statements, brochure, diary, commentary, journal, poster, narrative	newspaper report, encyclopaedia entry, fact file, advert, comic strip, recount, magazine article, email, survey	explanation, dramatic narrative, instructions, dialogue, persuasive writing, playscript, humorous narrative, timeline

Assessing writing

Words for spelling

The following lists of words represent the most common words children need when writing. The lists have been levelled into steps of increasing difficulty and could form part of assessment of AF8 (spelling). Most of the words are taught and practised in the Guided Writing sessions; however not all of the List 1 two-letter words are introduced in Writing Log 1 as it is expected that children will be able to spell many of these words.

List 1	List 2	List 3	List 4	List 5	List 6	List 7	List 8	List 9
am	and	all	can't	across	always	again	about	around
as	big	are	come	away	any	began	after	because
at	but	back	could	best	asked	catch	before	believe
do	can	down	don't	came	coming	does	caught	children
go	did	give	from	didn't	found	eat	every	everything
he	get	going	just	fast	having	first	friend	everyone
if	got	good	like	gave	know	getting	great	huge
in	had	have	look	little	lived	gone	heard	later
is	has	here	made	our	much	high	house	nothing
it	her	how	must	play	never	home	knew	opened
me	him	help	now	talk	next	last	only	people
my	his	new	one	that	over	near	really	yesterday
no	not	out	said	think	right	night	school	something
of	put	she	some	time	thing	other	shouted	sometimes
on	the	them	take	told	took	quick	slowly	started
so	saw	then	there	too	tried	their	stopped	suddenly
to	see	this	they	were	walk	which	thought	sure
up	was	went	very	who	when	wish	turn	those
us	yes	will	want	why	where	won't	under	through
we	you	with	what	your	would	year	wait	used

Assessing writing

My Writing Progress Chart Writing Log 7

Handwriting	
I write the letters neatly.	
I make a difference between the size of my upper case and lower case letters.	
I join some of my letters.	
Phonics	
I can segment and spell words with long vowels.	
Spelling	
I can spell 140 high frequency words.	
I can add 'ed' to words.	
I can add 'ing' to words.	
I know to use an apostrophe to show that a letter is missing.	
Sentence composition	
I can write a short sentence after hearing it.	
I can write longer sentences after hearing them.	
I know that a writer might choose to write a long or a short sentence.	
Sentence punctuation	
I remember to put a capital letter at the start of a sentence.	
I remember to put a full stop, question mark or exclamation mark at the end of a sentence.	
I know when to use dots to make a reader pause.	

© Pearson Education Limited, 2009

Assessing writing

My Writing Progress Chart Writing Log 8

Handwriting	
I make a difference between the size of my upper case and lower case letters.	
I join most of my letters.	
I usually write neatly.	
I leave an even space between words.	
Phonics	
I use my phonic knowledge to help me spell new words.	
Spelling	
I can spell 160 high frequency words.	
I can add 'ed' to longer words.	
I can add 'un' and 'dis' to words to change the meaning.	
I can write some compound words.	
Sentence composition	
I can write sentences joined with 'and' or 'but'.	
I can write longer sentences joined with 'then' or 'because'.	
I know when to write a long or a short sentence.	
Sentence punctuation	
I remember to put a capital letter at the start of a sentence.	
I remember to put a full stop, question mark or exclamation mark at the end of a sentence.	
I know that writers use commas to make the reader pause in a sentence.	

© Pearson Education Limited, 2009

Assessing writing

My Writing Progress Chart Writing Log 9

Handwriting	
I join most of my letters.	
I usually write neatly.	
I can write quickly and still keep it neat.	
Phonics	
I use my phonic knowledge to help me spell new words.	
Spelling	
I can spell 180 high frequency words.	
I know when to use an apostrophe.	
Sentence composition	
I can write a simple or compound sentence after hearing it.	
I can write a complex sentence.	
Sentence punctuation	
I remember to put a capital letter at the start of a sentence and for proper nouns.	
I remember to put a full stop, question mark or exclamation mark at the end of a sentence.	
I know when to use speech marks.	
I know that writers use commas in complex sentences.	